Raising Global Families

Raising Global Families

Parenting, Immigration, and Class in Taiwan and the US

Pei-Chia Lan

Stanford University Press
Stanford, California

Stanford University Press
Stanford, California

The Chiang Ching-kuo Foundation for International Scholarly Exchange has provided financial assistance for the publication of this book.

Library of Congress Cataloging-in-Publication Data

Names: Lan, Pei-Chia, 1970– author.
Title: Raising global families : parenting, immigration, and class in Taiwan and
    the US / Pei-Chia Lan.
Description: Stanford, California : Stanford University Press, 2018. | Includes bibliographical
    references and index.
Identifiers: LCCN 2017046837 | ISBN 9781503602076 (cloth : alk. paper) |
    ISBN 9781503605909 (pbk. : alk. paper) | ISBN 9781503605916 (epub)
Subjects: LCSH: Child rearing—Taiwan. | Child rearing—United States. | Families—Taiwan. |
    Immigrant families—United States. | Taiwanese Americans—Family relationships. |
    Chinese Americans—Family relationships. | Social classes—Taiwan. | Social classes—
    United States. | Taiwan—Emigration and immigration—Social aspects. | United States—
    Emigration and immigration—Social aspects.
Classification: LCC HQ792.C6 L36 2018 | DDC 306.850951249—dc23
LC record available at https://lccn.loc.gov/2017046837

Typeset by Newgen in 10/14 Minion

Contents

Preface

THIS BOOK USES PARENTING AS A LENS to examine cultural transformation and persisting inequality in the contexts of globalization and immigration. It focuses on ethnic (Han) Chinese families in Taiwan and the United States with class-specific experiences of transnational and cultural mobility. These parents come from distinct class backgrounds and choose various ways to raise their children, but they share one thing in common—they all feel anxious and insecure about raising children in times of rapid change and uncertainty.

Most of the parents in this book grew up in the 1970s and 1980s, around the same time as I did. Their parental anxieties look even more pronounced in comparison to our upbringings in a poorer Taiwan. During China's civil war, my father left his parents and boarded a ship to Taiwan; he later attended subsidized medical school and earned a modest salary as an army doctor. My mother grew up in a Taiwanese farming household and finished junior high school, already an achievement for women back then. She worked as an office clerk and later became a homemaker to raise the five of us. Although my family of origin could be broadly classified as the middle class, my parents delivered little cultural and global exposure by today's standards. My siblings and I often stayed home or played in the alley without adult supervision. We walked to school by ourselves, passing by bamboo forests and messy streets in not-yet-so-modern Taipei. Corporal punishment was common at both school and home. My mother threatened to "hang and beat" my naughty brother whenever I could not find him to get home for dinner.

However, when people in my generation become the new middle class and raise their own children, they shy away from the past and embrace new ideas of childrearing and education. They have fewer—mostly one or two—children and yet richer resources, economic and cultural ones. At the age of twenty, I applied for my passport for the first time in my life. Now, middle-class Taiwanese children make their debut overseas travel at the age of four or five, if not earlier. Given the increased parental attention and educational opportunities for children, I wonder, Why are today's middle-class parents feeling even more anxious about their children's future and constantly questioning whether they are making "right" choices for their children?

I attended public schools with pupils of mixed socioeconomic backgrounds. Many of my classmates' parents were street vendors and small shop owners, and we caught tadpoles in a pond together after school. Nowadays, the class gaps of unequal childhoods have become so substantial that the media calls it "Two Worlds, One Taiwan." The changing repertoire of childrearing also spreads parental anxieties across the class divides. Working-class parents worry about the legal consequence of leaving children at home while struggling with long work hours and the shortage of childcare. And they feel frustrated with new school curriculum and the increasing pressure that requires parental participation at school.

People in Taiwan widely share an ideal image of (middle-class) American family characterized by permissive parenting and happy childhood. US immigration is seen as a pathway for those lucky ones who are able to escape rote learning and academic pressure in the local regime of education. I recalled envying some friends who moved to the US as a parachute child or along with their parents in the 1980s.

My interviews with the current generation of immigrant parents, however, did not replicate such a rosy image. Professional immigrants worry about the so-called Asian quotas in college admission, and working-class immigrants feel frustrated to live up to the standard of the "model minority." The decline of the American economy and the rise of Asia further shatter their faith in the American dream. Juxtaposing parental experiences in Taiwan to those of the US, this book situates the emotional landscape of social class in a transnational context, showing how childrearing produces a myriad of hopes, desires, fears, and anxieties for parents living in an interconnected world.

I did not have the opportunity to become a mother. From time to time, I wonder what I have missed—an unknown adventure? The sweetest burden? I am grateful to have the chance to learn from my informants in Taiwan and the US, who generously shared with me their time and experiences. This book focuses on their parental insecurities and security strategies, but there are moments of joy and happiness that this book cannot fully record. Parenting is such a complex journey and daunting task that I must humbly say that this book can reveal only some of the thin layers.

The research process was funded by several research grants from National Science Council (NSC99-2410-H002-170-MY3) and Ministry of Science and Technology (MOST104-2420-H002-045-MY3) in Taiwan. During 2011–2012, the fellowship at Radcliffe Institute and Yenching Institute at Harvard University sponsored me to conduct data collection in Boston Area.

Although I am responsible for all faults in this book, the data collection and analysis involved an excellent team of research assistants. Juhan Chen, Hoching Jiang, and Winnie Hui-Tse Chang conducted class observation at the four schools in Taiwan and transcribed my interviews with parents; they also shared with me keen observations and insights based on their own upbringings. Ken-Jen She and Catherine Yeh assisted with coding the interview data; their insights greatly enriched my interpretation. Yun-Ching Chuan, Fei-Chih Jiang, Henry Su, Fu-Rong Yeh, Chu-Chieh Ko, Yu-Hsuan Lin, Yu-Hsiu Hsieh, and Yu-Chien Lee helped with literature, references and archival analysis over the years.

I am grateful to many colleagues who offered valuable insights during the revision process. Carolyn Chen, Sara Friedman, Miliann Kang, Kristy Shih, Ken Chih-Yen Sun, and Ting-Hong Wong read the whole manuscript. Special thanks to Ken Sun for directing me to the concept of global security strategy. Many others commented on particular chapters: Hae Yeon Choo, Nicole Constable, Katy Lam, Ming-Cheng Lo, Rhacel Parreñas, Hsiu-Hua Shen, Leslie Wang, and Brenda Yeoh. I also appreciate the feedback from the audiences during my presentations at several conferences, workshops, and lectures delivered at Academia Sinica, Chinese University of Hong Kong, Hong Kong University, Kyoto University, Melbourne University, National Taipei University, Toronto University, and Yonsei University. At Stanford University Press, Kate Wahl, Jenny Gavacs, Marcela Cristina Maxfield, and Olivia Bartz offered their guidance through the process. I also thank Jessica Cobb and Katherine Faydash for their super editing assistance.

The academic career is a lonely journey. I would not have survived without the friendship and support of my colleagues at Department of Sociology at National Taiwan University, especially Hwa-Jen Liu, Kuo-Hsien Su, Yen-Fen Tseng, and Chia-Ling Wu. Jerry Lin also helps me maintain sanity against work pressure, always reminding me to look at the beautiful moon and stars in the sky. Finally, thanks and love to my dog, Aga, who has taught me one or two things about parenting.

PCL
Taipei, Summer 2017

Notes on Terminology and Naming

IN THIS BOOK, I USE THE TERM *ethnic Chinese* to encompass people of Han Chinese cultural origin (*huaren*), whose nationality and ethnic identity vary. I use the term *Taiwanese* as a subcategory when describing parents in Taiwan (officially, the Republic of China). I use the term *Chinese* to describe immigrants in the United States who originate from both Mainland China (People's Republic of China) and Taiwan. The majority of them are naturalized American citizens except for a small number of green-card holders. Note that immigrants from Taiwan may identify their ethnicity as Taiwanese rather than Chinese. For instance, in 2010, Taiwanese American launched a "Write in Taiwanese" campaign to assert self-identity.

I employ pseudonyms throughout the book to protect individual identities. I use English first names for some informants, mostly immigrants in the United States and middle-class Taiwanese. It is common for middle-class Taiwanese to use English names in industries related to international business, and those children who attended a bilingual kindergarten generally acquired English names. It is now customary that women in Taiwan and China do not change their surnames upon marriage. So I gave pseudonyms for their maiden names.

I use the Pinyin system to romanize Mandarin Chinese words, expressions and names for those informants who originate from mainland China. I adopt Taiwanese romanization conventions for place names in Taiwan and personal names for Taiwanese citizens and immigrants. I adopt personal naming practice in Taiwan that inserts a hyphen between the two characters of a first name. Therefore, I refer to a Taiwanese individual as Pei-chia Lan, but a mainland Chinese individual as Peichia Lan.

Raising Global Families

Introduction

Anxious Parents in Global Times

IN HER CONTROVERSIAL BEST SELLER *Battle Hymn of the Tiger Mother*, Amy Chua, who was born and raised in the United States, used the label "Chinese mother" to describe her style of strict parenting in contrast to softer "Western" parenting.[1] Published in early 2011, soon after the financial crisis hit the American economy, *Battle Hymn* and the media sensation around it stirred both the American middle class's shattered sense of economic security and increasing anxiety about China's rise to global superpower. For instance, the *Wall Street Journal* published an abbreviated account of Chua's book with the title "Why Chinese Mothers Are Superior." A 2011 *Time* article asked, "Chua has set a whole nation of parents to wondering: Are we the losers she's talking about?"[2] The book's cover delivered an unmistakable reference to Chinese culture, with the title presented to resemble a red-inked woodblock stamp with the Chinese characters for "tiger mom" at the center in a stylized archaic script.

Ironically, when marketing a translated version of the book in China, the publisher "Americanized" the title and cover.[3] The Chinese title became *The Ways I Mother in the US: Childrearing Advice from a Yale Law Professor*, and the cover bore a picture of a smiling Chua standing before a US flag. Although Chua labeled herself a "Chinese mother," she nevertheless became an "American mother" once the book traveled to China. The book was promoted as a parenting guide from an expert whose credibility was based on her teaching position at an Ivy League university. It was only one among many translated childrearing guides from Western experts filling bookstores in China and Taiwan, where anxious parents are hungry for the knowledge deemed essential for raising a modern child in a global world.

1

The figure of the "tiger mom" frequently appeared in my conversations with ethnic Chinese parents in Taiwan and the United States. Many recalled growing up with or having heard of a strict Chinese mother who placed high demands on her children. However, for many of them, "tiger mothering" was not a cultural heritage to embrace but an archaic tradition to discard. Take, for example, Janice Chan, a fortysomething Taiwanese mother living in Taipei who was a human resources manager and now is a dedicated full-time mother and an avid reader of parenting guides and magazines. With a passion for innovative ideas and educational tools, Janice is determined to jettison the traditions of rote learning and strict parenting. She considers Western education an ideal pathway for her children to attain holistic development and to secure a niche in the global creative economy.

Every other year, Janice provides her two sons with a slice of the American middle-class childhood by enrolling them in summer camp in California. They stay in the spacious two-story house of her cousin who works in Silicon Valley as an engineer. On a recent trip, Janice was surprised when the cousin's wife asked her to bring over Taiwanese textbooks on math and physics. Yet this request was not unusual among Taiwanese immigrant parents to the United States. Just as Janice took her children to the United States for enrichment, many immigrant parents send their teenaged children back to Taiwan during the summer to improve their SAT scores and Chinese language skills. Feeling concerned about the depth of knowledge in American public education, as well as the rising opportunities in the region of Greater China, they use these trips to expose their American children to the culture and learning styles of their homeland.

In fact, most immigrant parents I interviewed in the United States tried to dissociate themselves from the controlling style of Amy Chua, but they could also relate to Chua's emotional struggle. They saw the tiger mom as an immigrant's tale—though Chua is US born—immigrant parents had little choice but to adopt a regimented parenting style in order to secure their children's educational success in an environment of racial inequality. Nevertheless, they were keenly aware that Chua was no ordinary Chinese parent; her childrearing style was more indicative of class privilege than ethnic upbringing. Only a few immigrant Chinese families could afford the tutors, private lessons, and elite school that Chua's daughters had access to.

Working-class Chinese immigrants, in particular, struggle with a shortage of economic and cultural resources in the new country. Mei-li Lin is a single mother and childcare worker living in a subsidized apartment on the outskirts of Boston's Chinatown. After winning the green-card lottery, she immigrated with her only daughter to the United States to seek a brighter future and a happier childhood. Still, she is confused by the different cultural scripts of childrearing between Taiwan and the United States and frustrated by the reversal of the parent-child dynamics: "People here always ask kids how they feel. In Taiwan, you just tell your kids to listen to you. In the US, kids will correct your English and say, 'Mom, you should listen to me!'"

When Mei-li brought her daughter back to Taiwan for a visit, her sister, a high school graduate like Mei-li, criticized her lack of parental authority. The sister, like many working-class parents in Taiwan, was mostly concerned about the looming dangers associated with drugs, gangs, and other social toxins in today's teenage world. She warned Mei-li that the American parenting style would have dire consequences: "If you were raising kids this way in Taiwan, they would have beat up their parents! They have no respect and no discipline." Mei-li resorts to the American rhetoric of freedom and justifies her hands-off approach to childrearing as a form of cultural assimilation: "We cannot control children in the US, and perhaps they would become more independent. This is the American way, isn't it?"

An increasing number of families around the globe are living their lives physically or virtually across national borders. I use the term *global family* to echo what Mike Douglass has called "global householding," which describes a dynamic process of forming and sustaining the households as a unit of social reproduction through global movements and transactions.[4] Globalization provides these families with expanded childrearing resources and cultural horizons, but it also brings new challenges and intensified anxieties. This book examines how these mothers and fathers navigate transnational mobility and negotiate cultural boundaries, through what I call *global security strategies*, to cope with uncertainties and insecurities in the changing society and globalized world.

Raising Global Families is the first book to compare parents of the same age cohort in the country of origin and in the adopted country, while also examining class variations in their parenting practices. It includes four groups of ethnic Chinese parents in Taiwan and the United States: middle- and working-class Taiwanese, and middle- and working-class Chinese immigrants in the Boston area. This research design allows for interrogating the intersection of ethnic culture and social class. It illuminates that ethnic culture is neither static nor uniform, but rather is constantly shifting across borders. Each group faced context-specific predicaments and employed class-specific strategies of cultural negotiation. The cross-Pacific comparison also demonstrates how class-based parenthood configures differently across national contexts. Parents' strategies of childrearing, which emerge from their class habitus and experience, take shape in reaction to public culture and local opportunity structure.

I propose the approach of *transnational relational analysis* to examine how parents develop strategic actions and emotional experiences of childrearing in relation to other parents. Well-resourced parents, who are inclined to "upscale" their perception of globalized risk, mobilize transnational resources and modify local norms to improve the security of their children. However, their global security strategies unwittingly magnify the insecurity of disadvantaged parents, who face increasing institutional pressure from the government and school to comply with the new cultural scripts of childrearing that privilege the middle-class nuclear family and Western-centric cultural capital.

Cultural Negotiation and Global Forces

The notion of tiger parenting, despite being overexaggerated in Chua's book, is rooted in the empirical research of cross-cultural psychology. Scholars in this field have described a Chinese style of authoritarian parenting in which parents hold high expectations for their children's achievement and use a harsh regimen to propel them toward excellence. Unlike white, European American authoritarian parenting, which is associated with distance, rejection, and lack of support, Chinese authoritarian parenting is accompanied by high involvement and sacrifice. The Chinese concept of *guan*, which connotes both "controlling" and "caring," encapsulates the Confucian emphasis on parental authority accompanied by intensive intervention of children's lives.[5]

Emphasizing cross-cultural variations in childrearing, the earlier studies are nevertheless vulnerable to the flaw of reifying ethnic and cultural boundaries. They widely adopted a comparative design—for instance, between Chinese Americans and European Americans—to illustrate marked differences across cultural origins.[6] Such binary comparison tends to present Chinese parenting values as being monolithic and static, leaving little room for "the more nuanced and contextualized portrait of Chinese mothers' parenting dilemma."[7]

Recent research efforts have challenged the tiger-mom stereotype with a more complex and dynamic portrait of Asian or Asian American parenting.[8] The practice of Chinese parenting not only varies within ethnic group and across social contexts but also transforms over time under the influence of local changes and global forces. It is more appropriate to describe the ethnic culture of childrearing as a multiplicity of cultural repertoires,[9] which can be habitual and unconscious, as being internalized and naturalized as taken-for-granted traditions and norms; yet parents also engage in *cultural negotiation* by reorganizing and revising cultural frameworks to adapt to new circumstances, especially during rapid social transformation and cross-border mobility.

East Asian countries stand as representative cases of "compressed modernity," which, according to Kyung-Sup Chang, describes "a civilizational condition in which economic, political, social and/or cultural changes occur in an extremely condensed manner in respect to both time and space." As a result, diverse cultural components (including both colonial and postcolonial components) and multiple social temporalities (e.g., traditional, modern, and postmodern temporalities) coexist and interact.[10] When raising children in such circumstances, parents feel augmented anxieties at the nexus of social change and global aspiration.

Taiwan is a strategic site for studying compressed modernity and global childrearing. Its "economic miracle" turned the impoverished island nation into a "tiger" of prosperity in less than half a century.[11] Taiwan also underwent a peaceful political transition from an authoritarian military state to a robust young democracy with a vibrant civil society. The past few decades have witnessed a great transformation in fertility behavior and cultural repertoire of childrearing. Taiwan promoted an organized family-planning program in the 1960s to mitigate the problem of overpopulation, but the government now perceives the plummeting birth rate, one of the lowest in the world, as a "national security threat."[12] Most families have only one or two children, and voluntary childlessness among married couples is increasing. People are hesitant to have more children, especially considering the rising costs of childrearing; meanwhile, shrinking family sizes have increased the resources available for each child and intensified parents' economic and emotional investments in both sons and daughters.[13]

For Taiwanese living in a national territory of only fourteen thousand square miles, transnational connections and mobility are critical means to achieve economic success and cultural advancement. New technologies and cheap travel have facilitated the suppression of spatial and temporal distances—which David Harvey calls "time-space compression"[14]—and contribute to a global convergence of childhood. Joining middle-class parents around the globe, Taiwan's newly rich parents seek inspiration and guidance from Western expert knowledge on scientific childrearing and child psychology.[15] They embrace the "sacralization of childhood" that Viviana Zelizer famously identified in the West, whereby children become "economically useless and emotionally priceless."[16] Moreover, commercial cultural products like McDonald's, Disney, and *Sesame Street*, have won global popularity and homogenized how children play and desire across the world.[17]

However, globalization is not a monolithic force that operates outside the fabric of culture; Carla Freeman urges researchers to examine the mutual constitution of culture and globalization: "What is 'cultural' about globalization and how does 'the global' work in and through the stickiness and particularities of culture?"[18] *Raising Global Families* takes a subject-oriented approach to investigate the dialectical entanglement between the global and the local, between the modern and the traditional.[19] By juxtaposing Taiwanese families to their immigrant counterparts in the United States, this book interrogates how parents reorganize and reshuffle ethnic culture in response to transnational flows of practices, knowledge, and people. Moreover, this book highlights that social class shapes parents' uneven capacities to mobilize time-space compression, digest global culture, and transform local traditions. Cultural negotiation and transnational mobility become critical forums for reproducing class inequality in global times.

Immigrant Parenting and Transnationalism

Immigrant parents raising children in the new country offer illustrative cases for cultural negotiation. In particular, the academic achievement of Asian Americans stirs debates about how cultural matters in the context of immigration. American cultural pundits widely credit the "Confucian heritage cultures" that emphasize hard work, filial piety, and strong family ties.[20] These popular stereotypes neglect historical and social variations, reducing ethnic culture to the product of bounded, timeless, and unchanging "traditions."[21] To shy away from cultural essentialism, recent scholars have examined how culture interacts with *structure*, including the contexts of immigrant incorporation and the racialized structures of opportunity, to affect parents' concerns and strategies of childrearing.

The very influential theory of segmented assimilation has demonstrated a trajectory of "selective acculturation" for immigrant youth, who can achieve social mobility and yet maintain strong ties with the immigrant community.[22]

Min Zhou has used the term *ethnic capital* to refer to an interplay of financial, human, and social capital in an identifiable ethnic community. The ethnic economy, which reproduces Asian-style supplementary education, helps the second generation to cope with parental constraints and attain academic success.[23] Ethnic institutions, such as Chinatown-based NGOs and Chinese-speaking Christian churches, not only deliver ethnic cultures and family values across generations but also help immigrant parents and children to absorb new cultural resources that are useful for them to adapt to the larger American society.[24]

Jennifer Lee and Min Zhou, in their recent book, invigorate the debate by identifying the class origin of the cultural framework that shapes Asian American achievement. They argue that, because the post-1965 stream of Asian immigration is a highly selected group in terms of socioeconomic status, the emphasis on academic success is actually a class-based mind-set that these highly educated immigrants selectively imported from their home countries and re-created in the United States. Additionally, the narratives of the "model minority" reinforce public perceptions in educational terrains, creating a "stereotype promise" that facilitates the success of Asian American youth.[25]

This groundbreaking study has encountered some noteworthy criticisms. Some scholars question how generalizable these findings are beyond the Los Angeles area. Chinese immigrants in other locations, such as New York City, are less affluent and more disadvantaged. The causal effect of immigrant selectivity is dubious, considering that Asian immigrants are bimodal in terms of socioeconomic distribution.[26] Lee and Zhou are also criticized for placing too much emphasis on social-psychological orientation.[27] Instead, Van Tran calls for a more dynamic analysis about "how the cultural scripts among immigrant groups are being refreshed, expanded and diffused as they come into contact with the American mainstream."[28] To achieve this goal, we must shift the focus from the second generation to immigrant parents and investigate class heterogeneity within an immigrant group.

Raising Global Families adopts a cross-class, cross-national comparison to enter the debate about how culture transforms in the context of immigration. The cross-Pacific comparison allows us to better identify the nuanced differences of cultural hybridization in both the home country and the receiving country. And the cross-class comparison demonstrates a complex picture in which immigrant parents harbor class-specific insecurities and develop context-sensitive strategies of cultural negotiation.

My analysis is built on the existing literature that has examined how parents navigate multiple cultural scripts to orient their actions of childrearing as they move across borders and encounter changing circumstances. Cati Coe, in her study of Ghanaian immigrants in the United States, describes immigration as "a liminal space of human experience" that generates a sense of uncertainty and ambiguity but also leads to partial recognition and creative adaptation.[29] Immigrant parents may selectively memorize and deliberately represent their "original" culture to cope with uncertainty and maintain a sense of dignity. Filipino immigrants, for example, elevate the patriarchal ideology of Filipina chastity to control the sexuality of their daughters and to assert the moral superiority of the Filipino community over white Americans.[30] Immigrant parents may also remake ethnicity as an act of everyday resistance. For instance, Ghanaian and West Indian immigrants, who feel deprived of their authority to discipline their children in the United States, project a nostalgic imagination of their cultural past to justify the exercise of corporal punishment.[31]

Social class has long been overlooked in many studies of Asian Americans, but a few scholars, including Vivian Louie, Jamie Lew, and Angie Chung, started to look into class divides among Asian American youth.[32] Despite their primary focus on the second generation, these studies show marked differences in educational strategies and cross-generational relations between middle- and working-class immigrant families. Zhou's concept of ethnic capital is criticized for carrying a risk to construct ethnic collectivities as homogenous and to overlook power relations within.[33] A class-based analysis allows us to examine immigrant parents' uneven capacities for cultural negotiation and to identify the specific components of ethnic capital that they enact and have access to.

Ethnic Chinese immigrants (born in Taiwan or China) constitute an ideal case for investigating class divides in immigrant parenting because the population is bifurcated by socioeconomic status and migration trajectory. Migrant members of the professional middle class first came to the United States for college or postgraduate degrees, whereas the less educated mainly immigrated via family reunification and they usually occupy lower-skilled jobs in the new country.

Raising Global Families further situates the cultural negotiation of immigrant parents in the context of transnationalism. Internet technology and cheap air travel assist bidirectional circuits of cultural and educational resources between home and host countries. Both immigrants and their children draw on transnational connections and practices to situate their cultural identities and even to facilitate their adaptation in the new country.[34] Meanwhile, transnationalism can also exacerbate emotional anxieties—a condition Diana Wolf calls "emotional transnationalism."[35] Immigrant mothers, in particular, struggle with feelings of ambivalence, confusion, and anxiety, because they straddle two cultural worlds in raising children and encounter multiple, sometimes conflicting, cultural repertoires of childrearing.[36]

Transnational contexts become more prominent in immigrants' search for identity and security in the current global climate, a historical conjuncture characterized by the prospect of Western decline and Asian ascendency.[37] The US recession after the 2008–2009 financial crisis rendered many professionals jobless and shattered a sense of economic security among middle-class immigrants. The rise of China also induced Chinese immigrants to maintain transnational ties with their home country and culture. Although affluent parents in Asia still see immigration to North America as a strategy for their children to become globally competitive, an emerging literature has exposed a recent trend of second-generation Asian Americans who pursue "return" migration to their ancestral homeland.[38]

By analyzing immigrant families in parallel with their counterparts in the home country, this book examines how the new global economy intensifies feelings of ambivalence and insecurity among immigrant parents who use class peers back home as their transnational reference groups as they arrange children's education, care, and discipline. Focusing on class difference within an immigrant group, this book explores why professional immigrants, as compared to working-class immigrants, are more likely to use educational resources back home for their American children. Childrearing becomes an everyday experience of emotional transnationalism for immigrant parents, who must navigate multiple cultural repertoires of education and childrearing in the homeland and the new country.

Parenting and Social Class

Following the seminal work of Pierre Bourdieu and Melvin Kohn, a large body of literature in sociology addresses the fact that parents' family origins and occupational cultures generate their preferences and priorities in the process of childrearing.[39] One of the most influential studies is *Unequal Childhoods*, an ethnographic study of twelve white and African American families. Annette Lareau vividly demonstrates two class-specific childrearing styles: middle-class parents engage in the style of "concerted cultivation" and cultivate a sense of entitlement with children, whereas working-class and poor families raise their children with the style of "the accomplishment of natural growth," and their children develop a sense of constraint from such upbringing. The family life as such reproduces class privilege or disadvantage across generations, including parents' and children's capacity, or lack thereof, to negotiate with institutional authorities like teachers and coaches.[40]

Anthropologist Adrie Kusserow attends to the intersection of national culture and social class and examines how social classes digest American individualism in different ways. Upper-middle-class Americans embrace "soft individualism"—they see the world as welcoming but competitive, and caregivers should protect the child's psychologized self like a delicate flower. Working-class Americans, in contrast, believe in "hard individualism"—they see the world as potentially dangerous and believe that caregivers should prioritize discipline and hard work to build the child's resilient self like a fortress.[41]

Heavily influenced by Bourdieu's theories, both Lareau and Kusserow see childrearing as a microcosm for the reproduction of parents' class disposition and habitus, that is, their unconscious and embodied ways of thinking, feeling, and acting built through cumulative exposure to repetitive situations.[42] Despite the insightful analyses, their focus on the middle class and the working class largely as two homogeneous groups overlooks variations in values and behaviors among parents who are similarly socially situated.[43] The middle class, in particular, is a notoriously fragmented class group.[44] In addition, Bourdieu's theory has been criticized for failing to explore how people may break from the passivity of habitus and change the status quo.[45] The shortcoming is salient when applied to circumstances in which people confront "unfamiliar and problematic situations" or "discontinuities in structure, culture and life experience."[46]

Raising Global Families advances theoretical discussion in this field in three major ways: First, parents in this book offer a critical case to explore how the transnational flows of culture and people destabilize the existing cultural order and social conditions, pressuring them to qualify or modify their ethnic and family habitus. The vocal and articulate middle class, especially, embodies the habits of self-refashioning and reflexive thinking in a time of late modernity.[47] Yet, I found that less-educated parents, albeit in a less eloquent or linear fashion, also develop a narrative of temporal sequence between the reconstructed past (their own childhood), the perceived present (their class experience), and their children's imagined future.[48] The structure of class inequality, however, constrains their capacities to justify their childrearing preferences and to put their security strategies into effect.

Paying attention to the narratives of parenthood also allows us to examine differences *within* a social class. Diane Reay and her colleagues look into a range of choices white middle-class parents in the United Kingdom made about their children's school: some of the narratives indicated a tenacity of family habitus, but the others made counterintuitive choices to enroll their children in urban, socially diverse public schools. Their findings reveal the flexible, dynamic dimension of class identity—people may reconstruct their family habitus by making a conscious reaction to the perceived limitation of their past.[49] Along the same line, this book examines how the structural influence of social class is mediated through parents' exercise of reflexive agency, including their various narratives and perceptions of what constitutes critical opportunities and potential risks in the globalized world.

Second, *Raising Global Families* situates parenting divides in a transnational geography of social inequality. *Unequal Childhoods,* along with many of the other studies on parenting and class reproduction, suffers from the pitfall of "methodological nationalism" by accepting the nation-state as a given unit of social analysis.[50] As critics have pointed out, Bourdieu's theory generally assumes that class distinction takes place in a relatively closed social system in which the pathways for status attainment are structurally stable.[51]

By contrast, scholars of migration and transnationalism have demonstrated various ways in which wealthy parents in the global South use spatial mobility as an educational strategy to secure their children's future. Aihwa Ong calls this "flexible capital accumulation"—resourceful parents convert financial assets into the next generation's cultural capital through the cultivation of Western degrees, foreign-language skills, and familiarity with cosmopolitan lifestyles.[52] Western education helps these children gain access to the global labor market or secure class privilege once they decide to return to Asia.[53] These educational choices often involve family separation. For example, in the "geese families" from South Korea, mothers accompany children studying overseas while fathers stay behind to earn money and fly to visit the family seasonally.[54]

Even for those parents who stay in their home countries, they imagine and aspire to a globalized future for their children. An increasing number of Asian families are choosing domestic private or charter schools with Western curricula to escape the rigidness and competitiveness of local education in Asia. At the same time, alternative schools such as Waldorf and Montessori are on the rise in Asia,[55] including in China, despite rigid state regulation of education at all levels.[56] These parents mobilize educational choices and transform childrearing styles hoping that their children can acquire "transnational cultural capital" and become cosmopolitan elites or global citizens.[57]

Finally, this book explores the emotional politics of family life in a time of rapid change and uncertainty. Instead of viewing parents as interest maximizers who pursue childrearing as a calculative action of class reproduction, an emerging literature has looked into parenting as coping strategies to deal with uncertainty and insecurity on many fronts, including enlarged economic risks offloaded by government and corporations and declining stability in the private spheres of intimacy and marriages.[58] What I found most inspiring is Marianne Cooper's concept of the security project, which describes the economic and emotional work done by a family to create, maintain, and further the family's particular notion of security. Families across the class spectrum are unevenly exposed to a multitude of risk, and they cope with insecurity in distinct ways.[59] While the poorer are "downscaling" risks in their lives and "holding on" as coping strategies, the richer are "upscaling" their anxieties about family finance and children's future.

Building on Cooper's idea, I coin the concept of *global security strategies* to highlight the global contexts that situate both parents' perception of risk and their strategies for mitigating insecurities. While Cooper's analysis focuses on class inequality within a society, my concept describes a transnational geography of social inequality, involving transnational mobility and cultural negotiation as class-specific and location-sensitive strategies. I prefer "strategy" to "project" to emphasize that the strategic conducts of parenting involve not only thoughtful plans and purposive actions but also emotional struggles with conflicting responsibilities and defensive reactions to the structural constraints they encounter.[60]

In sum, *Raising Global Families* adopts a transnational framework to examine not only between-class but also within-class differences in the emotional politics of childrearing. This book demonstrates that parents' concrete class experiences, in relation to the contexts of globalization and immigration, shape their particular notions of (in)security and direct their goals and preferences in childrearing and education.

Transnational Relational Analysis

Social classes are not separate categories but are constructed in relation to each other. Bourdieu suggests the approach of relational thinking to identify *real*, though not always visible, relationships in the structured social reality.[61] He uses the concept of social field, or social space of power relations, to illustrate how differently situated people bring in a variety of dispositions and capitals into a "game," which, in this case, refers to struggle for legitimation for the goals and strategies of childrearing. Several scholars, including Beverley Skeggs, Val Gillies, and Diane Reay, have revealed the emotional politics in which people make sense of their class positions in relation to others. Working-class women, shadowed by the moral discourses of motherhood and sexuality, display feelings of frustration, helplessness, and even shame, as well as longing for recognition and respectability.[62] Similarly, children from working-class families feel overlooked and disregarded at school, feeling like "an anonymous backdrop that middle-class children can shine against."[63]

Exploring the relational nature of social class on a transnational scale, *Raising Global Families* takes the approach of what I call *transnational relational analysis* by situating the four groups of parents in a transnational geography of social inequality.[64] Regardless of whether their members ever engage in personal interaction, these groups of parents are structurally interconnected in a variety of ways.

First of all, the various groups of parents are interconnected through their uneven links to the macroprocess of globalization. Geographer Doreen Massey has used the metaphor of *power geometry* to describe people's "differentiated mobility" as a consequence of globalization:[65]

> Different social groups and different individuals are placed in very distinct ways in relation to these flows and interconnections. This point concerns not merely the issue of mobility—some move and some don't, it is also about control over this differentiated mobility. . . . Some people are more in charge of it than others; some initiate flows and movements, others don't; some are more on the receiving end of it than others; some are effectively imprisoned by it.

Raising Global Families further demonstrates that intersecting social inequalities, including class and gender, mediate the profound effects of global forces by enabling or constraining people's access to rights, resources, and mobilities. Some forms of transnational mobility and connection generate cultural capital, whereas others are considered far less productive or legitimate by those who hold power and resources.

The globalization of production and markets facilitates the hypermobility of professionals, such as engineers and financial workers, and creates a globally oriented consumer lifestyle among the "transnational middle class" in the developing world.[66] The gendered division of labor is salient in these global households: while the frequent flyers for business and work are mostly men, their wives take on most of the responsibility of raising children in line with the ideals of modern childhood and global education.

Parents on the lower spectrum of social class are trapped in the local economy, but they are not immune from the impact of global forces. Capital outflow and the inflow of migrant workers have deprived job security for the working class, especially males. Many of these men in Taiwan, Singapore, and South Korea now seek foreign brides from China and Southeast Asia, organizing a different form of global family. However, as we will see in Chapter 3, the receiving societies usually do not recognize these immigrants' transnational connections as valuable or "cosmopolitan" as Western cultural capital.

Moreover, the transnational relational analysis interrogates the emotional experiences of global parenting in a relational manner, revealing visible and invisible links between those who move and those who stay behind. Recent scholarship on migration starts to investigate both mobility and immobility and to examine how different sorts of mobilities are interconnected across different locales.[67] In communities with high exposure to transnational migration, such as the Chinese border city in Julie Chu's study, those who are trapped and immobile actually best display the "longing and belonging" about "inhabiting the world in a particular cosmopolitan and future-oriented way."[68] In this book, I view the four groups of parents as parallel instances that illustrate how the global is imagined and lived differently across socioeconomic and regional variations.

Middle-class identity, in particular, characterizes the relational nature of class relations. The middle class constantly fears "falling off the class ladder" because their status is established on the basis of educational credentials, distinct from the hand-me-down wealth of the upper class and the shortage of cultural capital among the working class.[69] The neoliberal global economy further pressures them to seek transnational references—class peers around the globe—to define the benchmark for security and to measure the aspirations for their children's future. Both the Taiwanese middle class and the immigrant middle class in the United States compare, compete, and connect with one another, and they mobilize direct and indirect interactions across borders to exchange ideas and circulate resources in childrearing.

The hypermobility of the transnational middle class may inflict the injury of class on those families who cannot afford physical or cultural mobility. The state and school function as critical nodes in the social field of power inequality, validating class-specific cultural scripts of childrearing and stigmatizing those who lack institutionally sanctioned cultural capital and transnational experiences. The newly rich Taiwanese seek membership in the global middle class by consuming childrearing and educational styles they perceive as fitting a Western ideal. Their advocacy for education and curriculum reform, however, leads to a decline of parental confidence among the working class and immigrant mothers. In the United States, middle-class immigrants zealously invest in children's education to prepare them for competition in the United States and from the rising Asia. The stereotype of the model minority widely associated with Asian Americans can nevertheless pressure or even punish working-class immigrants and their children who cannot afford similar cultivation or who do not meet a high bar of attainment.

Global Security Strategies

I use the concept of *global security strategy* to describe a multitude of class-specific and location-sensitive modes of childrearing in which parents navigate transnational mobility and negotiate cultural boundaries in response to particular insecurities they identify in local and transnational contexts. Given the scope of this multisited study, this book does not aim to provide a comprehensive view of all practices utilized by all the four groups of parents. Instead, it uses the contrasts among and within these groups to illustrate the changing circumstances and practices of childrearing in the contexts of globalization and immigration. The chapters that follow address a set of core questions for each group of parents:

First, how do parents experience class mobility in relation to the macrocontexts of globalization and immigration in different ways? What kinds of risks and insecurities do they perceive as salient in their children's future and how do they thereby define their primary goals and responsibilities in raising children?

Instead of reducing parents' orientations to given traits of class habitus, this book examines how the concrete "class process"—the lived experience of class making that is simultaneously gendered and racialized[70]—shapes parents' capacity, preference, and strategies in raising their children. For parents in shifting circumstances such as immigration and intergenerational mobility, a narrative understanding between the past, the present, and their children's future helps them to cope with contextual discontinuity by giving life events a meaningful order. The narratives of parenting illustrate parents' goals and priorities in childrearing, their views of potential risks and opportunities for their children, and their perception of difficulties and challenges during intergenerational interactions.

Second, how do parents navigate spatial and cultural mobilities to arrange education, care, and discipline for their children? How do they negotiate ethnic culture and local institutions to maintain and achieve their particular version of security?

Parents of class privilege are more able to mobilize their global connections and resources to negotiate with the local regime of education. In addition to geographical mobility, I use the term *cultural mobility* to describe the practice in which parents make use of time-space compression to consume cultural goods and services across ethnic cultural realms or spatial territories.[71] Through either physical or virtual mobility, these parents are more capable to practice what Allison Pugh calls "pathway consumption" by purchasing *social contexts*—schools, camps, and extracurricular activities—to shape their children's trajectories into the future.[72]

Parents at the lower end of the class spectrum navigate transnational mobilities as survival and security strategies; they seek marriage partners, help with childcare, or even enforcement of child discipline through time-space extension. Lacking globally recognized human capitals, lower-class immigrants often suffer from economic entrapment and downward mobility. Because their own pursuits of spatial and cultural mobility cannot easily convert into advantages for their children's class mobility, these parents similarly invest a great deal in children's education despite that their strategies of pathway consumption are worlds apart.

Finally, how does the rupture between cultural scripts and institutional structure, and the disjuncture between the global and local, create unintended consequences in family lives? Why are parents' global security projects magnifying insecurities among themselves and other groups of parents?

When people and culture are in motion, frictions and disjuncture emerge between the global and local and between the cultural and the structural. Taiwan's new cultural scripts of childrearing, with marked influence from Western experts, are in conflict with school and workplace that still favor a collective culture. Parental education in the United States, which prioritizes a cultural model of therapeutic selfhood, alienates Chinese immigrants, especially those who struggle with economic stress. While parents encounter contradictions between their newly acquired cultural repertoires and the existing institutional reality, their value commitments and childrearing behaviors often turn into "paradoxical pathways."[73] Their global securities strategies—based on transnational and cultural mobilities—may lead to unintended consequences and magnify their parenting insecurities.

The Multisited Study

To study parenting divides that involve global processes and the increasing interconnectedness of people, I conducted a multisited ethnography, a method of data collection that brings the researcher to multiple field sites geographically and socially.[74] To capture class diversity and geographic particularities, I conducted in-depth interviews with ethnic Chinese parents across the socioeconomic spectrum in Taiwan and in the Boston area. The majority of Taiwanese parents were recruited from four public elementary schools where their children attended the second grade. The immigrant parents, recruited through snowballing referrals, had at least one child who was attending elementary school at the time of the interview. All interviews were conducted in Mandarin Chinese and translated into English when quoted. In addition, I conducted observations in some household activities, children's school activities, and parental workshops. For more details on the research methods and sample characteristics, see Appendixes A and B.

I divide the families into two broadly construed socioeconomic class categories based on education and occupational status. In the "middle-class" or "professional middle-class" families, at least one parent had a four-year college or postgraduate degree and held a professional position or a job with some managerial authority in the workplace.[75] In Taiwan, I conducted in-depth interviews with 80 parents from 57 households, including 51 mothers and 28 fathers. About two-thirds of my interviewees fell into the professional middle class, including 33 mothers and 19 fathers from 36 households.

About one-third of the Taiwanese households fell into the working-class category, including 18 mothers and 9 fathers from 21 households. None of the parents in this category had a college degree. Eight mothers were immigrants from Southeast Asia and Mainland China. Using the strategy of theoretical sampling, I deliberately included more cases of immigrant mothers to explore the effect of cross-border marriages.

I purposively recruited Taiwanese parents with a multitude of educational choices. With the exception of 11 parents (from 9 households) who sent their children to private schools, the majority of Taiwanese parents sent their children to public schools. I recruited parents through four public schools with distinct parents' socioeconomic profiles (see Appendix A for details), including an alternative school in the countryside that has attracted a wave of middle-class parents who emigrated from the city to escape mainstream education. When I recruited middle-class parents through schools or personal references, most of them responded positively, indicating their willingness to participate in interviews or household observations. Many assumed that they had been invited to join the study because of their success as parents. Some were eager to share their enthusiasm for innovative methods of childrearing and alternative education.

My experience with working-class parents was strikingly different. Many refused to be interviewed. A typical initial response to our request was "Did my child do something wrong at school?" This indicated a prevalent anxiety among working-class families about being labeled as misbehaving students or unsuitable parents. All the participants received my business card and a letter that explained the purpose of the research, but some working-class parents did not seem to fully understand what "professor" and "research" entailed. For example, one mother who worked with her husband at construction sites mistook me for a graduate student. Even after we had met a few times, she still asked whether I had finished my thesis for graduation.

For the immigrant samples, I categorize their social class on the basis of their education and occupation in the United States. It is important to remember that immigrants and nonmigrants in the homeland do not constitute "comparable" cases in a strict sense.[76] Immigrants are usually a selective sample because migration requires a sufficient amount of economic capital, human capital, and personal determination. Professional immigrants are generally more elite and privileged than their counterparts in the homeland.[77] Many working-class immigrants enjoyed a middle-class status back home and experienced downward mobility in the United States; they are thus equipped with more material and symbolic resources than the working class in their home countries. In addition, children's education is a major reason immigrants decided to emigrate or stay in the United States; this explains why Chinese immigrants across the class spectrum place premium emphasis on the next generation's academic performance, as previous studies have unfolded.[78]

I chose Boston as the site of research for two primary reasons. First, the area has accommodated a bifurcated population of Chinese immigrants because of the chain migration of family reunification and growing local employment in the sectors of science and technology. Second, the case of Boston allows us to examine how immigrant families are compelled to integrate into mainstream America. Most existing studies of Chinese immigrants were conducted in immigrant gateway metropolises such as California and New York, where the schools contain a substantial Asian population. In the Boston area, the children of middle-class Chinese immigrants attend schools in majority-white suburbs. Without living in proximity to a sizable ethnic community, these families find the strategy of segmented assimilation less plausible and the attainment of both ethnic pride and class mobility more challenging.

In Boston Areas, I conducted in-depth interviews with 56 ethnic Chinese immigrant parents (40 mothers and 16 fathers) of primary-school-aged children from 48 households. To have sufficient social class variation, the US sample included immigrants from both Taiwan and China (Taiwanese immigrants are largely concentrated in professional sectors). Compared to the sample in Taiwan, the sample of immigrant parents was much more polarized in terms of socioeconomic status, and residential segregation along class lines is more salient in the United States.

The professional immigrants I interviewed came from thirty-one households (twenty from Taiwan and eleven from China). All of these families had at least one parent who had acquired a postgraduate degree, and their occupations concentrate on the fields of science, technology, and management. Most of them own single-family homes in northern suburbs in the Boston area, known for high-quality public schools.

I also interviewed working-class immigrants from seventeen families (4 from Taiwan and 13 from China); they worked in Boston mostly as restaurant workers, caretakers, and other service workers. The majority were high school graduates, except for a few who had college degrees back home. Some lived in state-subsidized rental apartments in the city, while those who were financially better off purchased more affordable housing in southern suburbs.

All the Taiwanese and Chinese immigrant parents across the class spectrum sent their children to public schools, a pattern that has been identified by previous researchers.[79] I recruited middle-class immigrants through the references of Chinese-language schools, informal social networks, and advertisements posted in online immigrant forums. As in Taiwan, middle-class parents in the Boston area were happy to participate in the research. Most people kindly offered their help to me as a co-ethnic migrant. Some parents also saw me as a source of information about American universities since I was affiliated with an Ivy League institution.

I made contacts with working-class immigrants by attending community-based programs and activities held by a nongovernmental organization in Chinatown. I also made requests for interviews when I used services in ethnic business. It was harder to study working-class immigrants because they tended to work long hours and were unfamiliar with the research. Yet I also represented a possible source of access to social capital from the co-ethnic middle class. Thus, one working-class father addressed me respectfully as Professor Lan and used the interview as a precious opportunity to receive expert opinions on childrearing in the United States. He asked me for a reading list and even requested a copy of my interview questions. "So I can check if there is something that I've failed to do," he said earnestly.

Mapping the Book

The book is composed of five chapters. Following this introduction, Chapter 1 overviews the transpacific movement of ideas and resources that facilitated the spatial and cultural mobilities of Taiwanese and immigrant parents across historical periods. Transnationalism from both above and below alters the family lives of those who move overseas and of those who stay in the country of origin. The changes in the repertoires of childrearing, however, reach parents unevenly across the class spectrum.

Chapters 2 and 3 describe the growing divergence in parenting styles between middle-class and working-class parents in Taiwan. Taiwan's participation in globalized production has offered the professional middle class a ticket to intergenerational mobility in their lifetimes and opportunities to transnational mobility and career. By contrast, the working class, especially men, encounter stagnant mobility in the globalized economy; many seek foreign wives to escape their disadvantaged status in the local marriage market.

Chapter 2 describes the global security strategies of middle-class parents. To safeguard their children's happiness and creativeness, these privileged parents mobilize their economic and cultural capital to exit the local education system or to advocate for reform. Some seek transnational mobility to help their children to get ahead in the arms race of global education. Others turn to alternative and home education under Western influence to orchestrate their children's "natural growth."

Chapter 3 turns to the security strategies of working-class parents, who emphasize discipline and hard work to avoid the risks of children's going stray or stagnant mobility. With the new middle-class ideals of parental competency promoted by Taiwan's government and school, working-class parents, including immigrant mothers, suffer from a decline in parental legitimacy. Some parents reinforce harsh discipline to claim legitimacy while the others outsource education to improve their children's opportunities for class mobility.

Chapters 4 and 5 explore how immigrant parents across the class spectrum negotiate cultural differences and manage insecurities in the new country. People in Taiwan and China generally view US immigration as a pathway to social mobility, but many immigrants experience otherwise once they cross the borders. Those who lack English skills, local ties, and US-recognized degrees usually suffer from some degree of downward mobility. Even well-educated professionals may encounter racial discrimination and blocked mobility at American workplaces.

Chapter 4 describes the parenting styles of highly educated immigrants who widely experience a decline of cultural confidence. Their security strategies center on how to protect or achieve a sense of confidence among second-generation youth in a context of racial inequality. Some parents arrange "Americanized" extracurricular activities to orchestrate children's competitive assimilation, while others mobilize their homeland culture and transnational educational resources to cultivate ethnic cultural capital for the second generation.

Chapter 5 turns to working-class Chinese immigrants, whose narratives of parenting insecurity center on a decline in their parental authority, especially because corporal punishment is not recognized as a legitimate tool of child discipline in many parts of the United States. Some try to project an "American" outlook on their family lives by either interpreting the reversed dynamics of parent-child relations as an indicator of cultural assimilation or attending parenting seminars to learn about American knowledge and techniques of childrearing. The others seek resources from immigrant communities or transnational kin networks to sustain the ethnic practices of education, care, and discipline.

The conclusion compares the global security strategies among Taiwanese and immigrant parents across the class spectrum and identifies visible and invisible social connections between these four groups of parents. I end by discussing the theoretical and practical lessons we can learn from this research: why and how the global security strategies of childrearing unwittingly magnify parental insecurities and class injustice.

1 Transpacific Flows of Ideas and People

THE PACIFIC OCEAN HAS LONG been a vital conduit for flows of ideas, goods, and people. Waves of Chinese laborers began arriving in the United States during the 1840s gold rush, and the immigration reforms of 1965 expanded the population of Asian Americans. Taiwanese and Chinese migrant paths have never been limited to a single direction; instead, they involve reciprocal processes and circular movements across the Pacific, which not only bring renewed resources to boost industrialization in their countries of origin but also alter social structure and cultural practices back home, including the transformation of parenting repertoires.

The concept of transnationalism encompasses a variety of global forces, including international connections from above, such as foreign aid and investment, and transnational links from below, through travel, migration, cultural exchanges, and kinship networks.[1] This chapter lays out historical and geographical contexts for the later chapters by looking into transpacific flows of ideas and people in the following four sections: the geopolitical and immigration links between Taiwan and the US after World War II, Taiwan's changing scripts of parenting and transnational cultural circuits since the 1990s, immigration from postreform China to Taiwan and the US, and finally the current global economy and the increase of "return" migration among the second generation.

US-Taiwan Links: Geopolitics and Immigration

A vast majority of Taiwanese are the descendants of migrants from South China over the past four hundred years. Taiwan was a Japanese colony for half a century (1895–1945) and came under the rule of the Republic of China (ROC) after World War II. In 1949, the Chinese nationalist party Kuomintang (KMT) retreated to Taiwan after losing the civil war to the Communist Party of China. Chiang Kai-Shek brought in more than a million exiles from Mainland China with initial hopes of returning to the homeland soon. Taiwan's strategic location—less than one hundred miles east of China's southern coast—made it indispensable to American interest during the Cold War. The US wished to ensure Taiwan's social stability and economic prosperity and recognized the ROC as the only "free China" until 1979, when the US established diplomatic relations with the People's Republic of China (PRC).

Between 1951 and 1964, the US government offered Taiwan economic assistance totaling 1.5 billion USD. The aid covered a wide range of instruments and policies under the command of the Sino-American Joint Commission on Rural Reconstruction (JCRR). Although US aid to Taiwan officially ended in 1965, various forms of financial assistance from US state agencies and private foundations, including an organized campaign of family planning, continued to have a powerful impact on the nation's development and modernization. These transnational activities and connections "from above" paved the way for Taiwanese immigrants in the later decades to pursue opportunities for economic advancement, political security, and children's education in the United States.

Transnationalism from Above: US Aid and Family Planning

Taiwan of the 1950s was shadowed by nationalist sentiment and propaganda. Children were viewed as productive laborers for their families and future warriors for the nation. For example, a 1952 Taiwanese magazine article celebrating Children's Day described the meaning of the holiday as "cultivating young citizens with a sound mind and body to build a prosperous nation."[2] The magazine published pictures of child laborers shining shoes and pulling a rickshaw as role models, because children had to be "directed toward serious, disciplinary real life" and "trained for obedience and proper life habits."[3]

Taiwan's then-high fertility rate indicated a rich source of human power for KMT troops. However, US policymakers and demographers were concerned about the geopolitical impact of overpopulation in Asia, which threatened to breed communism through stagnant development.[4] In 1954, the US pressured Taiwan to become a "demographic laboratory" through the implementation of family planning programs.[5] Yet the campaign of birth control initially stirred local controversy and political resistance—if the KMT approved the

US's Malthusian diagnosis of overpopulation, the implication would be that the KMT rule was valid only within the territory of Taiwan and that the political claim to retake Mainland China was futile. Therefore, JCRR tactfully masked the promotion of birth control methods as part of "housewife sanitary education" and "pre-pregnancy health programs."[6]

Taking an incremental approach, JCRR established the legitimacy of family planning policy by producing large-scale fertility studies and disseminating scientific knowledge connected with the "soft power" of US experts and institutions.[7] The campaign reached success within a short period. Women's national fertility rate dropped from 5.6 in 1960 to 4 in 1970 and 2.5 in 1980.[8] The rapid change of fertility behavior in Taiwan was not simply a natural result of industrialization or an endogenous process of social change; rather, it was the consequence of geopolitical and cultural interventions.

The birth-control program was accompanied by a family education campaign that defined the "modern family" as having fewer children and ample parental love. Starting since 1951, the US Information Service (USIS) in Taiwan published the magazine *Harvest* to circulate news and knowledge among the rural populace. Because many Taiwanese farmers were more literate in Japanese than in Chinese, the USIS insisted on publishing *Harvest* as a bilingual magazine despite the KMT's rule that no books or newspapers could be published in Japanese after 1946 as a measure of decolonization.[9] *Harvest* produced a flood of articles about the shortcomings of big families with titles like "A Big Family Is Not a Good Fortune" and "Too Many Children, Too Much Pain." Parents were urged to offer their children quality care and advanced education, and they were advised that these investments were affordable only to families with two or three children.

In the 1950s, among a thousand newborns in Taiwan, about forty babies would die before reaching one year of age.[10] International public health experts attributed the high infant mortality to not only poor sanitation and widespread contagious diseases but also oversized families and outdated child-drearing styles. *Harvest* provided medical information about children's health, such as the necessity of vaccinations, and advocated against folk treatments and superstition (e.g., that children with measles can neither eat noodles nor have haircuts). Several articles introduced ideas about modern methods of childcare regarding household sanitation, children's sleeping habits, and home security; tips were offered for the purchase of children's toys, books, shoes, clothes, and food.

With the implementation of birth control and family education, the KMT political elites collaborated with US officials to practice their own political agenda and cultural mission. The KMT regime relied on the US aid to establish ruling legitimacy vis-à-vis Communist China through economic and social stability as well as moral and cultural hegemony in all areas, including the private sphere of family life. In 1953, under the advisement of US experts, the National Normal University established Taiwan's first department of home economics to promote the scientific management of domesticity. In 1959, Taiwan's provincial government started the annual tradition of electing and celebrating a "model happy family." This politically loaded celebration of family value took place just as the Chinese Communist Party was experimenting with the Cultural Revolution.[11]

Moreover, the KMT technocrats involved in JCRR and family planning were familiar with American culture and Western ideology through their personal connections. For example, Chiang Monlin, JCRR's director from 1948 to 1964, had received a PhD in education from Columbia University in 1917 under the advisement of John Dewey. Chiang described the duty of JCRR as "applying Western democratic thoughts to China."[12] Job interviews for JCRR officers were conducted in English and most of the recruits had graduate degrees from US universities.[13] The US aid also provided fellowships for higher education in the US to reproduce an increasing number of US-trained Taiwanese elites.[14] These political elites served as "agents of modernity" by appropriating and domesticating American cultural repertoire in Taiwan.[15]

While the few local elites enjoyed the privileged access to overseas studies and served as the agents of US aid, those at the bottom of the Taiwanese society became targeted groups for the inculcation of modern lifestyle. For example, the birth-control campaign specifically targeted rural women and the less educated.[16] The president of National Taiwan University Hospital commented on this matter: "People with lower education, mostly trapped in poverty, see reproduction as something natural and give birth to a dozen without thinking, and they also suffer from poor sanitary conditions and want to have more children as insurance."[17]

The Bureau of Health specified in its work plan that at least half of home visits by public health workers and nurses must take place in remote areas.[18] They organized small-group meetings in rural communities to teach personal hygiene and household sanitation and to advocate birth control and good parenting.[19] In sum, the US aid programs, which coincided with the KMT regime's interest in sustaining its ruling legitimacy, gradually established the norm of an ideal family featured by low fertility and modern parenting. This early phase of global parenting already indicated the power geometry of globalization, where the modernity project of birth control, as a measure of transnationalism from above, aimed at the lower strata of Taiwanese society.

Exodus of Taiwanese Immigration to the US

Migration paths across the Pacific were blocked for more than half a century after the Chinese Exclusion Act of 1882. American attitudes and immigration policies toward the Chinese began to soften after World War II, when the ROC (Taiwan) became an ally of the US. The Chinese Exclusion Act was repealed in 1943, but Chinese immigration remained limited under a quota system. The Immigration and Nationality Act in 1965 opened a wider gate to Asian immigration to the US, giving preference to immigrants with scientific and technical skills in order to compete with the Soviets during the Cold War. The law also allowed naturalized citizens and permanent residents to sponsor extended family members for immigration.

The post-1965 immigrants included a "hyperselective" group with much higher educational attainment than the average nonimmigrant American as well as the average citizen of their countries of origin.[20] Before the normalization of China-US relations in 1979, immigrants from Taiwan fulfilled most of the immigration quotas for China. Taiwan's political, economic, and cultural dependence on the US after World War II—including US aid, the influx of US investment in Taiwan's export-oriented economy, and the infusion of Taiwanese education systems with "the US modes of thoughts and patterns of actions"— predisposed the growing Taiwanese middle class to emigrate to the US.[21]

Taiwan's martial law lasted from 1949 to 1987, and travel outside the country was under state restriction until 1979. Yet throughout this period, an increasing number of students received scholarships from either the Taiwanese government or American universities to pursue graduate education in the US. A popular 1970s slogan, "Come, come, come to NTU, go, go, go to USA," described a common pathway for elite students who attended National Taiwan University (NTU), the highest-ranked university in the country, and later immigrated to the US. Over the period 1971–1985, a total of 62,430 Taiwanese students went to the US for graduate education; only 18 percent of these students returned to Taiwan.[22] In contrast to limited professional jobs in Taiwan's still developing economy, the US attracted them with more economic opportunities and a better quality of life.[23]

Taiwan's uncertain sovereign status was another push factor for emigration. When Taiwan (ROC) lost its seat at the United Nations in 1971, many citizens waited in line overnight outside the American Institute in Taiwan to obtain a visa application.[24] The same phenomenon occurred again in 1979 after the normalization of US-China relations. In 1982, the US passed the Taiwan Relations Act, which established an immigration quota of about twenty thousand per year for Taiwan, separate from China.[25] Taiwanese immigration to the US reached its peak between 1977 and 1990, with an average over ten thousand immigrants per year.[26] The fear of political instability increased emigration from Taiwan again in the late 1990s, when China threatened to attack Taiwan's democracy and silence the advocates for independence.

Highly skilled Taiwanese immigrants to the US concentrated in the fields of science and technology. From 1985 to 2000, 18,508 people from Taiwan received a doctorate in the US; more than 80 percent of these PhDs were in science and engineering.[27] Between 1988 and 1990, Taiwan produced more math and computer scientists than any other Asian country and was second in the number of immigrant engineers and natural scientists to the US.[28] The number of Taiwanese overseas students in the US hit a record high in the early 1990s.[29] Between 1990 and 2000, approximately 121,504 Taiwanese immigrants were admitted to the US; more than 60 percent of them worked in managerial and professional occupations.[30]

Taiwan's economic growth slowed down the outflows of economic migrants, but many continued to go abroad to find better educational opportunities for their children. Most of the Chinese "parachute kids" in the US during the 1980s and 1990s came from Taiwan; they migrated alone to attend elementary, middle, or high schools while residing with extended relatives or in rented homestay.[31] In other transnational families, the mother and children migrated while the "astronaut father" would fly back and forth to work or to manage a business in Taiwan.

Education in Taiwan was rigid and competitive, with national examinations at both the high school and the college level. By contrast, the US offered an abundance of colleges and widened opportunities for children who might not be eligible for a strong university education in Taiwan. Wealthy Taiwanese parents also seek educational migration for their children to realize the American dream. Maria Chee nicely summarized myriad motives in her study of Taiwanese transnational mothers in California:[32]

> Parents migrated to prepare a child for higher occupation and status than was possible in Taiwan given the child's scholastic aptitude and inclination, to free a child from rigid education, to give a foundering child a second chance, to broaden their worldview for a global era, or so they claimed. All of these goals shared one feature, one hope: that their children may move up or at least reproduce their parents' social economic positions in society.

Global Childrearing in Taiwan

Taiwan's high-tech industry boom of the 1990s halted the "brain drain" of professional emigration and induced a pattern of return migration. These return migrants established transnational social networks and cultural circuits that contributed to the globalized discourses of childrearing in Taiwan. After the termination of martial law in 1987, nongovernmental organizations mushroomed with the newly granted freedom of assembly and association. Social elites and highly educated parents introduced novel ideas about childrearing and advocated for education reform. While state-sponsored institutions gradually adopted and expanded parenting education, socioeconomically disadvantaged parents have been exposed to increasing state monitoring.

Transnationalism from Below: "Bigration"

To facilitate Taiwan's industrial upgrading in the 1990s, the government actively encouraged immigrants and overseas graduates to return by providing them with travel subsidies, job placements, and business investment assistance.[33] Some highly skilled immigrants decided to return home after having reached a glass ceiling for promotion or entrepreneurship in the US.[34] An increasing number of overseas Taiwanese students also returned upon graduation to capitalize on Taiwan's economic growth. The downturn in the US information technology industry in the early 2000s caused job losses among Taiwanese professional migrants. Even "millionaire migrants" who entered via investor visas were inclined to return because of a lack of business opportunities and social networks in North America.[35]

The new pattern of "brain circulation" was facilitated by the transnational social networks of high-tech elites. The Hsinchu Science-Based Industrial Park, which was established in 1980 and modeled after Silicon Valley, provided subsidized single-family housing and bilingual schools to help returned families transplant their American lifestyle to Taiwan. The community of US-trained Taiwanese professionals promoted reciprocal industrial upgrading in both Hsinchu and Silicon Valley through transnational flows of capital, skills, and knowledge.[36]

Shenglin Chang describes the transnational lives of these returned migrants as "two-way bigration."[37] They keep strong social ties across the Pacific thanks to reduced transportation costs and advanced communicative technology. Some Taiwanese engineers fly back and forth to sustain joint venture partnerships in both Taiwan and Silicon Valley. Some wives and children continue to live in the US while maintaining another home in Taiwan. These families live a "go-between" lifestyle, where wives mix and match cultural elements and material items from the two homelands.

The return of highly skilled immigrants and students to Taiwan established cross-border cultural and social networks. These social elites became "agents of modernity" in a wave of transnationalism from below. Unlike the earlier modernity project that was carried out by political elites in a top-down manner, this round of transnational project toward global childrearing was bottom-up in nature and mediated by civil society elites.

Modern Parenting and Education Reform

The Human Education Foundation (HEF), established in 1989, was the leading organization of education reform in Taiwan. HEF advocates, mostly college professors and intellectuals with substantial overseas experience, criticized rote learning and authoritarian school culture as outdated practices in line with "feudal" Chinese traditions. Instead, they promoted "humanist education" against the use of corporal punishment in classroom. They also worked closely with parents' associations, mostly in urban areas, to advocate for parents' rights to participate in school.

Corporal punishment from teachers and parents used to be a legitimate means of child discipline in Taiwan. A Chinese idiom similar to "spare the rod and spoil the child" describes physical discipline as an essential way to form children's moral character. In the post–martial law era, public discourses started to focus on children's rights under the protection of national laws and international treaties. Children were increasingly viewed as "subjects" or autonomous individuals instead of "objects" or productive laborers for their families and the nation.[38] The Western paradigm of developmental psychology, with growing popularity in Taiwan, cautioned parents about permanent damage that harsh discipline could impose on children. One HEF poster advertised the slogan "Give up your stick and use your brain" next to an image of a crying child. Physical punishment was no longer associated with "strict parents" but with "lazy parents" unwilling to learn new methods of childrearing.

HEF reformers criticized parents at polar ends of the class spectrum as either irresponsible or incapable. They blamed elite parents for pressuring their children to treat education as a competition. Working-class parents with limited time at home were criticized for their failure to acquire new parenting skills. To address these problems, HEF offered parenting education, including evening courses in the city and workshops in less urban areas, to instruct parents on how to become "modern parents" who attend to their children's needs and express love.[39]

The HEP reformers turned to the child-centered paradigm of permissive, liberal parenting, which has dominated American childrearing since the 1930s,[40] as an alternative cultural model. It views parents' physical company and emotional attendance to child's needs and desires as a critical means to the child's cognitive and emotional development. The ideals of the parent-child relationship are marked by the rhetoric of cooperation, equality, and trust instead of authority, obedience, and discipline.

The broader political and social contexts partly explained why education reformers in Taiwan were inclined toward a more permissive style of childrearing. Joining the vibrant civic advocacy to expand democracy in Taiwan, the reformers promoted students' rights and freedoms in school. They advocated progressive education as a form of political resistance against KMT political censorship and ideological control. This backdrop also channeled their preference for deregulation and free-market principles as a means to achieve a humanistic education.[41]

A critical event on April 10, 1994 demonstrated the strength of civil activism and pushed the state to enact an official campaign of education reform. In alliance with 219 social organizations, HEF led a crowd of more than thirty thousand Taiwanese marching on the streets of Taipei and angrily shouting slogans like "We want happy childhood!" Shortly afterward, the government held a National Educational Congress meeting in June and appointed the Educational Reform Deliberation Committee in September. The committee was chaired by the Nobel laureate (in chemistry) Yuan-Tseh Lee, who had returned to Taiwan after working in US academia for thirty years.

Absorbing many reformist ideas, the government made tremendous changes in the educational system over the years, including the deregulation of textbooks, the prohibition of corporal punishment at schools, and, most important, the expansion of higher education to alleviate academic pressure. Parents won the legal entitlement to participate in school committees. They also gained some autonomy over school choice or the choice to educate children at home, as the parliament gradually lifted legal barriers to experimental education and homeschooling.[42]

Meanwhile, an increasing volume of parenting guides and magazines introduces innovative and mostly imported ideas about childrearing.[43] From the sales records of Taiwan's largest online bookstore, Book Your Life, I compiled the best-selling books on parenting during the five-year period of 2006–2011. Among the ninety-two best sellers, only sixteen books focus on more traditional ways of Asian parenting, such as how-to guides on cultivating children's learning ability or academic performance; some are parents' testimonies to their children's success from authors like Bill Gates's father, a Korean mother whose son became a global elite, and a Taiwanese mother who helped her daughter gain admission to Ivy League universities.

The other best sellers demonstrate the new cultural trends under the influence of global experts. Twenty-five books focus on the parent-child relationship, emphasizing parents' communication skills—how to encourage, compliment, and reason with children—and cross-generational bonds through activities like story reading and cooking together. Another twenty books explore the topic of character building, highlighting children's autonomy, independence, and nonacademic exploration.

This book list displays high aspiration for scientific parenting and cosmopolitanism. Over a quarter of the best sellers are authored by experts like doctors, teachers, scientists, and professors. One-third of the books were translated from English or Japanese, and eleven books were written by Taiwanese authors who either lived abroad or introduced overseas childrearing ideas and educational systems to Taiwan. A book series on global childrearing won market success in 2012, with titles like *German Mothers Teach Discipline*, *American Mothers Teach Confidence*, *Japanese Mothers Teach Responsibility*, and *Jewish Mothers Teach Thinking*.

The new cultural scripts of childrearing, marked with the influence of Western child psychology, advise parents to perform an increasing amount of emotional work.[44] Emotional intimacy expressed through verbal and physical communication is not stressed in traditional Chinese parent-child relationships. However, many of the younger generation of Taiwanese mothers purposively use words and actions (e.g., hugging and kissing) to express affection for their children.[45] These types of oral expression and body language are not habits inherited from the previous generation but rather are newly acquired skills of "modern" parenting. Some parents tell their children "I love you" in Chinese, but even more say the phrase in English because it sounds more "natural," revealing how this kind of intimate interaction is not inherent in local culture but rather more closely associated with Western culture and practice.

In sum, the new repertoire of childrearing defines parental competency as involving emotional sensitivity, expressive communication, educational involvement, and international exposure. Yet the new script of global childrearing and the expansion of parents' rights to choose children's schools have empowered only select groups of parents. As we will see in Chapter 2, the families who benefit most from the deregulation of education are those who can afford to send their children to private or alternative schools in Taiwan, followed by universities overseas. While school curricula and national policies increasingly treat intensive parenting and child-centered family life as the norm, working-class parents with limited exposure to global culture or new pedagogies face intensified institutional pressure.

State Monitoring of "High-Risk Families"

Parenting education began in grassroots campaigns by civil organizations but was gradually adopted by state-sponsored institutions. In 2003, Taiwan promulgated the Family Education Act with the aim of "promoting family values, increasing knowledge and skills of family life, improving mental and physical health, building happy families, and creating a peaceful society."[46] The law established family education centers in over twenty cities and counties throughout Taiwan. Today, soon-to-be-married couples are encouraged to participate voluntarily in at least four hours of family education from their local government.

The Family Education Act was originally enacted to stabilize marital relations and lower the divorce rate,[47] but implementation gradually shifted focus to cross-generational relations. Section 102 of the Protection of Children and Youth Welfare and Rights Act mandates that parents or guardians who abuse or neglect children must receive between four and fifty hours of parental education.[48] In 2008, Legislator Chou Sho-shun proposed an amendment to the Family Education Act that would make parental education mandatory for parents whose children seriously misbehave at school.[49] The proposed monetary penalty won support from the teachers' association but received severe criticism from parents' groups.[50] Instead of imposing a fine, in 2011 the Taiwanese legislature gave family education centers the power to make home visits if parents receive three notices of absence from mandatory parental education.

The Ministry of Education proudly presented the Family Education Act as an ideal mix of the global and the local. It was allegedly based on extensive research into related policies and laws in "Germany, the UK, the US, Japan, Hong Kong, China and other foreign countries" in combination with "our traditional culture and family values."[51] Notably, the state project of parental education does not endorse the paradigm of permissive, liberal parenting that has dominated the transnational-middle-class-infused HEF discourse. Instead, the state project privileges a "warm and authoritative" model, which emphasizes responsiveness and a clear boundary between parents and children.[52] The programs also include filial education, designed to strengthen children's respect for parents and grandparents.

Meanwhile, the instability and dysfunction of family life are exposed to greater regulation by public authorities. The phenomenon of "latchkey children" was fairly common until Taiwan's government outlawed the practice in 1993.[53] Leaving children alone at home, especially those younger than six, is now seen as an act of neglect. Although corporal punishment is still lawful in the home,[54] punitive acts inflicting physical injury on children would be considered by the authority as maltreatment or child abuse. The reported cases for suspected incidences of child abuse increased three times from 2006 to 2016, although many cases turned out to be unfounded.[55]

In the early 2000s, a few high-profile cases of child abuse attracted widespread media attention. The nation was also shocked by incidences of entire families tragically lost to murder-suicide committed by impoverished parents. The Ministry of the Interior responded by expanding "preventive" care for vulnerable children and families, instituting the Special Care and Counseling for High-Risk Families program in 2005. A wide range of agents, including social workers, schoolteachers, daycare staff, police, medical personnel, immigration officers, borough chiefs, and even community security guards are mandated to report to the local government if they observe children in possible high-risk environments.

The so-called high-risk families exposed to this mandated reporting are defined as "those families who encounter economic, parenting, marital, and medical problems and thus fail to offer adequate care for children and adolescence."[56] The working guidelines offer a list of risk indicators that fall into three categories: First, unstable or atypical family relations, including single-parent households and grandparent-headed families; second, families that lack adequate or functional caretakers, such as families where the parents suffer from addiction or other psychiatric illnesses; third, families impoverished by parents' unemployment, illness, incarceration, or other causes. Social workers and NGOs find that these indicators are vaguely defined and difficult to identify, leading to misreporting and misapplication in practice.[57] As Chapter 3 shows, parents of lower socioeconomic status and of immigrant backgrounds are exposed to increased monitoring by the state.

The PRC Connections to Taiwan and the US

Emigration from Communist China was strictly prohibited until the economic opening in 1979. The exodus of Chinese immigrants took off to multiple destinations, including a bifurcated stream to the US. The newly rich Chinese pursue transnational mobility for their families and especially a global education for their children. Even the less privileged are equipped with increased assets to partake a journey of immigration even if without legal documents.

Meanwhile, after decades of separation during the Cold War, Taiwan (ROC) and China (PRC) resumed exchanges in the 1980s, leading to class-specific and gendered streams of migration across the Taiwan Strait. A tidal wave of capital-linked migration consists of small business owners and professionals, mostly men, working for Taiwanese firms with operation in China.[58] Cross-border marriages composed of Chinese women and Taiwanese men, mostly the working class, have also grown rapidly in Taiwan during the past two decades. Both types of global households create conundrums for marriage and childrearing.

Capital-Linked and Marital Migration Across the Taiwan Strait

It is estimated that about 1.5 million Taiwanese citizens frequently travel across the Taiwan Strait and maintain simultaneous connections in both societies.[59] The number is significant for a country with a population of 23.5 million. According to the 2010 Taiwan Social Change Survey conducted on a random household sample, about 7 percent of the respondents had spouses, parents, children, or siblings currently working in China.[60] Taiwanese investors use their linguistic and cultural ties to play a mediate role in the global production chains connecting Western buyers and cheap labor in China. Taiwanese professionals also capitalize on their "exceptional membership" to pursue flexible mobility in China,[61] where Taiwanese enjoy some entitlements that ordinary foreigners are not eligible for, especially rights of residency and employment.[62]

The majority of Taiwanese entrepreneurs and professionals working in China are married men; most of their families reside in Taiwan for reasons such as children's education, spouse's jobs, lifestyle preferences, or the need to care for aging parents.[63] The popular magazine *CommonWealth* estimates that the current number of such split or "left-behind families" could be as high as 1 million.[64] According to the research of Hsiu-Hua Shen, these couples' extended time apart reinforces the conventional gendered roles—while Taiwanese husbands who relocated to China are better able to fulfill the male role of financial supporters, Taiwanese wives who stay behind take responsibility for the daily care of children and family elders.[65]

Meanwhile, Taiwan has become a receiving country for labor and marriage migration from Southeast Asia since the early 1990s. Immigration from Mainland China, including workers and students, is nevertheless subject to tight control and exceptional regulation.[66] Despite their linguistic and cultural affinity with Taiwanese, Mainland Chinese are stigmatized by their association with poverty or backwardness and distrusted because of political tension across the Taiwan Strait. Shu-mei Shih calls this paradox "the threat of similarity": Taiwan's migration regime excludes Chinese because Mainland Chinese lack "the *difference* necessary to maintain and police the boundaries of national identity."[67]

Marriage migration is the only path for Chinese nationals to gain permanent residency and citizenship in Taiwan. Over the past two decades, about half a million of immigrant women entered Taiwan through marriage, including more than three hundred thousand from Mainland China.[68] Compared to declining marriage rates among Taiwanese citizens, cross-border marriages increased over the 1990s and peaked in the early 2000s. The number of "Chinese brides" outnumbered their Southeast Asian counterparts after the discriminatory regulation against Chinese spouses was lifted in 2008. Each year some twelve thousand to fourteen thousand cross-Strait couples register their marriages in Taiwan, constituting on average 9 percent of all marriages.[69] Many of these Taiwanese husbands are undesirable partners in the local marriage market—elderly veterans, divorcees, the disabled or working-class men, but there are also middle-class men who met their Chinese wives through trade or tourism in China and work or study in a third country.

Chinese spouses are subject to more stringent regulation compared to marriage migrants from elsewhere. Taiwan's Immigration Law stipulates that foreign spouses receive residency upon the first arrival and become eligible for naturalization after four years of residency in Taiwan. Chinese spouses, in contrast, obtained residency after two years of marriage and waited twice as long for citizenship. The policy reform in 2008 lifted the quota control and shortened the residency required for naturalization to six years for Chinese spouses. Prior to this change, a Chinese wife could expedite the process only by becoming pregnant and skipping the two-year probation. Childbirth enabled Chinese spouses to assert marital authenticity in the eyes of the state and thus to gain preferential treatments that helped them to acquire residency or citizenship sooner. In other words, migrant women are perceived as worthy citizens and loyal members only after they become mothers of Taiwanese nationals.[70]

The growth of cross-border marriages stirs social anxieties in a time of low fertility and intensive parenting. Taiwan's media coined the term "New Taiwanese children" to describe these mixed children of cross-border marriages. In 2003, the birth rate for children of immigrant mothers reached its peak of thirteen for every hundred newborn Taiwanese babies.[71] In the 2013–2014 academic year, nearly 10 percent (or about 210,000) of all students enrolled in primary and secondary school were born to an immigrant mother (40 percent of these had mothers from Vietnam, 37 percent from China, and 12 percent from Indonesia). This proportion is significant partly because the number of children born to a Taiwanese mothers continues to decline.[72] Chapter 3 examines how immigrant mothers from China struggle to be good parents when economic, social, and cultural marginalization truncates their capacity to raise children in Taiwan.

Bifurcated Chinese Immigration to the US

The inflows of Taiwanese and Chinese immigration to the US have diverged in recent years: Taiwanese immigration has slowed down since the 1990s while immigration from China is on the rise. The demographic profiles of these two immigrant groups are also different. According to the 2010 US Census, documented immigrants from both Taiwan and China had higher household incomes and educational attainment than the US national population. Taiwanese immigrants mostly belonged to the professional middle class with a median household income close to 80,000 USD and over 70 percent were homeowners. Almost 70 percent of Taiwanese immigrants held a bachelor's degree or above, and nearly 40 percent had a graduate or professional degree. Over 85 percent of the population worked as professionals or office employees; the poverty rate was slightly above 7 percent.

Immigrants born in China were more heterogeneous with respect to educational attainment and socioeconomic status. Although over 40 percent received graduate or postgraduate education, a quarter did not finish high school. Nearly half of Chinese immigrants were employed in professional occupations, but a quarter were service workers. Their median household income was close to 52,000 USD and more than half were homeowners; still, a sizable proportion of Chinese immigrants lived in poverty (12.2 percent) (see Appendix C for details).

After China and the US resumed normal relations in 1979, Chinese students began traveling to the US to study. The number has continued to rise since the 1990s. During the 2014–2015 academic year alone, more than 304,000 Chinese international students attended American universities.[73] Even the volume of Chinese teenagers studying in the US has risen dramatically.[74] The most common channel for Chinese students to adjust their immigration status is the H-1B visa program created by the 1990 Immigration Act. In the decade that followed, the US economy recovered from a recession and entered a period of prosperity. The fast-growing IT industry, in particular, welcomed foreigners to meet its need for highly skilled professionals.[75]

Investment immigration from China to North America also rapidly expanded during this period. To stimulate the local economy with an infusion of foreign capital, the US government introduced investor immigration in the Immigration Act of 1990.[76] The EB-5 investor visa program is particularly attractive to people from newly industrialized Asian countries such as Taiwan, Hong Kong, South Korea, and recently, China. Newly rich Chinese pursue immigration for multiple reasons: to protect their assets, to improve life quality, and to seek a better future for their children.

In addition to the wealthy and highly educated, a substantial population of working-class Chinese emigrated to the US through family reunification and asylum seeking. As of 2014, over half of Chinese immigrants who obtained permanent residency in the US were sponsored by family members or immediate relatives, and 16 percent were refugees or asylees; by contrast, 30 percent of permanent residents achieved their status as employment-sponsored immigrants.[77] A significant proportion of working-class Chinese immigrants have no legal status in the US; the number was estimated to be at least 325,000 in

2014.[78] Some eventually gain legal status by seeking asylum, with the one-child policy and Falun Gong membership as the two most popular claims.[79] This book focuses on documented immigrants only.

Less-educated Chinese immigrants are often employed in ethnic enclave economy, doing manual labor like construction, domestic work, and restaurant staff. It is estimated that a quarter of the Chinese population in the US works in the fifty thousand Chinese restaurants throughout the country.[80] Many Chinese immigrants struggle to enter the mainstream job market because of language barriers and a refusal to recognize their degrees or qualifications from China. Many rely on personal networks or coethnic agencies that advertise exclusively in Chinese and require minimum training or English proficiency.[81] These employers depend on the "Chinese work ethic" to support their businesses because immigrant workers are willing to endure long hours with poor pay, little protection, and substandard conditions.[82]

The class bifurcation of Chinese immigration leads to the divergence of intergenerational relations. In her study conducted in New York City in the late 1990s, Vivian Louie divided her respondents into "uptown Chinese Americans" growing up in suburban America and "downtown Chinese Americans" from urban ethnic enclaves. The middle-class youth were expected by their immigrant parents to assimilate into the (white) mainstream even at the cost of diluting ethnicity and losing Chinese literacy. Working-class children, in contrast, often had to work in ethnic family business but felt a profound sense of disconnection from their parents' world.[83] Chapters 4 and 5 in this book extend the discussion and examine the class-specific practices of immigrant parenting facing new challenges in the current global economy.

New Challenges, New Directions

The twenty-first-century global economy carves new directions for transpacific flows of people and ideas. A growing number of second-generation Chinese Americans are moving to the booming Asian markets, especially the economic superpower of China, while the American economy has suffered from stagnant growth and depressing employment after the financial crisis of 2008. Western educators and parents also started to look into potential merits of Asian education. The new landscape of global power shifts stirs anxiety among Chinese immigrant parents in the US, especially those who live in predominantly white neighborhoods like in the case of Boston.

What If "White Is Just Alright"?

For many among the older generations of ethnic Chinese immigrants to the US, the assimilation of the second generation meant emulation of white middle-class America in terms of language, manner, and lifestyle. In the 1980s, many Taiwanese immigrants living in white suburbs deliberately discouraged their children from speaking Chinese to avoid an accent in English. In a newsletter published by the Lexington Chinese-language school, an immigrant father recalled that an older-generation Taiwanese immigrant once instructed him: "Learning Chinese is not that important. The next generation has to become Americans after all."

Yet the experiences of non-European immigrant families prove that Americanization is neither a linear nor a racially blind process. Asian Americans confront an assumption of "forever foreignness," where they are seen as somehow more Asian than American.[84] Their ethnic identity is not a voluntary option as it is for white ethnics,[85] but it is imposed by virtue of their physical appearance through a structural process of racialization. "Selective acculturation" offers a segmented path of assimilation for immigrant youths, who can achieve both social mobility and cultural preservation by making close ties with the immigrant community.[86]

Chinese immigrant communities nowadays take shape in new locations. Traditional Chinatowns no longer serve as primary centers of settlement, and more than half of all Chinese Americans live in suburbs.[87] Suburban communities with reputable schools, like Los Angeles's San Gabriel Valley and Cupertino in San Jose, received an influx of professional immigrants from Asia, leading to a new, distinct phenomenon of "ethnoburbs."[88] After-school programs and educational consultants of Asian styles have mushroomed in these ethnoburbs; even white families are moving out to escape the intense academic pressure (the so-called new white flight).[89]

In their recent article entitled "When White Is Just Alright," Tomás Jiménez and Adam Horowitz argue that at schools with a dominant Asian population, teachers often associate Asianness with academic success and hard work while linking whiteness with academic mediocrity and laziness, leading to a new "ethnoracial encoding of academic achievement."[90] Jennifer Lee and Min Zhou's study in Los Angeles similarly found that Asian students are likely to experience a "stereotype promise" that boosts their academic performance as a self-fulfilling prophecy.[91]

However, few areas of the US resemble Silicon Valley and Los Angeles; many Asian Americans live in places with a smaller Asian population or a different ethnoracial composition. As of 2010, California (37 percent) and New York (17 percent) accommodated more than half of Chinese Americans, but significant growth of the population has also occurred in Texas, New Jersey, Massachusetts, Illinois, and other states.[92] In these areas, the Chinese immigrant population is numerically significant but geographically dispersed.

Boston has a long history of Chinese immigration dating back to as early as 1870. Chinese immigration stopped with the Exclusion Act but resumed after World War II, and most immigrants found jobs in Chinatown's growing restaurant and garment industries. The community further expanded with the arrival of immigrants who reunited with their families on the basis of the 1965 law.[93] Meanwhile, Boston has attracted an influx of professional immigrants working in the sectors of science and technology. It was the fourth most popular place of intended residency among Asian natural scientists in the late 1990s.[94]

The Boston area, including the city's adjacent suburbs, has grown popular among wealthy Chinese and Taiwanese immigrants in recent decades. They prefer Boston for the city's reputation for academic excellence, given the presence of Harvard, Massachusetts Institute of Technology, and other universities. The state of Massachusetts is also praised for having an excellent system of public elementary and high school. Boston is considered the seventh most attractive city for Chinese real estate investors; wealthy Chinese look for housing near good schools, sometimes buying a home even before getting married or having children. The local media has described this phenomenon using the phrase "Boston: China's Town."[95]

Class divides, rather than national divides, shape the settlement patterns of Chinese and Taiwanese immigrants in the Boston area. Although Boston's Chinatown continues to provide markets, educational services, and social affiliations, especially for working-class newcomers, immigrants across the class spectrum are moving to the suburbs because of the lack of adequate housing in and around Chinatown.[96] Professionals and entrepreneurs often choose to reside in the best school districts, such as the northern suburbs of Brookline, Lexington, and Newton. Working-class immigrants settle in less expensive suburbs, such as Quincy and Malden with a substantial population of racial minorities.[97]

Unlike their counterparts in Los Angeles and New York, Chinese and Taiwanese immigrants in Boston are compelled to integrate into mainstream

America. Attending schools in majority-white suburbs, the children of professional immigrants are more likely to encounter racial ridicule, which can harm self-esteem or produce identity crises.[98] These parents are also concerned about a hidden racial bias in college admissions and the dubious existence of "Asian quotas." In other words, Asian stereotypes are not always a promise; they can also function as a *threat* to these children of immigrants. As we will see in Chapter 4, professional immigrant parents living in white-majority neighborhoods face a dilemma in childrearing: can they instill an ethnic cultural identity in their children while also fostering class mobility? They are also concerned whether raising their children like white Americans will result in mediocre academic performance and weakened capacity to compete globally.

The "Return" Migration of the Second Generation

The earlier literature often associates return migration or transnationalism with the first generation, but the "new second generation" that came of age in multicultural societies also engage in transnational practices.[99] Younger cohorts of Asian Americans are strongly affiliated with Asian popular cultures, such as music and television drama. Mandopop, Mandarin-language pop music produced largely in Taiwan, has a large fandom among young Chinese Americans; in fact, many singers are second-generation returnees who established their popularity based on the hybrid of "diasporic closeness" and American cool.[100] Both the Chinese and Taiwanese governments sponsor activities like summer camps for overseas youth to connect with their ancestral homelands for language education or cultural exchanges.[101] Children in higher-socioeconomic-status immigrant families are especially likely to maintain frequent visits to their countries of origin.[102]

There is an emerging trend of "roots migration" or "ancestral homeland migration" among 1.5 or second-generation Chinese Americans and Canadians who are moving to China, Hong Kong, and Taiwan to pursue jobs and careers.[103] Similar inflows of second-generation youth who "return" to their parents' homeland also are happening in India, Japan, Vietnam, and South Korea.[104] They attempt to grab opportunities in the booming Asian economies while escaping the depressed labor markets in the West. Some are also pressured to leave by institutional racism in North America, where they personally encounter racial discrimination or anticipate barriers to promotion based on their Asian identity.[105] Although their primary motivations for migration tend to be economic, other factors also influence their migration decisions, including reunion with family, taking over the family business, looking for a spouse, and seeking cultural roots in the ancestral homeland.[106] The children of transnational families are even more likely to return because they usually have family members in Asia and maintain strong language ties and personal networks with their countries of birth.[107]

Many of the second-generation returnees are postgraduate degree holders with a sufficient stock of cultural and social capital.[108] They engage in what David Ley and Audrey Kobayashi call "strategic switching" between countries to complete the migration cycle of flexible capital accumulation.[109] While many of their parents brought economic capital earned in East Asia to North America to cultivate cultural capital in the next generation, the youth now return to East Asia and convert their ethnic heritage and cultural advantage into market gains. Their English proficiency and Western education are increasingly valued in Asian workplaces.[110] Meanwhile, their ethnic heritage serves as a form of social capital, which helps them make business liaisons more quickly than nonethnic foreigners. Leslie Wang coins the term *strategic in-betweenness* to describe how Chinese Americans consciously maneuver the "socially ambiguous space between cultures" to their own benefit. Notably, many of the second-generation youth do not position themselves as return migrants; they still prefer a North American lifestyle and maintain a strong American or Canadian identity.[111] They tend to see their sojourn in China or Taiwan as a temporary career stage or part of an ongoing process of circular migration.[112]

The reverse flows across the Pacific involve not only people's migration to the East but also the movement of Chinese or Asian ideas about education to the West. In 2012, Programme for International Student Assessment (PISA, a study by the Organization for Economic Cooperation and Development that compares the math, reading, and science skills of secondary school students around the world), Shanghai students scored at the top of the global class in all three subjects. Other Asian countries, including Singapore, Hong Kong, Taiwan, South Korea, and Vietnam, were also highly ranked, leaving the US and the United Kingdom far behind.[113]

The PISA test results raised concerns among American and British educators and stirred debates about the value of Chinese or Asian styles of education. In 2013, the British education minister proposed extending teaching hours and cutting the length of school holidays to improve students' performance.[114] In August 2015, the BBC broadcast a controversial documentary series titled *Are Our Kids Tough Enough? Chinese School*. The program centered on an experiment in which five teachers from China were invited to teach a class of British high school students in the "Chinese style" for a month. At the end of the month, the students showed higher test scores than another group who received a standard British education. In 2016, the government provided £41 million of funding to help eight thousand primary schools in England to adopt an Asian mastery approach to math teaching.[115] While some commentators criticize Asian's high-performing system for neglecting critical thinking and holistic development, others emphasize that Asian schools excel because they continually work to reform their long-standing traditions by combining "Eastern academic rigor" with modern pedagogy.[116]

Meanwhile, after-school programs with foreign origins, such as the Japanese learning center Kumon, the Russian School of Mathematics, and the Indian programs of online math education are becoming widely popular in suburban America. The import of Asian-style education reflects a deep anxiety among Western upper-middle-class parents about the globalized competition their children will face in the future. Immigrant Chinese parents in the US feel even more unease with the limitation of American education; some turn to their culture of origin as a source of ethnic cultural capital.

Conclusion

The movements of people and ideas across the Pacific demonstrate variegated forms of global-local entanglement. The US, as a geopolitical superpower with cultural hegemony, has greatly influenced the transformation of parenting discourses in postwar Taiwan through both transnationalism from above (through US aid and family planning) and transnationalism from below (through cultural transmission and education reform). Affluent parents in Taiwan and China use immigration as a strategy for their children to become globally competitive or to escape academic pressure. Yet the stagnant economy in North America, compared to the booming Asian markets, stirs anxiety among immigrant parents and induces a recent trend of second-generation ancestral homeland migration.

Transnationalism from above and below transforms the family lives of migrants and of those who stay behind. Families across the social class spectrum, however, have uneven access to the effects of time-space compression. Both during the US aid period or in recent decades, state controls on fertility and childrearing in Taiwan suspected lower-educated parents of lacking modern knowledge and parental competence. By contrast, middle-class parents in both

Taiwan and China can appropriate transnational connections and global re-sources to reform or escape local systems of education. Class inequality shapes not only people's uneven ability to achieve the American dream of immigration but also how they imagine, aspire, and practice "the global" in the everyday practice of childrearing.

2 Taiwanese Middle Class

Raising Global Children

A handsome young man wheels his suitcase into the airport Arrivals lounge. His parents, gray haired and elegantly dressed, greet him with passionate hugs. They step into a chauffeur-driven limousine. In Mandarin Chinese sprinkled with English words in a crisp American accent, the son talks excitedly about his experience studying overseas. As the car passes a private school, memories of his upbringing flash by, including his college years in Taiwan's most distinguished university and a special father-and-son holiday spent hiking together. The father's voice, solid and warm, cuts in: "I've simply expected you to get the grades in college; exploring your interests is more important. You've graduated from Harvard now. You don't need to make a lot of money, but you need to have a dream." The slogan appears: "Every father's dream is to give his child a bigger world."

THIS VIDEO NARRATIVE ADVERTISES expensive condominium homes in a development near an elite private school in Taipei. Selling at around 1.5 million USD for a three-bedroom unit, the condominiums are marketed to appeal to "modern" parents who aspire to a global future for their children. The commercial captures the ideal parent-child relationship in such families, which involves affective displays and emotional bonding with not only the mother but also the father; all these elements were alien to the Taiwan of yesterday. As familial dynamics have shifted, so have parents' expectations of their children. Success is no longer measured solely by good grades and a high income: children are encouraged to explore their interests and unknown possibilities. However, an Ivy League education and fluency in English are still considered to provide a smooth route to a life of happiness and fulfillment.

This chapter examines how middle-class Taiwanese parents raise "global children" and, on the other side of the same coin, how they aspire to become "global parents." My analysis situates their childrearing strategies in the emotional politics of social class and expands Pierre Bourdieu's thesis of cultural capital accumulation to a global scale (see the introduction). These upwardly mobile parents aspire to be liberal, open-minded parents by exposing themselves to the cultural scripts of Western childrearing. They encourage their children to explore the world and discover unknown possibilities, and yet they feel responsible for managing the uncertainties that loom large in the global economy and local environments.

The Taiwanese middle class is not a monolithic category; their class experiences involve a variety of career tracks and different relations with globalization. Despite sharing a similar cosmopolitan aspiration, they make a range of educational choices and display a spectrum of childrearing styles to negotiate with the local regime and to secure their children's global future. Parents on one side of the spectrum strive to cultivate their children's capacity for global competitiveness and mobility, while those leaning toward the other end orchestrate an environment where they achieve their children's "natural growth" as a desired way of life. These parents draw on their class-based resources to facilitate the different strategies of cultural negotiation, but their endeavors often magnify anxiety and insecurity among parents themselves.

Intergenerational Mobility and Lost Childhood

Middle-class parents in this book, most of whom came of age in the 1980s and 1990s, have achieved intergenerational mobility during Taiwan's compressed development. Thanks to industrial upgrading and educational expansion, people in these cohorts generally attained higher education and earning than their parents.[1] They are usually the first generation of their family to attain higher education or even study abroad. Few of their parents ever received a tertiary education; many worked as farmers, factory laborers, and small shop owners. The better-off ones ran small businesses and accumulated wealth during the economic takeoff, allowing the next generation to seek cultural capital and even transnational mobility.

However, many of these upwardly mobile parents lament their "lost childhoods," lacking in joy or opportunity. Growing up, many suffered under a heavy burden of schoolwork and parental pressure to achieve academic success. A childhood deprived of leisure time and extracurricular activities turned them into adults who lack hobbies and who don't know what they might really enjoy. Those who grew up in financial difficulty were envious of better-off classmates who had access to learning resources that nurtured their talents.

Many also attributed the deprivation of a happy childhood to their upbringing under strict parenting. When I asked the interviewees if their childrearing styles are influenced by their parents, many answered with a firm "not at all!" followed by explanations like "My parents' influence on me is that I don't want to become like them" or "My wife and I have only one thought on this: Don't continue in the way the previous generation did." Several interviewees lament their distant relationships with their parents, who were either occupied by work or culturally constrained with regard to emotional communication and affective displays.

Male informants, in particular, recall a childhood in the shadow of harsh discipline and swear not to become an authority figure or an emotionally distant father to their own children. Fong Wang, an engineer father in his late forties, moved his family to Yilan in pursuit of an alternative style of education and family life. He described his childhood relationship with his late father, who served in the army:[2]

> My father was very strict. He treated his children like a military officer would [laughs]. . . . Whenever I did something wrong, it was just spanking, spanking, and more spanking. . . . By the time I reached adulthood, there was a lot of misunderstanding, a lot of resentment. I hated my father because he had no sympathy and didn't reason with us. . . . I've gone through a lot of therapy sessions and I can finally let it go.

The past, as reconstructed in a narrative of lost childhood, channels middle-class parents toward a particular version of the ideal present: they want their children to enjoy the childhood they never had, and they feel protective of it. They embrace the ideal of "joyful childhood"; that is, children should be happy and carefree before they enter the pressure-ridden teenage years and the harsh realities of adult life.

Middle-class Taiwanese parents also use a narrative of "generational rupture" to describe their agency in initiating changes that remodel the local traditions of childrearing. Many emphasize the limited value of suggestions made by their own parents, who grew up in a poorer Taiwan and attained limited education. Instead, the opinions of parenting experts, and even children, have become the primary sources of guidance. A mother of two and full-time homemaker said: "I don't ask my parents [about childrearing]. I'm inclined to judge by myself, to read books. . . . The older generation's ways aren't suitable nowadays. . . . Actually, I ask my children for the most part." This echoes Sharon

Hays's observation in the US that parenthood, and motherhood in particular, has become labor intensive, emotionally absorbing, and child centered in the sense that "the child (whose needs are interpreted by experts) is now to train the parents."[3]

Global consumer culture offers a bridge for these adults to intimately participate in kids' world. Some parents use cartoon characters or mythical creatures, mostly imported from Japan and the US, to construct a fantasy world that upholds the image of an innocent childhood. Halloween celebration has become a regular ritual in many kindergartens, especially in those offering bilingual curriculums; parents purchase cheap costumes made in China and dress their children as Princess Elsa from Disney's *Frozen* or Batman. In several non-Christian families, the parents try to create childhood memories full of festive cheer by leaving presents under a Christmas tree with tags signed by Santa Claus; some even fake footprints around the tree to nurture their children's belief that Santa visited the subtropical island.

Despite their concerted effort to break from the earlier generation, many parents also admit that, to some extent and on an unconscious level, their own ways of raising children are still influenced by their upbringing. Half-jokingly, some informants said, "I've been possessed by my parents without realizing!" or "I'm just like my mother's mirror image!" This is what Bourdieu calls "habitus": individual values, lifestyles, and dispositions that are acquired through repetitive experience and cumulative exposure, such as in one's childhood. Habitus is mostly embodied and unconscious, seemingly constituting one's "nature."[4] The individual can "denaturalize" the habitus accumulated from her family of origin through later experience and reflexive intervention,[5] but this requires a concerted effort at self-monitoring and emotional work.

Julie Huang, a mother of two at Garden School, has a college degree and works in the insurance industry. Her own parents achieved only a primary education and struggled to raise five children by running a small diner. Julie was committed to offering her sons a different childhood from her own, but her instincts and actions do not always follow her beliefs:

> JULIE: One day, I was saying something to my sons, and all of a sudden I realized that, damn, I was doing exactly what my mother had done. I was shocked and I thought, no, I don't want to become a strict mother like her. . . . I'm actually a mother who quite likes to reflect. I do a lot of thinking about how I can do better next time and how I can avoid the things my mother did to me.

LAN: Do you mean that you would consciously avoid repeating your mother's ways of behavior?

JULIE: All the time . . . [pause] but you only become aware of it after you've already done it [embarrassed smile]. I can only keep reminding myself: "Oh, don't do that again."

"Reflexive monitoring" is a salient feature of middle-class parenthood in a time of late modernity.[6] Parents are exposed to the expanding intervention of expert knowledge and scientific discourses, which, in the word of a mother I interviewed, may "wake up" parents and turn their "unconscious influences" into an object of reflection. To avoid repeating the mistakes of past generations and to live up to the new cultural norms, parents feel impelled to constantly monitor their own behavior in everyday parent-child interactions. The rapidly changing environments, including the local education regime and global economy, stir even more uncertainty and anxiety among these parents.

Education Reform and Schooling Choices

As Chapter 1 showed, Taiwan's education reform in the late 1990s dramatically altered the opportunity structure faced by the younger generation. Before the reforms, higher education in Taiwan followed an elitist model; the national entrance exam was so competitive that people referred to entry to universities as a "narrow gate." With the official plan of expansion, the number of four-year universities and colleges rapidly increased from 28 in 1986 to 127 in 2000.[7] College admissions no longer center on standardized entrance exams, and multiple tracks of admission are open, including applications based on individual merit. With fewer pupils as a result of declining fertility, the gate to tertiary education opened wide. In 1985, the gross enrollment rate (GER) for Taiwanese youth aged eighteen to twenty-one was only 20 percent, but the rate increased to 56 percent in 2000 and 83 percent in 2010.[8]

Middle-class parents perceive and respond to the consequence of education reform in different ways. On the one hand, many become concerned about the depreciation of higher education or local diplomas. The unemployment rate among college graduates has risen continuously since 2000.[9] Job insecurity is on the rise as a result of the recent global financial crisis and Taiwan's stagnant domestic economy. To secure their children's futures, resourceful parents relocate the front of competition to the admission to elite universities, or they send their children to study abroad as early as college or even high school.[10]

On the one hand, with the relief of educational pressure, some parents believe that an alternative environment of holistic education will provide their
children with an advantage in the track of individual applications. The number
of alternative schools, which adopt a nontraditional pedagogy and design their
curriculums without following the national guideline, grew from one in 1992 to
over a hundred in 2018. Steiner (Waldorf) schools are by far the most popular
in Taiwan; the first Steiner elementary school was founded in 2002, and almost
twenty similar schools were established by 2018.[11] Half of them are private institutions that charge students high tuition, while the other half includes public and charter schools that provide low-cost enrollment through government
funding. Despite that the total number of pupils receiving alternative education
is still limited,[12] some of the charter schools have become so popular that the
intended parents need to relocate to the school district years before their child
reaches school age.

Middle-class parents make a range of educational choices to enrich their
children's futures at the conjuncture of global aspirations and local institutions.
Some parents choose international education and private schools so that their
children can exit the local education system and pursue a pathway to global
mobility. Some send their children to alternative curriculums (like "Garden
School," described in this chapter[13]) as a strategy of cultural mobility to escape
the tradition of rote learning and to connect with the global community of humanist education. The majority enroll their children in regular public schools
(like "Central School" described in this chapter) and struggle to achieve a balance in a tug-of-war between a happy childhood and global competitiveness.

Cultivating Global Competitiveness

In 2007, Taiwan's *Business Weekly* magazine ran a cover story titled "The
Global Education Arms Race" that investigated how parents plan their "educational investments" in the face of increased global competition. Writing for
its financially minded readers, the magazine employed the language of investment, benefit, and reward to analogize the timing, purpose, and effectiveness
of education, claiming that "investing in children's education is like investing in
funds: the earlier the better."[14]

The target readers of *Business Weekly* are Taiwanese professionals, managers and financial workers, who have established careers and wealth in Taiwan's
global economy participation. Capital outflows to China and Southeast Asian
since the 1990s further increased their cross-border mobility, whether they

take an overseas post or fly back and forth frequently. Scholars have called them "the transnational middle class," who embraces cosmopolitan consumption and global education to identify with the Western middle classes. Members of this class are mostly private-sector professionals who play a key role in globalized production and the neoliberal transformation of developing economies.[15] Their career paths and consumer lifestyles set them apart from members of the locally oriented middle class, such as public servants and schoolteachers, whose employment and consumption are more limited to the local market.[16]

The rhetoric of global education arms race sounds more urgent than ever, partly because of the new rules of the educational game, including differentiated tracks for applying to universities. *Business Weekly* reminds parents that they need not only economic resources to fight the "financial battle" of educational investment but also cultural resources to comprehend college admission applications as an "informational minefield."[17] Parents need to cultivate in children "visible abilities" such as English proficiency, a second foreign language, and professional skills as well as the "invisible abilities" of global competencies such as self-confidence, communication skills, flexible thinking, and cross-cultural sensitivity.[18]

In addition, many parents, especially fathers whose employment or business is tied to the global production chain, feel disheartened by the global talent competition their children will face in the future. In particular, mainland Chinese youth, who grow up in a high-pressure education system, are perceived as formidable competitors. These parents believe that their children's prospects of success are largely determined by their exposure to Western education and their capacity for transnational mobility. To quote *Business Weekly*: "In this day and age, one must be able to move horizontally in order to move vertically."[19]

Building on Allison Pugh's term *pathway consumption*,[20] I suggest that professional middle-class parents, especially in the Global South, engage in "global pathway consumption" to purchase contexts for their children to gain the experiences, opportunities, and skills necessary for their future pursuit of global mobility. When growing up, most of the parents did not enjoy similar access to these contexts, such as international school, overseas camps, and enrichment programs; therefore, they rely on market agents to attain these pathways. This section examines how their strategies for global pathway consumption vary depending on their access to economic, cultural, and social capital.

Recent literature has shown that affluent parents in North America and Europe also attempt to equip their children with multicultural capital—to become "culturally omnivorous and globally knowledgeable"[21]—so they can join the ranks of new global elites who "feel at ease" with both non-Western and non-elite cultures.[22] Children are encouraged to attend bilingual education or spend a gap year abroad to cultivate "cosmopolitan" or "transnational cultural" capital.[23] Wealthy parents in the Global South share a similar strategy of cultural mobility, but the "ease" they seek to cultivate is largely directed toward comfort with Western elite culture and lifestyles. By contrast, even though Southeast Asians constitute a sizable minority through marriage and labor migration to Taiwan, parents rarely recognize these transnational connections as valuable multicultural liaisons. The seemingly neutral rhetoric of cosmopolitan parenting glosses over power hierarchies in the global village and reinforces a sense of Western superiority.

Flexible Citizenship and Western Cultural Capital

Jessica Chang is a thirty-nine-year-old full-time homemaker with a US master's degree in accounting. Her husband, Vincent Huang, works as a sales manager in an IT company and spends on average two weeks per month away for business travel. Witnessing the rapid economic growth and intensive talent competition in China, Vincent believes that Taiwanese children can develop an edge over youngsters from China only by developing their individuality and creativity. Jessica reiterated her husband's point of view:

> My husband talks about this with me all the time. He feels that this generation of Taiwanese isn't as competitive and aggressive as the Chinese. But he also says that he doesn't approve of Chinese education, which pushes children to study narrow subjects. He says, "Could you have imagined something like Google or Facebook before?" He tells me just to let the kids explore and find their own passions.

The couple considers exposure to Western education and culture a necessity for cultivating these desired qualities in their children. They began taking steps for their children to acquire "flexible citizenship" as soon as they learned about the pregnancy.[24] Jessica traveled to Los Angeles to give birth to her two children so they could acquire US passports and gain an "extra advantage" in the future. She also arranged a variety of nonorthodox learning activities during their preschool years, including a "brain development" class at the age of three and a board-game class at the age of four. The children, now seven and eleven, attend a private elementary school. A British tutor visits them at home twice a week for English conversation and uses Lego bricks to instruct them in physics, math, engineering, and other scientific principles. The children have golf and table-tennis lessons on the weekend.[25] Every summer, Jessica takes the children to attend summer camps in California.

Through careful consideration and planning, what Lareau calls "concerted cultivation," Jessica foresees a globalized future for her children:

JESSICA: I want both of our children to go abroad for college. I don't really care where exactly. My husband says that Japan's pretty good, and so is Singapore.

LAN: So anywhere abroad is good?

JESSICA: We want them to have an international perspective because when you look for a job in the future, you won't just look within Taiwan. We want them to have an international career so their lives will be different.

Parents who have studied in the West claim that those experiences opened their eyes and shaped their eventual practices as parents. Andrew Tseng, a fifty-two-year-old architect with a master's degree from the US, sends his two daughters to a bilingual private school. Andrew explains his educational preference:

You know, US schools don't give students textbooks. They only give you a reading list, and you do group discussions and presentations. In Taiwan, for the most part, we just read and study. To put it bluntly, we were just a bunch of parrots, right? You believe and follow what the textbook tells you, so it's like memorizing the answers. Going to school in the US, we felt like their method is better. Why wait until they go to university or grad school to learn this? Isn't it better for them to start young?

Andrew's priorities for his children's development include independent thinking and presentation skills, and he codes these qualities as the outcomes of Western education. The acquisition of "Western cultural capital" not only refers to *institutionalized* forms of cultural capital, like Western degrees and credentials; it also involves *embodied* cultural capital, such as familiarity with upper-middle-class Western ways of thinking and living and the acquisition of long-lasting dispositions in the mind and body.[26]

To avoid the sacrifice of family separation in the arrangement of "parachute kids," the current generation of elite parents prefer the strategy of "studying abroad at home" by acquiring foreign passports so their children can attend international schools in Taiwan. David Guo and his wife are both corporate lawyers in their forties with US law degrees. Like many professionals in Taiwan, especially those in multinational companies or the high-tech industry, David and his wife need to communicate with foreign partners or clients in English. These work experiences make them appreciate the value of English-language skills, and they do not want their children to repeat any shortcomings they have had. Sitting in his office overlooking Taipei 101, then the third-tallest skyscraper in the world, David explained why he chose an international school for their only daughter, Monica:

> When you do this line of work [international business], your English becomes an instant problem. It was a very painful experience. When I first started at a foreign company, it was like I was on another planet. I couldn't understand a thing. . . . If you wait until you're older [to learn English], the accent will never go away. I talk to foreigners at work but they'll always know I'm not native. I sent her there [an all-English school] for the accent.

Living in a pricy neighborhood with a sizable population of Western expatriates, David and his wife sent Monica to an all-English kindergarten run by the former teachers of Taipei American school. Later they decided to "buy" a foreign passport before Monica reached school age. They invested roughly 40,000 USD in a shopping mall in Burkina Faso in exchange for three passports for the entire family. When I asked David if he had ever been there, he shrugged and smiled: "[The immigration agency] just showed us a picture of this mall being built. They stopped contacting us after that. Even if they did, I suspect it burned down last month or something." With a foreign passport, Monica is able to enroll in an international school with an annual tuition of 15,000 USD. Half of her classmates are Taiwan-born "fake foreigners." David joked: "I'm pretty sure Burkina Faso is where most of these families come from."

David is proud of Monica for her crispy English accent and knowledge of European culture and history—when the family traveled in Europe last summer, Monica served as their knowledgeable guide. In optimism, David projects a bright future marked with cultural flexibility and brain circulation:

> Many people talk about brain drain. I don't object to that. . . . You let her explore the outside world for ten or twenty years; she will eventually come back. So we think it's important that she identifies with the homeland but, with the language skills, she can go wherever she wants. I think the future world will be like that.

Like many highly educated and mobile parents, David considers flexibility the road to opportunities at work and in private life in a time of insecurity.[27]

However, he also feels ambivalent about what Monica may have missed out, such as Chinese-language skills, local social networks, and ethnic cultural identity by attending an international school. He can only hope that family ties can help to maintain her cultural identity and keep return migration as an ultimate option.

Private School and Subtle Symbolic Struggle

In addition to international schools, private bilingual schools with the goal of US college entrance began to pop up in Taiwan during the last decade. These schools advertise English-language immersion or an Americanized teaching style, and their tuition fees are about twice those of standard private schools.[28] Some work in partnership with foreign high schools or apply for international school certification so pupils can gain a transnational diploma as extra leverage toward overseas college applications.[29] The growth of private education is especially salient in metropolitan areas.[30] Private schools also help parents to arrange extracurricular activities, such as Western sports activities like horse riding and rowing, and overseas homestay programs with an aim to equip their children with cosmopolitan tastes and dispositions.

Cheng-yi Li and his wife, Yen-fen, are both in their late forties and send their two daughters to an elite private school in Taipei. Cheng-yi received his medical degree in Taiwan and completed a PhD in Germany; Yen-fen is a full-time homemaker with a master's degree in music. The Li daughters, both talented musicians and straight-A students, easily cope with the pace of elite education, but they find it emotionally stressful to be surrounded by pupils from very wealthy families. Even at a young age, classmates made fun of the Li girls for not knowing brand names in English. Cheng-yi, who works at a public hospital, joked painfully: "Medical doctors are at the bottom of the heap when it comes to the parents [at the school]." He and Yen-fen are thankful that both of their girls were born in the summer so they can avoid hosting fancy birthday parties. Their daughter once attended a birthday party at a five-star hotel where the favor was a foreign-certified, handmade teddy bear.

Professional middle-class parents who socialize with an affluent upper class highlight their stock of Western cultural capital to make up for their relatively modest economic capital. Cheng-yi describes the several years he spent studying in Europe as an eye-opening experience. Although they lack the funds to travel frequently, he and his wife try hard to inject European cultural elements into their family life. Yen-fen believes that European culture cultivates a taste more refined than that of America, which helps their daughters stand out among their classmates:

> We try to expose them to a lot of European cultures. . . . We talk to them about it, let them read books. . . . They grew up listening to European songs, songs in German, French, and Italian. . . . For me, I think European culture is where the advantage is, so we don't really follow American values or lifestyle, because Europe is more cultured. A lot of the parents at the school have experience of the US, but they don't have any experience of Europe. They can speak English very fluently, but they don't know any other language. So we make ourselves distinct through Europe, and this is how I build confidence in my children.

Professional middle-class parents like the Li family strategize to mark social distinctions based on subtle shades of cultural difference. For example, the summer homework required by the Li children's private school asks each student to make a poster about their holiday travels. To distinguish themselves among classmates with the funds to fly to New York, Paris, and other destinations around the world, the Lis' poster claims that they travel independently, "never with tour groups." Cheng-yi and Yen-fen teach their daughters to research their travel plans on the internet so to cultivate "the fun in discovery." At their destinations, they encourage their daughters to "experience the local lifestyle, shop at local markets, and interact with local people." They hope to foster an embodied mode of multicultural capital, as opposed to a financial confidence, which they believe will secure their children's place in the global middle class.

The Li daughters have a busy life attending to both heavy school homework and exposure to European culture. Yen-fen described herself a Type A personality, joking that she was one of the school's most infamous "tiger moms." She set high standards for her daughters' academic performance and paid particular attention to their piano practice. Yen-fen saw time control and progress monitoring as a mandatory in a contemporary Taiwanese lifestyle:

> I feel like this is the only way when you live in Taiwan. If we were in the US, we could take our time and slow [piano practice] down, because there'd be little schoolwork and I wouldn't have to worry about this or that. Taiwanese children have so much homework, and time's of the essence. They get off school at four and it takes another forty-minute car ride to get home. Once they get home, they rest for a bit, but there's homework waiting. I've got to supervise them this way because they only have one hour for piano practice. . . . They've got to make

so much progress in that one hour. American children get off school much earlier and their weekends are really weekends. They have the luxury of time and can take time to enjoy life, and the parents and teachers use negotiation and communication to teach [music] more often. But in Taiwan, teachers don't have the time to talk to you, parents don't have the time to talk to you.

Taiwan's public narratives widely portray the US as a "paradise for children." Drawing on these narratives, Yen-fen viewed learning at children's own pace as a privilege of middle-class American families. Even that, as we will see in Chapter 4, Chinese American middle-class family life is not as relaxing or stress-free as Yen-fen assumed. The imagined American styles of happy childhood and permissive parenting become an unrealistic ideal for middle-class Taiwanese parents to emulate and distinguish at the same time. Notably, Yen-fen portrayed herself as an unwilling tiger mom not to reproduce ethnic cultural heritage but to adapt to the new cultural script of holistic education that still includes intense academic pressure. Most middle-class parents I interviewed in Taiwan projected a self-image as "liberal" and "democratic" parents and dissociated themselves from tiger moms who are obsessed with children's success. Still, they felt they had no choice but to prepare their children for globalized competition, resulting in a whirring family rhythm and a sense of perpetual time crunch.

Micromanagement of Holistic Development

On parents' evening at Central School, a public elementary school located in a well-off neighborhood of Taipei City, a dozen commercial reps stood outside the campus gate, bowing, smiling, and handing out flyers to parents rushing to attend after work. Some also gave away educational toys. They came from the nearby cram schools and educational centers that offer a wide range of supplementary education and extracurricular classes, including math, science, English, music, art, sports, and writing composition. The names of these schools often mimic the names of famous Western cities or educational institutions, such as Juilliard Art School, Boston English, Little Harvard, and Oxford Math. They promise to train the next generation of elites: one school offers "premedical" biology classes for fifth and six graders. Another center provides "international math tests" as early as kindergarten. Many flyers quote the famous Chinese slogan "Don't let your children start behind the others," and one adds the promise "We will help your children lead ahead all the way." To appeal to parents torn between the pursuit of global competitiveness and a happy childhood, these advertisements are sprinkled with words like *fun, play, inspiration*, and *creativity*.

For parents who send their children to regular public schools, extracurricular activities are a critical place to micromanage children's holistic development. Social surveys in Taiwan show that children's participation in after-school activities are highly associated with parents' social class, especially the father's occupation and the mother's education.[31] Middle-class parents feel responsible for identifying their children's strengths and engineering the development of their talents. The reform of college admissions to include individual applications produced the unintended consequence of transforming the learning process into the accumulation of recognizable credentials. The commercial sector exacerbates the institutionalization and commoditization of "competitive childhoods."[32] Children are encouraged to participate in various competitive activities and to keep a record of their learning progress that may become a useful part of the child's future portfolio. Even learning to ride a bicycle is transformed into a documentable achievement at training camps where children can earn a certificate upon graduation.

English is widely considered by parents to be the most important of extracurricular activities. Wealthy parents have sufficient funds to send children to study abroad or to international schools in Taiwan to learn English. Not-so-well-off parents seek less costly ways to broaden their children's familiarity with English, such as enrolling in all-English kindergartens, going abroad for camps during summer vacation, or staying with relatives abroad for a short period. If parents cannot afford expensive trips to North America, Australia, or the United Kingdom, they send their children to Singapore or the Philippines at half the cost.

All-English summer camps in Taiwan provide an even more economical way for children to have a virtual experience of transnational mobility. Yet parents who have limited experience abroad and weak English skills struggle to evaluate which camps are authentic or effective. Some mothers nervously asked me: "Should I send my child to study in the Philippines? His English is terrible. Will it work?" or "Do we really need to start fostering an international perspective at a young age? Is it too late if we start in elementary school?" Other parents were disappointed to learn that their children frequently speak Chinese at one of the English camps. One perplexed mother said: "I don't think they learned anything there. Do American children simply play like that?"

Compared to wealthy parents who can afford international education for their children as early as primary education or at least from college, parents who send children to public schools experience even more friction between cultural scripts and family life. Many of them belong to the locally oriented middle class—unlike the transnational middle class, their employment and lifestyle are more oriented to the local economy. Although they want to offer their children something distinct from their own childhoods, facing continued competition for admission to leading universities in Taiwan, these parents still fall back to traditional educational methods such as disciplined learning and repetitive training.

Time management is a clear feature of life routines in many of these middle-class homes. Children are subject to a busy schedule that coordinates their multiple organized activities. Some mothers set up a timetable for evenings spent at home, including Pei-ing Lai, who quit her job as a sales manager after giving birth to Yun, now a second grader at Central School. Yun's father, Wu-han Yao, works as a real estate manager. The couple decided not to have more children so they could concentrate the resources on their only daughter.

Wu-han was occupied by work and usually returned home around nine or ten in the evening. Even on the weekends, he attended training seminars or business-related social events, or went on long bike rides by himself to relieve the pressure from work. Often as the sole parent at home, Pei-ing arranged Yun's daily activities in minute detail. After dinner, Yun did homework for at least thirty minutes, followed by violin practice for twenty minutes. Then she was allowed to use the computer for fifty minutes (or thirty-five minutes when her grades drop). Pei-ing skillfully relied on machines for time management: the computer was set to automatically shut down after the designated time. While playing on the computer, Yun had to wear a helmetlike machine with special glasses to protect her sight. Pei-ing also used the timer on her cell phone to remind Yun to take a shower at 9:45 p.m., and she used different alarm tones for the father's and daughter's wake-up times.

Habituated to a full calendar arranged by adults, Yun expected her mother to answer readily, "What should I do next?" whenever there was a break between the designated activities. Middle-class children like Yun, who are frequently turned into objects of adult micromanagement, grow up to internalize a sense of time constraint. A frown on their young faces, the children at Central School often said to each other, "I'm really busy" or "I'm running out of time," sounding like their time-crunched parents. Ironically, they also said, "I'm bored" or "This is boring"—feeling impatient with the shortage of stimulation or entertainment—more often than children we observed at other schools.

Similar to what Lareau observed among American middle-class families, children's weakened capacity for self-direction and self-entertainment is an unintended consequence of concerted cultivation in Taiwan. However, the micromanagement of holistic development often turns into a "regimented growth" that prevents Taiwanese children from developing what Lareau calls "a sense of entitlement." Instead, it fosters a sense of obedience and respect toward their parents.[33] When facing a time deficit, the decisions regarding the priorities of extracurricular activities are usually up to parents rather than children. Children are often forced to drop activities that are "simply fun" and keep those parents consider more intellectually inspiring, such as Chinese checkers and abacus. Parental authority becomes even more salient as children enter middle school and academic pressure increases. The emotional ties between parents and children, which are validated in the new cultural repertoire, may ironically become a means for parents to reinforce "soft authority" that eclipses children's autonomy.

Educational Mothers and Astronaut Fathers

The mother remains the children's primary caregiver in most middle-class Taiwanese families. She collects up-to-date information on new methods of childrearing and education, absorbing this material before providing a summary to her husband before bed at night. The Japanese use the term *kyōiku mama*—"education mother"—to describe the many middle-class women who quit their jobs to focus on raising their children. This phenomenon is not unusual in Taiwan, where some women see this sacrifice of career as necessary because, as one Taiwanese mother and full-time homemaker who also has a master's degree put it: "What costs the most in children's education is not money, it's the mother's time."[34]

Still, only a third of Taiwanese middle-class households have one parent who is a full-time homemaker.[35] It is difficult for single-salaried families to afford to live in Taipei, a city with stagnant wages and rising housing costs. Instead of staying home, mothers tend to choose jobs with stable or flexible work hours, so they can attend to children's education and provide a bulk of emotional work involving almost all areas of the children's lives.[36]

Taiwan's government, school, and community have encouraged fathers to get involved in their children's growth and education.[37] Middle-class fathers, in particular, are more likely than working-class men to have jobs with some degree of time flexibility and become emotionally invested in today's family life.

Several of the middle-class fathers in this study assign themselves the duty of cultivating children's cognitive and linguistic skills through conversation and games. For instance, when an engineer father learned that his seven-year-old daughter did not like to drink water at school, he solved the problem as if it were an engineering project. Together with the daughter, he designed experiments to formulate a standard operating procedure (SOP) for her water consumption. Together, they concluded that she must drink thirteen drops during each class break. These fathers view interaction with children as an extension of their professional training or occupational culture, and they expect to foster an embodied habitus that may improve their children's future opportunities in the professional labor market.[38]

However, most parents face a workplace culture that is not family-friendly, as Taiwan ranks among the countries with the longest working day.[39] Even young children have a clear sense of the time crunch faced by their overworked parents. In December 2010, a teacher at Central School asked a class of second graders to write down their Christmas wishes. In addition to the predictable ones ("I wish to grow taller," "I wish to have better grades," and so on), several children wrote: "I wish my parents didn't have to work so late," "I wish my dad could come home for dinner," and "I wish my dad could come back to Taiwan [from working in the PRC] more often."

Work and family are most difficult to balance when the father's firm expands its operations across international borders. Time-space compression technologies such as the internet and cellphones also increase their work hours. Emails and conference calls during off-work hours are common. One father even keeps his cellphone next to him when he showers, afraid that he will miss an important call from clients in different time zones. Some fathers are stationed overseas, mostly in China or Southeast Asia, and return home on every one or two months. In one Central School classroom, four out of twenty students had a father working in Mainland China. Another father was laid off from a managerial position when he refused a transfer to a factory in the PRC, and at nearly fifty years of age, he wound up driving a taxi. Many fathers chose to relocate in China to enhance the economic welfare of the family, because expatriate packages allowed them to receive between one and a half and two times their previous salary in Taiwan.[40]

Eric Cheng is a well-built forty-one-year-old man who works as a manager in the PRC and returns to his family in Taiwan once a month. He feels torn between fulfilling the responsibility of breadwinning and sustaining emotional ties with his two sons. In a soft voice, he sadly admits: "I know little about what goes on in my children's lives. I can only imagine from what the kids tell me." He brings up what one son once said to him when still in kindergarten, "Daddy, why do you have to do this job? Can't we just sell red bean soup [a traditional dessert]?" He sighs and says: "It hurts, you know. Children are simple. They just want you to be there and spend more time with them. But I can't even do that."

Middle-class fathers in contemporary Taiwan feel a tension between two conflicting constructs of "hegemonic masculinity":[41] in the public sphere, they are rewarded for being frequent flyers who navigate the global business world and proudly represent "transnational business masculinity."[42] Yet in the private sphere, they are expected to conform to a new, gender-sensitive masculinity by sharing the housework and childrearing.

Professional fathers use different approaches to resolve conflicts of masculinity in the situation of transnational breadwinning. Some highlight their financial contribution and divide parenting labor along traditional gender lines. Unlike mothers who leave their families for work, such as migrant domestic workers, face the social stigma of "abandoning" their children,[43] transnational fatherhood does not seem to present the same threat to the family routine. One mother described her engineer husband's work in the PRC by saying: "His living in China doesn't really affect the children. Even if he weren't in China, I'd take care of 95 percent of the kids' stuff anyway."

Some other transnational fathers try hard to provide paternal companionship with the assistance of technology. For example, Eric frequently uses Skype, phone calls, and text messaging to maintain his virtual presence in the family life. When his sons were small, he would pretend over the phone that he was their favorite Japanese cartoon character Ultraman to "create some space of imagination for the kids." Now, every morning when Eric gets up and before he goes to bed every night, he uses text messaging to see how his two boys are doing: "Go to bed early and have a good night! Keep up the good work everyone, Dad has to work now." "Good morning kids, time to go to school now!" "Don't sleep in tomorrow. When you get up, remember to text dad to say good morning so I know you're up."

The pedagogical, labor-intensive, high-cost project of global parenting has the unintended consequence of magnifying the gendered division of labor in childrearing. While the mother's main duty is to convert her cultural capital to enrich the child's holistic development, the father is mainly responsible for maximizing household income to meet the rising cost of childrearing. Feeling pressured to invest more time and energy in breadwinning, some middle-class fathers take the overseas high-salaried jobs but suffer from the emotional cost of physical separation.

The "Transitional": Engineering a Happy Childhood

Watching his two daughters playing in a camping tent set up in their fashion-ably decorated living room, Jason Liu calmly said, "I don't want them to become too successful." Jason is a forty-two-year-old computer engineer who achieved financial success during the spike in Taiwan's high-tech industry. He earns an annual salary close to 100,000 USD, plus generous stock options. Yet he feels that his career is too stressful, and he laments his own childhood as "lost" to intensive academic pressure. Feeling confident about the family wealth he has accumulated, he prefers for his daughters to "enjoy life." He hopes that as adults, they will find "easy jobs" such as work in public service.[44] He even has started to research about capacity training related to the civil service exams.

Unlike their class peers who embrace global pathway consumption, parents like Jason Liu steer their children away from bilingual kindergartens and overly competitive schools. I call this group of parents the "transitionals" because they are still indecisive and struggling in the middle range of the spectrum.[45] They aspire to build a pressure-free childhood for their children, yet they still micro-manage their children's lives to avoid the risk of sliding down the class ladder.

Jason actively "engineers" a happy childhood for his two daughters, five and eight years old. He finds watching television and playing computer games dis-tasteful. Instead, he carefully plans to fill the weekend with activities that "nur-ture children's bodies and minds." The family often goes hiking so the children can escape the busy city and breathe in the fresh air. Yet Jason later confessed to me that he dislikes outdoor activities: "Before having children, we [he and his wife] spent the weekends in department stores and air-conditioned rooms. Getting in touch with nature, this is all for the kids." He also feels ambivalent about the effects this concerted planning has on his two daughters: "I'm not so sure if this is good or bad. For instance, they don't know how to play by them-selves. They open their eyes and ask: 'Dad, where are we going today? Take us out to play!' They make me feel that I need to make more plans [pause]. This seems, um, a bit odd. We're often trapped in a dilemma."

Jason and his wife, Catherine Wang, were college sweethearts at the school of engineering. After their younger daughter was born, Catherine quit her en-gineering job and started working as a university administrator. The change greatly reduced her salary, but she is glad to get off work on time. Catherine is a music lover who learned piano during her childhood. She wanted her eldest daughter, Penny, to follow in her footsteps, but she carefully avoided forcing her to learn:

> I want to give her a gift. It's not for me. It's for her. I want her to have a hobby she really likes. But I won't force her to learn piano. I was waiting for her to open her mouth and say "I want to learn." How did I do it? Since she was little, every month I collected information about all the concerts in Taipei. I arranged, like an investment for her, whatever performance—as long as children were allowed, we went to it. I thought gradually she would [pauses] . . . I was waiting for her to say it. Finally, we went to a concert by Lang Lang. She turned around and told me: "Mommy, I want to learn piano."

During our interview, Catherine repeatedly used the analogy of a gift to describe her motherly contributions to her children, including both her affective care and the arrangement of enrichment programs. The gift analogy, which prioritizes the needs of the recipient (the children), helps Catherine dissociate herself from the traditional role of Chinese parent as an authority figure who dictates children's lives. Catherine firmly believes that parents should give their children choices instead of orders, even as they work hard in the background to channel the formation of these "choices."

Instead of directives and punishment, Catherine follows expert advice that parents should reason with their children and encourage them to negotiate with the rules. However, Catherine told me in a worried tone: "You see, Penny is a child with strong opinions. We give her a lot of space to make decisions on her own. But when she grows up, she's going to find out that lots of things aren't up to her, and she might turn around to us and ask how come she can't decide on this and that." Parents like Catherine are concerned about whether their outspoken and opinionated children will adjust well as an adult to institutions that still emphasize loyalty, hard work, and respect for authority.

Janice Chan is another devoted mother at Central School. Her husband, Eric Cheng, whom we met earlier, flies back and forth to China, so she quit her job at an insurance company to become a full-time homemaker raising their two sons. In their spacious apartment piled with books on parenting and education, Janice talked at length about her belief in the model of developmentally adaptive education as opposed to the traditional Chinese method of pushing children to learn early. She sent her two boys to a public kindergarten that offered only play-based learning, with no academic teaching. However, when her younger son seemed to lag behind the other elementary students, Janice started to question this decision:

> He was just playing all the time and learned nothing [at the kindergarten]. I believe that you shouldn't push children to learn before they reach the right age for learning. . . . But now he learns really slowly. Sometimes I wonder, perhaps this is my fault? Did I make him lag behind like this? I've been worried [about] whether we should send him to an after-school program now.

Worried about her son's school performance, Janice searched for alternative educational venues. She and her husband also considered the possibility of immigrating to the US, although they were not sure if they could manage it financially. They were also attracted to alternative education and had even visited Garden School a couple of times. Yet they were hesitant to move to that end of the parenting spectrum out of fear that their children would not be able to integrate into a mainstream high school.

These transitional parents experience a tug-of-war between the polarized goals of childrearing. Despite their earnest pursuit of happiness and autonomy for their children, they still worry about whether their children can survive the cruel reality and secure material comfort in the future. Many of the transitional parents are likely to move toward the right end of the spectrum, when children reach teenage years and face more intense competition at high school. An increasing number of middle-class parents, albeit still a minority, are moving toward the other end of the spectrum and practicing a security strategy I call orchestrating natural growth.

Orchestrating Natural Growth

The loaded term *natural growth* repeatedly appeared in my interviews with parents who are leaning toward a more permissive way of childrearing. The notion is vaguely defined against three interventions parents deemed "unnatural" and harmful: First, children should enjoy free time for playing and pressuring them to learn is destructive to their development. Second, parents should avoid too much "hands-on" guidance so children can develop independence and autonomy. Finally, the family should live an organic life, in connection with nature, to protect children's purity and health from commercialism and chemical toxins.

This middle-class version of a "free-range childhood," which I call orchestrating natural growth, bears a superficial resemblance to the childrearing

approach of working-class American parents that Lareau calls "the accomplishment of natural growth." These American working-class children are granted
an autonomous world apart from adults in which they are free to try out new
experiences and create their own entertainment, because parents are occupied
by work and the family has insufficient resources. In contrast, middle-class
Taiwanese parents who orchestrate their children's natural growth engage in
concerted efforts and invisible work in the background. While consciously re-
fraining from much intervention in children's free play, they thoughtfully design their home space and carefully remove commercial toys so to encourage
children to pursue more "naturally oriented" or "developmentally appropriate"
activities. This section shows that their strategy of natural parenting relies heavily on middle-class financial capital and Western cultural capital.

This style of childrearing is best exemplified by those who choose alternative
schools for their children. These parents prioritize the pursuit of what Andrew
Sayer calls "internal goods," such as a happy childhood and natural development,
and consider "external goods" like gaining credentials as secondary.[46] Garden
School in Yilan follows a humanistic approach to learning based on the Aus-
trian educational philosophy of Rudolf Steiner, the founder of anthroposophy.
Garden School jettisons textbooks, examinations, and other formal assessment
methods. The staff members there enjoy a high degree of autonomy to design
their curricula, incorporating instruction in arts, crafts, music, dance, cooking,
farming, and nature-oriented activities. The educational goal is to accomplish
children's natural and holistic development. Parents are advised to curtail their
urge to "teach" children and to wait until the children grow ready to learn.

Early Garden School parents included many lifestyle migrants who moved
to the countryside to engage in organic farming, a trend related to the growing environmental movement in Taiwan. With increased media exposure and
a growing student population, Garden School now attracts a more heterogeneous group of parents. Drawing on a narrative understanding between the
past (their childhoods), the present (their work experience), and their hopes
for the children's future, these parents choose alternative education to avoid the
risks they perceive as salient in children's lives and recalibrate the priority goals
of childrearing.

Narratives of Alternative Pathway

The majority of Garden School parents are former urbanites who emigrated to
Yilan for the purpose of children's education. Attending school in the 1980s,

when grades rather than personal interest were treated as primary concerns, many of these parents recall emotional trauma from conflicts with authoritarian teachers or unhealthy competition with peers. They are thus determined to protect their children from these harms by seeking an educational environment that privileges individuality and well-roundedness.

Tim Huang, a thirty-seven-year-old civil engineer who wears heavy glasses and has a quiet demeanor, described his learning experience: "I just went with the flow. I did whatever people asked me to do. I didn't know what I wanted, what I liked." His wife, Julie Chen, a college graduate of a similar age and now a full-time homemaker, was selected for a special "chorus class" at an elite high school in Taipei. She recalled this environment as suffocating for her self-esteem:

> Only people with good grades could get into the chorus class. But we were singing not for fun, only for competition. If you didn't sing well, the teacher just told you to shut up—you were to move your lips but make no sound. My classmates weren't playing during the breaks; they were competing for grades. The teacher didn't care about you; they only cared about your grades. All of the nonacademic subjects—art, sports, cooking—turned into math and English.

Some parents originally intended to cultivate global competitiveness but came to realize that some of their children's personality traits—such as being hyperactive, talking out of turn, and lacking focus—made it difficult for them to adjust to a mainstream education. Meg Kao and her husband, Wen Lin, fall into this group. They are both in their forties and have master's degrees from the US. When Meg was six months pregnant with her son Tom, she quit her accounting job and went to Los Angeles to give birth so that Tom could benefit from "flexible citizenship." They initially enrolled Tom in a bilingual kindergarten and elite private school in Taipei, but their plan to raise a global elite child fell apart when Tom was diagnosed with attention-deficit disorder. Meg searched for up-to-date information and resources, reading every book she could find about raising children with ADD, attending dozens of parenting and educational psychology lectures, and looking for online parental support groups. All these efforts "opened her eyes" to alternative options, and she "did a complete one-eighty" with her educational preference.

The family moved to Yilan for Garden School. They purchased a house with a yard and carefully decorated the interior based on the Steiner school style— painting the walls and dying the curtains in warm pastel colors, using natural wood furniture, and setting up a hammock in the playroom. Although Wen has to commute three hours to work in another city, he fully supports the decision to move. He is thankful that Tom's condition helped him "see through" the individualist façade of meritocracy and appreciate the structural bias inherent in mainstream education:

> After we had found out that our child couldn't fit into the system, we started to realize that we were actually lucky because we'd got good grades back then. Those naughty classmates of ours who got bad grades, we thought it was their fault, but it was actually the education system, which isn't suitable for every child. . . . We were winners in the system; many others became losers, and their difficulties we simply ignored and overlooked.

Some parents draw on their work experiences to question whether educational achievement is worth sacrificing happiness. Jia-ming Lin is a forty-year-old father and a graduate of a middle-ranked college in Taipei. After toiling for a few years in the city, he decided to return to Yilan to live with his parents and work in the family's lumber business. His wife, Shu-fen, graduated from the same college and now also helps out in the factory. Both of them had to retake the college entrance exam given their average grades. Becoming parents, they no longer believe that academic performance has a direct correlation with actual ability. Sitting in the yard of their house with the four stray dogs they adopted running around, Shu-fen said:

> We suffered a lot to make it into a mediocre college. So what? Now, I don't think degrees are the be all and end all. . . . We only expect him to learn basic language and math skills. These should be enough for one to survive in the world. This would be good enough for us. It would be great if he could master a skill. If that's not working, at least we have the family business; he can work here.

A significant number of Garden School parents, especially those who are originally from Yilan, operate family businesses such as restaurants and shops. They do not prioritize a college education for their children as much as their own parents did. Instead, they emphasize the cultivation of social skills and personality traits over degrees and certificates. Having a family business places them in a secure class position such that they can feel more relaxed about the uncertain outcome of alternative education.

Finally, some parents, especially those working in technology and the creative industries, expect alternative education to provide the upbringing they were unable to acquire when they grew up. By escaping the rigid structure of mainstream education, these parents hope to cultivate alternatives to competitiveness—such as creativity, autonomy, artistic expression, and social competence—that can help their children to thrive in an unknown future marked by innovation.

Cultural Mobility: Reconstructing the Global and Local

Parents who choose alternative education encounter criticism from middle-class urbanites who cultivate global competitiveness. In the absence of standardized tests and textbooks, alternative methods are suspected of being "too easy" and "only about having fun." The skeptics question whether these children can survive in the "real world" and gain admission to decent universities. Locals in Yilan are also skeptical of Garden School. Many are puzzled as to why so many urbanites favor a school that, in their eyes, embraces an "outdated" style of education. Instead, most local parents enroll their children in more "competitive" schools in the city. Also, Garden School children are easily labeled as "problem children" who are "too wild," "difficult to control," and "have no respect for rules." This section shows how Garden School parents justify their educational choice by reconstituting the meanings of the global and the local and defining their pursuit of alternative pathway as a practice of cultural mobility and global parenting.

Leah Tao and Ming-chih Chang both struggled academically and only made it to technical college in Taiwan, but they became successful sales managers and worked in Shanghai for several years. Although their oldest daughter, Katie, attended one of the most expensive, prestigious international kindergartens in Shanghai, the parents were uncomfortable with the school's political education. When Leah was pregnant with their second child, she stumbled upon an article about Garden School in a Taiwanese magazine. She excitedly told Ming-chih, "Oh, if our children could go to a school like this, it would be wonderful!"

After some research and deliberation, Leah decided to quit her job in Shanghai and move to Yilan with the children. Her Taiwanese friends in the PRC voiced serious concerns about the decision: "Everyone's trying to go abroad, why would you take your kids to the middle of nowhere?" Leah responded to similar objections with confidence: "A lot of people worry for us, but we don't worry. I believe children will grow on their own, and what matters most is that the education makes them happy." Ming-chih, however, retains an orientation toward future competition, hoping that alternative education will help his children "think outside the box" and cultivate an innovative mind to adapt to the flexible global economy.

Leah described her friends' views: "They say that only two types of people send their children to Garden School—those who are highly educated and super rich and can send their children abroad and those who are idiots." In other words, peers who object to alternative education do so for two distinct reasons related to children's globalized future. Some opponents view alternative education as a backward step, going against the trend of global pathway consumption. Conversely, others believe that alternative education is suitable only for wealthy families who can afford higher education abroad.

In spite of criticism from others, parents like Leah turn to Garden School that provides an abundance of cultural resources to bolster parental confidence. Many mothers sign up for the two-year teacher-training course not with the goal of becoming teachers, but simply to better understand Rudolf Steiner's educational philosophy. Unlike other alternative schools, Garden School emphasizes a Western-based curriculum that helps parents feel confident in the school's educational legitimacy. Many parents express sentiments similar to these: "Garden School uses a philosophy and a curriculum that's well thought out and proven, not something they just invented." And, "The founding father is a famous professor, and there's an organization in Switzerland that provides resources to schools all over the world."

Garden School parents view their choice of an alternative pathway as a practice of *cultural mobility*. Although no transnational mobility is involved in their pursuit of global parenting, they rely on Garden School to access and consume cultural goods and services across spatial terrains. Globalization creates a global "imagined community" of humanistic education for like-minded parents to identify with across borders. From time to time, Garden School receive overseas visitors who are educators utilizing the same pedagogical approach; the school also organizes tours for students, teachers, and parents to visit similar schools in other countries and attend training sessions in Switzerland.

The global curriculum of Garden School also helps parents to see their rural hometown and the older generation's lifestyle in a new light. While urban parents at Garden School move to the countryside in search of pastoral bliss, those who grew up in a rural area see their move to Yilan as a journey of "returning to their roots."

Ying-jer Wang, a forty-two-year-old father and a high school administrator, shares a nostalgic hope that a lifestyle of voluntary simplicity will preserve children's innocence and happiness. He and his wife, also a teacher, decided to move back to his hometown of Yilan for his two children to attend Garden School. Ying-jer described his academically focused childhood with a sense of anguish: "When I was a child, my parents did everything for me so I could focus on my study. Now I feel angry sometimes. They know so many things about farming, but I know nothing. They didn't allow me to do anything." After surviving educational competition and hectic urban life, Ying-jer now aspires to tranquility in the countryside.

However, Ying-jer's father, a longtime farmer in Yilan, opposed his decision: "Why are you sending the children to a school where they learn how to climb trees and play with crafts, not reading and writing?" Ying-jer's parents, like many in their generation, viewed educational achievement and social mobility (both occupational and rural to urban) as the primary goals of childrearing. They still do not consider a farmer's skills and knowledge as cultural capital worthy of passing on to the next generation. Nevertheless, Garden School has sufficient symbolic capital associated with the glamour of global education to redeem the values of farming, carpentry, and even tree climbing by incorporating them as parts of the official curriculum. Even though limited transnational mobility is involved, Garden School parents engage in cultural mobility in a local, even rural, context, a process that globalizes the local and modernizes the traditional.

"Natural Mother" and "Weekend Dad"

Many parents tell me: "Children can adjust to Garden School very easily. It's us parents who had a difficult time making such a big change!" Among families who relocated for Garden School, most fathers still work or operate businesses in the city, and they join their family only on the weekends. These mothers jokingly call themselves "pseudo–single parents." The split household also places a burden on the family finances, because most mothers gave up their careers to become full-time homemakers. Although everyday expenses in the country are lower than living the city, the family's spending increases because of the cost of commuting and maintaining two homes.

Mothering duties become even more intense when these families pursue a Garden School–approved organic lifestyle that discourages the use of commercial products. Scholars have argued that the ideologies of the "organic child" and "natural mothering" have reinforced a neoliberal notion of motherhood that holds women individually responsible for protecting their children's health and purity through vigilance over food consumption and vaccine refusal.[47] Similarly, the discourse of children's "natural growth" has become so dominant at Garden School that mothers are pressured to engage in the practice of "natural mothering" and to build an organic home for their children.

Garden School serves organic, vegetarian lunches and advises families to cook at home with fresh produce and organic ingredients. In addition, the school requests that parents prepare materials for the children's craft activities at school, which include weaving yarn dolls, hand-dyeing classroom curtains, sewing indoor shoes, and knitting bags to hold school supplies. Not surprisingly, most of these duties fall on the shoulders of mothers. My informants respond to these expectations with both positive and negative emotions. Some mothers, especially the few who are gainfully employed, perceive these requests as a time-consuming burden that challenges their maternal competence. One mother describes the challenges of hand-sewing slippers in her first school assignment: "We spent the whole three days. Oh my God, that was terrifying for me! I haven't done anything like that since high school. And nowhere could you buy such shoes! Nowhere indeed!"

However, the majority of my informants, mostly full-time homemakers, perceive their participation in these activities as a confirmation of their motherly devotion. One mother proudly showed me her cooking calendar, which documented the contents of three family meals, as proof that she had carefully managed the nutrition and diversity of her children's food intake. Another attended a Garden School workshop for two years and regularly volunteers at the school. When I asked about her family separation (her husband works in Taipei), she answered: "I don't mind it. Probably because after moving here I had more to do, like getting to learn more about the philosophy of Dr. Rudolf Steiner." Pausing for a few seconds, she added: "I need to get involved in things, so it makes sense that I don't work." Although being a full-time homemaker implies a social status with financial comfort, in Taiwan, it is also viewed as a waste of human capital for highly educated women. These mothers try to elevate the mundane routines of housewifery to the level of "scientific motherhood" marked by substantial contribution to the family's welfare.[48]

The remaking of family life has also led to some unintended consequences for spousal relationships, including reinforcing a gendered division of labor and disparate parenting styles between mother and father. Annie Liao and her husband Gary Wu have organized one such split family. Gary lives in Taipei during the week, and his work requires frequent travel to mainland China. The family's home in Yilan completely abides by the Garden School's motto. There is no television in the living room, only a set of handmade wooden play furniture; the mother also purged all the plastic and metal toys from their old home in Taipei. In the foyer stands the "seasonal table" recommended by Garden School, decorated with seasonal items such as acorns, rocks, and other natural objects as well as wool dolls handmade by the mother.

During my visit to their townhouse in Yilan, my cellphone rang. After I had finished my call, Annie's daughter came to me with a mischievous smile and asked, "What games do you have on your cellphone?" Remembering the school's policy restricting children's exposure to electronic devices, I felt incredibly awkward, and her knowledge of cellphone games surprised me. Annie complained that Gary was becoming a corrupting force: "It's all his fault. Every time he comes back from Taipei, he lets them play with his cellphone and iPad, and it's all against our house rules. . . . The teachers keep telling me, you have to tell your husband to give your children affection, not these grown-up games." Gary, sitting next to us, innocently voiced his disagreement: "Is it really that big a deal? I just want to show them the apps I downloaded. It's just a bit of fun, even educational. When I've got nothing to do in Taipei I browse the Internet and find things like this."

"Weekend dads" attempt to build intimate ties with their children using familiar tools and technologies or they try to compensate for their absence by indulging their children with the consumer goods they have easy access to in the city. Yet these commercial objects are exactly what Garden School prohibits. Leah's husband, Ming-chih, remains in Shanghai for work and visits the family every two months. Before every return trip, Ming-chih arms himself with plenty of gifts for the children—Disney dolls, Hello Kitty backpacks, a toy knife for his son, and so on. He uses material consumption to express fatherly love and perform long-distance fatherhood. When Leah voiced her disapproval, Ming-chih interjected to defend himself: "Then what am I earning money in China for?! I mean, the whole point is to make money and spend it on them. . . . I miss them and I just think about what they need. When I've got nothing to do on weekends I just go to the department store and buy things for them."

Isolated from the physical presence of their husbands, Garden School mothers gain a sense of belonging and community support by connecting with like-minded mothers. Annie Liao describes the isolation of her former time spent as a full-time mother in the city: "I felt very lonely in Taipei. I had no community, no support. I was shut in at home taking care of the children. I was very emotional all the time." Garden School mothers, with their shared ideas and lifestyles, are able to build extensive social networks to exchange information, organize group activities, and collectively purchase nonmainstream commodities. Such social capital helps them accumulate the cultural and material resources to practice childrearing styles that are distinct from their upbringing, reinforcing their commitment to alternative pedagogy against the suspicions and disapproval of others.

The Unnaturalness of Orchestrated Natural Growth

The pursuit of an alternative pathway creates uncertainty regarding children's educational outcomes. Thus, Garden School parents carefully scrutinize their children, as well as older students at the same school, for signs of positive changes that confirm the value of alternative education. At the end of each school year, Garden School puts on a play in English and a student showcase performed by its middle school students. Many parents encouraged me to attend: "The students are really amazing and they look so confident. It really isn't like anything you see at regular schools." "Have you seen the final showcase? Every time I see it, I feel good about my decision."

Feeling insecure about their children's futures, Garden School parents feel pressured to constantly and reflexively monitor their childrearing practice. Some parents, especially mothers, apologetically told me, "Our family isn't very Garden School." They question themselves whether they have made the necessary transformations to their family life, and they worry that their failure to do so may incur negative and irreversible consequences for their children. In some cases, their micromanagement of family life unintentionally leads to a fixation on the notion of natural growth.

Steiner education identifies child development by stages and prescribes "developmentally appropriate" learning models. For elementary school pupils, extracurricular classes are not recommended; these children should simply enjoy free play after school. To achieve the "natural rhythm" the school prescribes, some parents as wholehearted followers even make their children "unlearn" things or discourage them from learning certain skills. For example, some children attended bilingual kindergartens prior to Garden School, and their parents deliberately let their English skills get rusty. One second grader was very interested in learning piano, but his mother discouraged him because she had heard that, according to the Steiner theory, playing the piano at that age impeded children's growth. In other words, the very idea of orchestrating natural growth is an oxymoron—instead of unfolding naturally, children's "growth" is carefully planned; the natural growth orchestrated as such is rather unnatural.

Garden School advises parents to create a natural environment and to lead an organic lifestyle. Household items, especially children's clothes and toys, should preferably be made of natural materials like cotton and wood. Plastic toys, commercial games, and televisions should be removed from the home. Some parents, suspicious of childhood vaccines and Western medicine, prefer herbal treatments, homeopathy, or Chinese medicine. Garden School parents carefully build a haven, but they cannot fully insulate their children from the broader environment in which aggressive corporate advertising stimulates children's consumerist desires. Garden School pupils are exposed to commercial culture when interacting with fathers, grandparents, and other relatives, although they are keenly aware that they must present themselves "correctly" at school. We observed that some boys secretly exchange game cards in the school bathroom. Likewise, a second-grade girl who loves her T-shirt of Princess Elsa from *Frozen*, a gift from her auntie, astutely told me: "Garden teachers don't like this! We can't wear things like this to school."

The orchestration of natural growth produces another paradox: children's independence and autonomy, which these parents desire as the outcome of their childrearing, are still largely dependent on parents' class privilege. Parents with greater economic capital can afford to send their children to study overseas if they fail to gain admission to local universities, or they can secure their employment at a family business as a backup plan. Parents with greater cultural capital tend to provide supplemental education to bolster their children's academic abilities. They seek lenient, flexible private tutors or small-group English classes that do not jeopardize their pursuit of a "happy childhood."

A teacher at Garden School describes these families: "Strangely, some children come to our school to play, and go home to study." For example, Maggie Wei, who works as a college lecturer, chose Garden School to avoid the negative elements of mainstream schooling, such as constant testing and excessively stern teachers. Yet she still has reservations about the effectiveness of alternative education. When she noticed that her children were making spelling errors, she started to make them practice at home. She told me, self-assuredly: "It's okay. If the school doesn't teach it, we can do it at home. Whatever they don't do, we can do ourselves."

Garden School parents swear to safeguard a happy childhood and respect the natural rhythm of children's growth, but their pursuit of alternative education and cultural mobility leads to uncertain outcomes in local institutional contexts. It is at this intersection of determination and perplexity that the paradox takes place. These parents, mothers in particular, feel driven to micromanage their family lives and even fixate on the notion of natural growth. They aspire to raise confident, autonomous children, but their orchestration may controvert their purpose.

Conclusion

Globalization brings in a mixture of hope and fear for middle-class Taiwanese parents. They are optimistic about their children's expanded access to transnational and cultural mobility, but they feel insecure in this dynamic, interconnected, and unpredictable world. This chapter uses two Weberian ideal types to characterize the opposite ends of the spectrum that describes middle-class educational choices and security strategies. In reality, many parents are still struggling and indecisive, falling somewhere among "the transitionals" who perform a delicate balancing act between preparing children for global competition and protecting childhood as a time of natural development.

Parents at one end of the spectrum prioritize cultivating their children's capacity for competition and mobility in global arenas. They view their own childhood having been deprived of material resources and opportunities for transnational or cultural mobility. Their career paths are embedded in global capitalism and dependent on their educational credentials, rendering them sensitive to the value of Western cultural capital. Their intricate knowledge of globalization produces an "upscaling of insecurity" about their children's future,[49] which they predict will be marked by increasing competition and heightened uncertainty in the global labor market. Their strategies of global pathway consumption rely heavily on their financial capital and the cultural capital that favors Western language and social skills.

Parents at the other end of the spectrum take great pains to guard their children's "natural growth" from academic pressures and other social toxins. They describe their own childhood as clouded by academic pressure and educational trauma that led to a lack of interests or hobbies in adulthood. Many choose alternative education considering their own work experiences marked by a disjuncture between credentials and careers. They pursue cultural mobility by subscribing to the Western paradigm of alternative education so their children can enjoy widening access to future possibilities. Globalization helps these

Taiwanese parents connect with the global community of humanistic education to establish symbolic legitimacy for their choice of an alternative pathway.

Middle-class Taiwanese parents across the spectrum seek transnational references—class peers around the globe—to define the benchmark for security and to imagine their children's future. Although institutional changes have allowed flexibility in schooling choices, parents who embrace global childrearing or alternative education encounter frictions between cultural scripts and institutional reality. Despite the celebration of children's independence and autonomy in the globalized discourses of parenting, Taiwan's institutional environments, including mainstream schools and workplace, are still dominated by a culture of collectivism and Confucianism, which rewards obedience, seniority, and hierarchy.

In tension with the local institutional contexts, these global security strategies result in unintended consequences in the family routines, parent-child dynamics, and gender division of parenting labor. While middle-class parents lament their lost childhood and authoritarian upbringing, many unwittingly repeat what their parents did—controlling their children through micromanaging the environment and depriving of opportunities for children to explore and fail. Despite embracing the idea of happy childhood, they arrange education in ways that ultimately and continuously serve to generate a promising adulthood with instrumental goals.

3 Taiwanese Working Class

Affirming Parental Legitimacy

My husband and I run a food stall at the night market so we're both very busy. A couple of days ago, my son misbehaved so I hit him and he got a bruise. The day-care teacher found out and called the police without telling us. I promised her that we would never hit the kid again, . . . but the next morning, the police knocked at our door. And then the day after social services called and wanted to talk to us. I was so confused and started to panic. . . . I'm very scared that they're just going to come at any moment and take my kid away with no warning. Who can help us? What do we do? Whom can we talk to? Can the city councilor or some reporters help us? I feel very scared.

AN ANXIOUS MOTHER POSTED this plea for help in an online forum at around midnight.[1] She had just finished a long working day; her hair and clothes were probably stained with grease. She rushed to seek advice from strangers, but the online community was far from sympathetic. Commenters accused her of "poor emotional management" and "lacking knowledge of childrearing." Some posters even questioned whether she was fit to parent: "Your food vendor business is a terrible place to have kids around. . . . Do they even get enough sleep?" "I get that you need to make money, but you can't save time by hitting and yelling at your kids." "You don't know how to educate your children. Why do you even bother having kids? What can you offer them anyway?"

Instead of receiving help and advice, this desperate mother was targeted by online bullying. She added a second post to defend herself as a capable parent: "Running your own small business is a hardship that most people do not understand. . . . The minute I get free time, I give my children a shower, and they are in bed by 9 p.m. They always get a full night's sleep." Although she occasionally used spanking to discipline her children, she swore that this punishment was very different from abuse: "I would never injure my children. When they misbehave and I have to hit them, I'm heartbroken and crying too." Likely with shaking hands and tears in her eyes, she begged for sympathy from the other posters to the online forum: "Please . . . You can have your opinions. But don't make me sound like a criminal."

This chapter examines the childrearing practice of working-class Taiwanese as their security strategies to cope with increasing economic insecurity and cultural uncertainty. Taiwan's outflow of capital and inflow of labor in recent decades created employment insecurity for many working-class men. Many of them feel pressured to go to Mainland China and Southeast Asia to find wives and organize a new form of global household. Meanwhile the social campaigns of schooling reform and parental education are promoting a new repertoire of childrearing that is middle-class-centric and developed under a substantial Western influence. Conventional practices such as corporal punishment and the accomplishment of natural growth are labeled as problematic conduct indicative of parents' shortcomings in knowledge and skills.

The working-class parents I interviewed in Taiwan develop a variety of security strategies to cope with a decline in parental legitimacy. Some reinforce the tradition of harsh discipline as an act of responsible parenting or a way to compensate the father's emasculated manhood. Some parents, especially immigrant mothers, seek pathways across class divides, including relocating to better school districts and building wider social connections, to improve their children's opportunities for class mobility. Southeast Asian immigrants' cultural heritages and transnational connections were seen as a burden that impeded the assimilation of mixed children but the recent state policy to invest southbound turned them into a valuable ethnic capital.

Stagnant Mobility and Cross-Border Marriage

When Taiwan's economy took off in the 1970s and 1980s, the prevalence of small and medium-sized businesses offered plenty of opportunities for the working class to pursue entrepreneurship. After the economic structuring of the 1990s, Taiwan was no longer the "boss island."[2] Capital concentrated in the hands of the few and most small entrepreneurs were unable to remain competitive. Today, over half of Taiwanese business ventures end in failure.[3]

Many of the working-class fathers in this study once had dreams of microentrepreneurship as a pathway to class mobility. They borrowed money to try their hand in establishing businesses in Taiwan, China, or Southeast Asia, but their dreams clashed in the end. The more fortunate ones were able to sell family land to pay off their debts, but most found themselves in deep financial

trouble. These families appeared economically stable, but it was only after getting to know these families that I learned about their struggles with debt. Many
depended on credit cards to make ends meet and to avoid the humiliation of
asking for loans from friends and family members.

The working class faces not only stagnant social mobility but also increased
vulnerability and precariousness in the globalized economy. The outflow of
Taiwanese capital to China and Southeast Asia broadened opportunities for
professionals to pursue transnational mobility, but for working-class people, it
produced only job loss and competition with migrant workers from Southeast
Asia. Contract labor visas were introduced in the early 1990s to mitigate the
capital outflow and have since continued to grow in the manufacturing and
caregiving sectors. The current population of foreign workers is over 650,000,
or more than 5.5 percent of Taiwan's working population.[4]

Taiwan's unemployment rose substantially at the beginning of the current
century, reaching its peak after the 2008 financial crisis. In general, Taiwanese
men suffer more job insecurity than women.[5] The unemployment rate is highest for younger cohorts of men across all educational levels because many are
temporarily jobless as they search for better positions or prepare for examinations. The rate drops significantly for college-educated men above thirty years
old, but for those with less education, unemployment remains high even as they
increase in age.[6] Thus, middle-aged men with lower levels of education appear
most susceptible to involuntary unemployment. In addition, employment benefits and job security are deteriorating. Blue-collar and low-end service workers are increasingly subject to short-term contracts, temporary jobs, part-time
work, and other forms of contingent work.

In addition to their labor market disadvantages, working-class Taiwanese
men are also viewed as undesirable husbands in the local marriage market.
Because of this, many farmers, fishermen, and factory workers look for spouses
in Southeast Asia and China.[7] Cross-border marriages help working-class Taiwanese men meet their traditional obligation to reproduce the patrilineal family. Immigrant wives also provide unpaid labor to family farms or as caretakers
for their husband's aging parents.[8]

Men who experienced prior marital disruption also tend to engage in cross-
border marriages. Taiwan's divorce rate has risen rapidly since the late 1990s.
During this period, the educational gradient in marital dissolution reversed
from positive to negative. That is, prior to the 1990s, college-educated men and
women were most likely to divorce, but today men with a high school diploma
or less are most likely to divorce.[9]

Cross-border marriage is a union of "spatial hypergamy,"[10] in which the groom's nationality turns into an elevated rank to compensate for his socio-economic status, rurality, disability, or other social disadvantage. The encounter with foreign women who are seemingly trapped in the third-world poverty temporarily boosts the masculine ego of Taiwanese bachelors. A semiemployed father married to a Vietnamese woman twenty-five years younger smilingly describes the moment when the commercial broker brought him to Vietnam to interview dozens of women in a hotel room: "I felt like an imperial emperor selecting his empress!" However, many immigrant wives found out about their husbands' meager income only after they moved to Taiwan; because of the age or employability of their husbands, some immigrants reluctantly become the primary breadwinners. As we will see later, the transgression of national borders and gender roles stirs marital stress and childrearing difficulties in these families.

State Monitor and Lost Legitimacy

Chapter 1 showed that the increased exposure to global culture has transformed the dominant repertoire of childrearing in Taiwan. Parental competency is now defined and measured in terms of emotional sensitivity, expressive communication, and educational involvement. Family education, which covers marital and parental issues for adults, has become state-sponsored institutions. For those parents who fail to supply their children with financial comfort and cultural inspiration, the media and institutional authorities frequently remind them of their deficiencies.

Children's development has also come under the scrutiny of public health and medical experts. In the 1990s, Taiwan's government introduced an "early intervention" program and began using the category "developmentally delayed" to identify young children who need additional health and education services. Nearly every child under the age of six is incorporated into a network of assessment involving kindergarten and nursery school teachers, pediatricians and nurses, social workers, and parents.[11] Starting since 2005, the preventive program for "high-risk families" involves a wide range of agents, including the police and borough chiefs, as institutional gatekeepers with a mandatory responsibility to report on observing children in possible high-risk environments.

Families that deviate from monoethnic, dual-parent, middle-class normalcy are vulnerable to the label of troubled home. For instance, many medical staff members attribute children's stunted growth to family conditions such as parents' low socioeconomic status and cross-border marriages.[12] State bureaucrats have considered making parenting education a prerequisite to means-tested welfare benefits. The head of the Division of Welfare, Chang Siu-yuan, recently suggested that such a requirement was necessary to prevent child abuse. She said: "Statistical evidence shows that low-income families are more likely to have cases of child abuse. In order to receive welfare benefits such as low-income housing, parents should be asked to attend parenting classes."[13] Although such a provision has not been passed, low-income families are generally perceived as a potentially risky environment for children.

Schools have placed increasing pressure on parents and produced a disciplinary effect upon family life. Schoolteachers expect parents to attend students' activities and field trips and to help children with homework. The learning sheets children take home carry hidden assumptions about the normative ideas of family life and parental competency. In addition, schools also function as a site of family education. Primary and secondary schools are required to offer at least four hours of family education each year. Parents are encouraged to attend lectures by invited experts prior to parent-teacher meetings. Though well-intended, these forms of state paternalism can lead to social labeling and exclusion for the disadvantaged families.

Immigrant mothers, for their shortage of local language skills and cultural knowledge, are similarly targeted as a group of parents who are in serious need of parenting knowledge and skills. Starting in 2005, local governments began collaborating with nongovernmental and community organizations to offer parenting seminars and households visits to instruct immigrant mothers about scientific and hygienic childrearing practices. The Ministry of the Interior prints and gives out free copies of "Guidance for Children's Growth" and "Handbook for Parenting Education" in Indonesian, Vietnamese, Thai, and English. Special funds are allocated to the family education of immigrant parents held at children's schools.[14]

Recent policy has nevertheless changed the social perception of immigrant mothers' cultural differences. With the inauguration of independence-leaning President Ing-wen Tsai in 2016, the New Southbound Policy became an agenda of priority. With rising concerns about Taiwan's overdependence on China's economy, the government is encouraging business to "go south" by investing in Southeast Asia to diversify political and economic risk. The Ministry of Education has earmarked 1 billion TWD (33.2 million USD) for the New Southbound Talent Development Program to facilitate the two-way flows of transnational cultural exchange. Southeast Asian languages will receive further institutional recognition after they are included as parts of the "mother-tongue" language curriculum in all elementary schools from the academic year of 2018. The New Southbound Policy targets children of Southeast Asian immigrants as the beneficiaries, but as we will see later, the new policy also brings them with a mixed blessing.

Problematization of Natural Growth

Many Taiwanese working-class parents raise children in a manner similar to what Lareau calls the "accomplishment of natural growth."[15] Parents keep children safe, enforce discipline when necessary, and allow them to grow. Their efforts are directed toward the care and nurturing of children rather than educating or inspiring them. These parents pay attention to grades, but they do not demand high performance. Children are expected to finish basic education, but a college education is viewed as an option dependent on children's "born with" capacity. Parents will support a child to pursue higher education if he or she shows academic ability.

Although the style of hands-off parenting is partly attributed to their limited time and resources, my research also shows that working-class parents similarly undergo reflexive assessment on their past to anticipate their children's future. Despite not being as articulate as the middle class in narrating their ideas of childrearing, they reflect upon their own childhoods and their regrets as adults to identify the risks they perceive as salient in children's lives and thus define their parental responsibility. Considering their negative experience in education and social mobility attempts, many try to protect their children from early exposure to academic and other pressure in adulthood.

This section situates the emotional experiences of working-class parents in the broader contexts of cultural transformation and institutional changes. The middle-class campaigns to "modernize" education and childrearing, including advocating curriculum reform and parents' participation in school activities, unwittingly exacerbate the decline of parental legitimacy among the working class. The latter's encounters with medical and school authorities inflict the injury of social class filled with feelings of frustration, helplessness, and self-doubt.

"My Mom Is a Better Parent Than We Are"

The Ho family lives in an old apartment at the outskirts of Taipei, which they were lucky to inherit from the father's family. The forty-year-old father, Gu-ming, drives a taxi and earns an annual income about 20,000 USD. His wife,

Bi-fen, five years younger, used to work at an electronics factory but opted to stay at home after having three children. Both of them grew up in poor farming households and started work right after vocational high school. Raised by a strict father, Gu-ming felt like he "was not valued much at home." Now he avoids spanking his children, and Bi-fen tries to satisfy her children's material desires. The living room of their apartment is strewn with cheap toys from the night market, and a variety of snacks are piled on the dining table, within reach of the children.

The Ho children come home directly after school, and they play with each other after they finish homework. Unlike many children in this study who rush their dinner before or after many extracurricular activities, the Ho family enjoys home-cooked dinner together every evening when the father takes a break from driving. Bi-fen disapproves of the long hours her neighbor's only son spends at cram school: "Wouldn't that make school boring? It must be very hard for the kids. All I want for them at this age is to have a painless childhood."

Like many working-class parents, she and Gu-ming experienced frustration at school and failed attempts at entrepreneurship. A few years ago, they tried to open a convenience store, but the business failed and they lost all their savings. Bi-fen comments on her expectations for the future of her children: "We only want them to grow up safe and healthy. Good conduct is more important." Gu-ming shares a similar view and emphasizes that children, rather than parents, should take responsibility for their own learning:

> I told the children, "Learning is your own business, not mine. I won't force you." . . . I just don't want to pressure kids to do what they don't want to do. Of course, I want them to have a good future. But I think for the most part it's still up to them. We try our best to bring them up. What they can handle is really up to them.

Less-educated parents also find it increasingly difficult to help with children's homework, especially with the recent reform of the national curriculum. For example, the new mathematics curriculum is influenced by "constructivist mathematics," a paradigm that emphasizes theoretical reasoning and conceptual knowledge instead of structured drills and repetitive practice. This abstract type of knowledge is more familiar to college-educated parents; it is challenging for shop owners and workers, despite their practical skills in arithmetic. Gu-ming is frustrated with the new curriculum and worries about confusing his children if he gets involved in teaching them: "I have no idea how to teach the math they're learning now! It's too complicated. It was much easier before. I don't understand why they made it so hard now. This way, we don't know how to teach our children."

When I asked Bi-fen how her upbringing influenced her childrearing, she looked down and said in frustration: "I think my mom was a better parent than we are. At least they knew how to discipline children, how to control their material desires." When Bi-fen picks her children up from school, she often gives in to their pleas to buy potato chips, chocolate bars, and sugary sodas at convenience stores on the way home. Her lack of confidence in her parenting is particularly salient in the matter of children's education. Bi-fen frequently compares herself to peers on this matter, asking me questions like "What are the other parents doing? Do they all send children to cram school?" And "My neighbors asked me why our kids are not learning English . . . Do you think if it's too late to learn English at the fourth grade?"

Bi-fen's younger daughter Bei-bei is a second grader at Riverside School. At home, her behavior is largely typical for her age, but at school, she does not speak. When the teacher calls on her to answer questions, Bei-bei freezes. At recess, she stays quiet and keeps to herself. There are a few girls she communicates with nonverbally, and she occasionally whispers a few words. The teacher recommended that she should see a doctor who diagnosed Bei-bei with selective mutism, a childhood anxiety disorder characterized by a child's inability to speak and communicate effectively in particular social settings, such as school.

The mother listened to the teacher's advice and took Bei-bei to several therapy sessions subsidized by the government, but the free sessions ran out before Bei-bei was able to make substantial progress. Bei-bei no longer receives any treatment for her mutism and she continues not to speak at school. Neither of her parents worry about her condition, nor do they consider it a developmental disorder. Instead, they tell others that Bei-bei is introverted and has a quiet demeanor, saying, "This is just the way she behaves," "She is just shy," "She gets nervous easily," and "She simply has an odd personality." Bei-bei's parents believe deeply in children's "natural growth" and perceive medical intervention as unnecessary. Untroubled, Gu-ming comments: "I was like that when I was a child. She will grow out of it, eventually."

Gu-ming and Bi-fen's attitude toward Bei-bei's mutism may strike many experts and middle-class parents as "lazy" or "irresponsible." I, too, was concerned. I tried to broach the subject with caution to avoid making the parents feel criticized. Bi-fen shared that she was concerned when the free treatments ended. She pulled a book about mutism off the shelf, which she bought after the first visit to the doctor who treated Bei-bei. With an embarrassed smile, she confessed: "I could barely finish a few pages. I guess I'm pretty lazy. It's just been sitting there." But Bi-fen is not a lazy parent. Rather, reading has never been a part of her daily routine, and the medical language of the book is particularly difficult to access. Bi-fen also feels alienated from health-care professionals. She describes their first visit at the hospital: "I didn't even know what kind of doctor to see" and "I didn't quite understand what the doctor said."

Bi-fen also shows resistance to her daughter's diagnosis because of the social stigma associated with psychiatry: "They make it sound like she's crazy, like she has a big problem." But ultimately, financial concerns were the primary factor influencing the Ho family's turn toward the narrative of natural growth and the idea that Bei-bei would "grow out" of her mutism. Although Taiwan has universal health care that covers many types of treatment, Bei-bei's follow-up therapy sessions were not covered. Lacking financial resources for the expensive treatments, Bi-fen became convinced that the sessions were futile, saying, "I didn't even think the treatments were working."

Two other working-class families in this study have children with symptoms of behavioral disorders—in their cases, attention-deficit hyperactivity disorder (ADHD). The mothers in these families similarly use a logic of natural growth to counter the teacher's suggestion that the child should see a doctor to obtain a medical diagnosis. One mother flatly refused the suggestion, saying, "The teacher only told us to go to the doctor because she's too lazy to discipline him." The other mother said that the teacher was pathologizing her son to cover the teacher's own deficits: "He just cannot sit still. It's the teacher making excuses for not being able to control students."

To working-class parents, educating children is mainly the job of teachers, and discipline is a necessary part of school education. Even though corporal punishment is now forbidden in the classroom, many parents still offer teachers the privilege of hitting their children for misbehavior. Yet the labels of "ADHD" and "developmental disorder" turn children's behavior problems into a psychological or medical abnormality and shift the burden of discipline onto the shoulders of parents.

Some middle-class parents in this study also have children with ADHD symptoms or other learning disabilities. They keep close eyes on their children's development; once with a susceptible problem, they have sufficient resources to see developmental specialists and hire private coaches. Some parents send their children to alternative schools or get involved in parent-teacher association committees because they have the cultural confidence to question whether mainstream curricula and classrooms are set up to support their children. Likewise, Val Gillies finds that middle-class British mothers with misbehaving children often invoke their children's individuality to claim a special exception or entitlement, whereas working-class mothers have no such "legitimating power and resources" and tend to emphasize their children's commonalities to the others.[16]

Working-class Taiwanese mothers face a double bind when seeking help from medical experts. On the one hand, they are subjected to the stereotype that they are incapable of providing adequate care to their children because of their lack of education. On the other hand, these mothers are rarely able to receive as much information or assistance as they need from professionals because they are assumed to lack sufficient cultural ability or emotional capacity to navigate these complicated health problems.[17] In the face of this conundrum, working-class mothers turn to the cultural logic of "accomplishment of natural growth" to legitimize their limited intervention and avoid being blamed as irresponsible or lazy parents. The narrative of natural growth bolsters their claims of commonality—their child should be treated as "normal" and not differentiated by their unique conditions.[18]

"Who's Going to Have Time to Help Me?"

Atai Chen is usually the last to leave the second-grade classroom at the end of the school day. Until his father or grandmother shows up, Atai's round, bright eyes are anxiously fixed on the window. Wednesday is the father Wu-long Chen's turn to pick him up. When arriving in his gray, stained work clothes, Wu-long always quietly waits by the door. He rarely comes inside to speak to the teacher, and he avoids making eye contact with other parents.[19]

Wu-long was twenty-seven years old when he met Nam at the factory where they both worked. Nam was a contract worker from Thailand. They quickly fell in love and married, and Nam gave birth to a beautiful son. The family of three lived with Wu-long's mother and brother in a run-down three-bedroom apartment. But when Atai was in kindergarten, Wu-long had an affair. Nam angrily left with Atai.

Grandma Chen, who is not yet sixty years old but looks much older, grew up poor and completed only elementary school. After her husband died twenty years ago, she brought up her two sons by working construction and factory jobs. But as she got older, finding a job grew more difficult. She had been un-employed for quite some time before her current job of dishwasher in a restaurant. While Atai was away, Grandma Chen spent her afternoon breaks visiting each day-care center near Nam's factory until she found her grandson. After the divorce, Wu-long gained sole custody and raise Atai together with Grandma. Nam continues to work in Taiwan. She calls Atai nearly every day and visits him on her days off.

Wu-long and Grandma Chen both work long hours. They try to coordinate their schedules so that one of them can take Atai to and from school. At 7:00 a.m. each day, Wu-long takes Atai to school on his motorcycle before hurrying off to work at a lumberyard almost an hour away. He starts work at 8:00 a.m. and usually returns home around 10:00 p.m. He frequently works overtime on weekends to meet the rushed deadlines of international clients. Most days, Grandma Chen picks up Atai from school. She works six days a week and uses her two-hour afternoon break to run household errands and pick up Atai from schools before returning to the restaurant. But on Wednesdays, school ends around noon while Grandma Chen is still at work. Wu-long must commute all the way from the factory to pick up Atai. Occasionally, a great-uncle living nearby takes Atai out for dinner, but on most days, he waits for his grand-mother to get home from work with leftovers or takeout food.

Atai frequently stays home alone after school. His grandmother reminds him not to go outside or answer the door to strangers. The legal regulation against "latchkey children" overlooks the challenges faced by single parents and parents with long or odd work hours, a condition prevalent in the service sector.[20] To avoid violating the regulation, Atai's family might have sent him to after-school care, but Wu-long does not want his son to go through the same ordeal as he did. His teenage years were mostly spent in cram school—after-school programs that prepare students for drilling and exams—even though he was not able to go on to postsecondary education.

When the global economy crashed in 2008, both Wu-long and Grandma Chen were forced to take three months of "unpaid holidays." When Grandma Chen eventually returned to work, all the employees at the restaurant had their pay reduced by 10 percent. The family has trouble making ends meet with their meager income.[21] To alleviate the stress of a mortgage and other bills, Grandma Chen applied for a credit card to help them get by whenever there is a shortfall. Together, Grandma Chen and Wu-long have accumulated 400,000 TWD (13,000 USD) in credit-card debt. In addition to her financial burdens,

Grandma Chen shoulders most of the care duties for Atai. Disheartened, she told me: "I take care of everything at home. This family depends on me for everything. There's no way I can change that."

Despite their resource constraints, Atai's parents use consumption to show affection for their only child. Whenever Nam takes Atai out, she buys him a gift to celebrate their precious time together. Wu-long often picks up extra shifts on weekends, so when he finally has the day off, he takes Atai to the movies at the upscale theater and buys him soda and popcorn. A plastic movie-theater soda cup with a cartoon Iron Man logo still sits on Atai's desk as a memento of a special day between father and son.

Although parents in financial struggle cannot satisfy their children's material desires on a regular basis, they occasionally splurge on symbolic gifts or special occasions for their children. Allison Pugh describes this kind of parental spending as "symbolic indulgence"—lower-income parents are willing to disregard their economic difficulty when buying objects with emotional value to satisfy children's needs for social acceptance among peers.[22]

Atai's parents and grandparents try their best—within their time and financial limits—to take care of him, but they can hardly meet the expectations from schools and teachers. Take-home worksheets are usually structured with middle-class, dual-parent family life in mind, and it is difficult for families like Atai's to comply. For example, Atai's summer homework required families to engage in four "special activities." First, children were to ask their parents about their experience of barbecuing. Second, children were to cook a dish together with the family that included protein but no meat. Third, children were to clean the bathroom together with at least two other family members. Fourth, children and parents were to engage in a scavenger hunt involving twelve tasks. Upon seeing these assignments, Atai complained, "Who's going to have time to help me?" He helplessly showed the homework to his grandmother. After putting on her glasses and reading it carefully, she said, "I'm going to work now, we'll deal with this when I get back." Atai later told me that Grandma Chen simply signed the form and wrote down the name of a dish, even though they never had the time to cook anything together.

The expert advice on childrearing generally assumes the nuclear family as the prototype,[23] but it is still common for Taiwanese families to rely on grandparents (mostly grandmothers) to help with childcare.[24] Even the government offers a moderate allowance for grandparents who take care of young children once they have completed some training in childcare.[25] The school's requests for parental participation, however, fail to consider that families come in all shapes and sizes. Those who are already short on time or cultural capacity are burdened with further pressure to get involved in children's education, and their failure to do so leads to the questioning of their legitimacy as suitable caregivers.

Reinforcing Harsh Discipline to Claim Legitimacy

While we were recruiting research participants at Riverside School, the teacher kindly explained to the parents, "They want to go to your home and observe your interactions with your children." Upon hearing this, parents often responded frankly: "What's there to see? We just hit our children." Many working-class parents still embrace the traditional models of harsh discipline and authoritarian parenting. They communicate with their children through commands, and they leave little room for negotiation in their methods of punishment. They sometimes reinforce discipline by citing external authorities such as teachers or police ("Your teacher will come and tape your mouth shut!" or "If you don't behave, I will call the police and have them take you away"). Even their body language indicates a power hierarchy between parent and child: when parents speak to children, they often stand up and look down. This is distinct from middle-class parents at Central School, who mostly squat down while talking to small children.

Why do working-class parents continue to use, even prefer, corporal punishment as their main method of childrearing? The existing literature, especially the seminal work of Melvin Kohn, explains this tendency as related to the spillover of values from parents' occupational experiences. Working-class parents in jobs that reward obedience rather than autonomy tend to convey similar values to their children. Unlike middle-class parents who emphasize self-direction and communication as vital capabilities for their children, working-class parents emphasize hard work, proper conduct, and conformity to external authority.[26]

In addition to the explanation of working-class habitus, I found that many parents choose to use corporal punishment in a more conscious, reflexive manner. Some consider it a more effective way of correction than verbal reasoning, and they disapprove of their middle-class relatives' permissive parenting styles. As one mother states: "You need to punish [children] and talk sense into them at the same time. My sister-in-law only talks to her kids, 'Please don't do this, don't do that.' But I don't think that kind of attitude works. You need to have some authority and make them feel small."

Some working-class parents also emphasize that their methods of corporal punishment are different from their parents' and less likely to result in injury. In many cases, corporal punishment and affective expression are not mutually exclusive but rather complementary methods of childrearing. We were present when some mothers moved from hitting their children to embracing them tearfully, saying things such as, "I hit you because I love you, you know that right?" and "I'm so sorry, please forgive me. Mommy loves you very much. You need to listen to me more, OK?"

Harsh discipline also serves as a security strategy for working-class fathers and mothers to cope with the decline of parental legitimacy and the challenges of marriage instability and emasculated manhood. Their use of corporal punishment reveals multiple vulnerabilities and predicaments faced by working-class families. Economic insecurity leads to emotional turmoil, cognitive constraint, and marital tension in family lives, pushing parents further away from the new repertoire of childrearing.

Economic Insecurity and Compensated Masculinity

Forty-year-old Yan Zhang is a pretty, articulate woman from Canton Province in southern China. After graduating junior high school, she earned her living as a sales clerk. When she was twenty-five, a friend introduced her to a Taiwanese blacksmith, Hong-chang Liao, a vocational high school graduate six years her senior. Yan was attracted to his gentle voice and calm demeanor. Hopeful for the future, Yan quit her job and moved to Taiwan.

Yan had always fantasized about life in Taiwan from what she read about in Taiwanese romance novels. "If I were to do it all over again, I would have never married him," Yan said with a regretful sigh on multiple occasions. Only after getting married did she learn about Hong-chang's heavy debt. Some friends had encouraged him to do business in Cambodia, a country he knew nothing about, and the investment failed. At first, Yan was optimistic about their prospects for paying down the debt, but bad luck continued to strike the family. A few years ago, Hong-chang had an accident at work and injured his back. He can no longer perform the high-skilled labor of ironsmith. In a context of economic decline, possibilities for other employment are few and far between.

Yan was forced to become the family breadwinner after Hong-chang's accident. For a while, she ran a breakfast cart, but this work was difficult to balance with childrearing. She gave up the business and looked for jobs with a stable schedule. As a new immigrant, Yan found herself at the bottom of the labor market hierarchy. She currently works odd jobs at a small factory. The job provides no benefits but minimum hourly wage and her monthly earnings barely exceed 16,000 TWD (530 USD).[27] "Lower than the wage of an illiterate old woman!" Yan complained about the unfair treatment.

After I knew the Liao family for some time, I finally had the courage to ask Hong-chang about the size of his debt. He shook his head and said he wasn't even sure, given the interest rates on his credit cards. Banks do have payment plans for debtors like Hong-chang, but he lost faith in the banking system and was confused by the complicated financial provisions. He saw the repayment plans as unrealistic and mismatched with his family situation: "To be honest, in the end you're getting screwed anyway. Sometimes your family needs to spend more money, or sometimes your job situation changes all of a sudden and you don't have an income anymore. What can you do? It's not like I don't want to pay them." He abruptly went into the bedroom and returned with an envelope full of receipts from his money transfers. Spreading them on the table, he said vehemently: "You see? I kept them all. See here? I did pay when I could!"

With their unstable income, the family struggles to maintain daily life in order. Their apartment is on the third floor of an old building. The public hallway is messy and cramped, but Yan keeps the inside of their home meticulously clean. Seven-year-old Abu and his nine-year-old brother Adong share a room with few amenities. On the wall hangs Yan's handwritten list "House Rules." The books on the shelf, mostly hand-me-downs from neighbors and relatives, do not match their age level. Despite living a thrifty lifestyle, the family needs low-income assistance to make ends meet. Yan feels ashamed of their dependence on government welfare, which to her indicates a poor work ethic and loss of dignity:

> I really don't like receiving low-income assistance. It makes me feel so small. I'm a proud person. Why can't we provide for ourselves? But it's the way the economy is. It's not like we don't try. I mean, with my husband's condition there's not much we can do. . . . I really don't want a handout. All I want is a job.

Deliberately or inadvertently, working-class parents like Yan make their financial situation known to their children. They want their children to understand why the family cannot afford certain activities or toys. One day, Abu came home from school holding a field-trip notice. Quietly he muttered to himself, "We can't afford to go." Yan even took her sons to visit an orphanage and showed them TV news about starving children in Africa. She wants her children to see worse conditions so that they are grateful for what they have. And she hopes to motivate the children to work harder so they can achieve an adulthood free from their parents' financial struggles.

Abu and Adong took the initiative to help with housework and cooking, a situation I rarely saw in middle-class households. But they got into trouble a few times at school. Abu once stole stationery from a classmate, and on another occasion, both brothers vandalized their classroom and skipped school. Yan responded to these incidents with harsh discipline, using objects such as a belt, pipe, broom, and toy sword to hit her sons. Hong-chang did not agree with his wife in this matter. His own parents used corporal punishment on their children, causing his younger brother to run away; he did not want the same thing to happen with his sons. Yet he did not know another way to enforce discipline. He once asked the boys to write down the house rules ten times. Another time, he angrily poured water over their textbooks, and twice he took his sons to the police station. Yan thinks these methods are useless and urges the father to conduct more assertive discipline:

> YAN: You better think about it more carefully. Don't kid around. If you can't figure out how to get them in line now, later when the police are after them for real, it will be too late for you to teach them anything and you're going to have to live with it.
>
> HC: You could ask my wife how angry I was that time. I literally took them to the police station. . . . I didn't know what to do, so I thought I'd try it and maybe it would scare the crap out of them. I was really, really frustrated with them . . . I didn't actually want to report them to the police because they're so young. But I didn't know what else to do, so I took them to the police [station].

Working-class parents are frustrated over not knowing "how to parent." They do not have as much access to parenting books, magazines, classes, and other informational materials as middle-class parents do. Feeling that his attempts at soft discipline are useless, Hong-chang is shifting toward the old script of harsh discipline. He warned his sons: "I've told you millions of times, and you never listen. By fourth grade, I'm going to make you good. I'm going to start hitting. If you're still acting this way in fourth grade, I'm sorry, I will for sure treat you the way your grandfather treated me."

Under these circumstances, the use of corporal punishment paradoxically becomes a way for working-class parents to claim legitimacy as responsible

parents. Despite his decent grades, Abu has been labeled a "bad student" because of his misconduct. Whenever Yan goes to school, she feels judgment and
coldness from other parents, particularly middle-class ones. She is reluctant
to attend parent-teacher conferences and other school activities for parents.
Either intentionally or unconsciously, she uses the disciplinary acts to show
that she is trying her best to correct her children's behavior. During interviews,
she described in detail the extent of her anger and the severity of her punishment. Even during our home observations, she does not hold back from using
physical force.

Behavioral psychologists have argued that a lack of time or money limits
cognitive capacity and constrains people's everyday decisions and behavior.[28]
Many working-class parents face cognitive overload and emotional turmoil,
which erode their self-control and push them toward disciplinary actions that
deliver immediate results. With a sigh, Yan said: "Our family life certainly has
an impact on our emotions, on the way we raise our kids . . . When your job is
unstable, you constantly worry. I'm trying to raise my kids right but I have to
think about many other things too. My head just never stops spinning; it never
gets time to calm down. It's like a movie and I have to play all the roles. This one
is due, that bill needs to be paid, and there is always another thing that costs
money."

Marital tensions also influence parents' interactions with their children.
Hong-chang is too proud to accept unskilled jobs that pay minimum wage,
so Yan carries most of the burden of providing for the family. Yan feels increasingly fed up with her husband as he watches television all day. She derides
him as "useless," as "pretending to be the boss when he's not," and "as lazy as a
donkey." The conjugal dynamics of cross-Strait couples are complicated by the
racialized images of Chinese femininity and Taiwanese masculinity. Taiwanese
men often complain about Chinese women as direct, forceful speakers while
Chinese wives generally characterize their Taiwanese husband as gentle and
soft.[29] Yan's derisions contribute to a cycle in which Hong-chang feels too frustrated and disheartened to continue his job search. He said to me when Yan was
not present: "She pushes me into a terrible mood and I don't want to do it even
more. Why do I have to do so much?"

Trouble with the children can also exacerbate tension between parents.
Hong-chang recalled one scenario in which his boys misbehaved, and instead
of punishing his sons, he slapped his wife. Hong-chang explained his rational
to me:

You listen to me: I didn't hit her very hard at all. It was a weak slap and I was in control. I just wanted them [the boys] to understand: "If you're bad, isn't it your mom's fault!" I wanted them to know how I feel. "It's because your mom does not know how to teach you two, that's why you're so bad." I threaten them like that on purpose. "If you act out again, I'm going to do that to your mom and hurt her. You understand?"

Hong-chang's violent act toward his wife was a symbolic act of "collateral punishment" that conveyed two messages. First, he threatened his sons with the consequence of hurting their mother. Second, he reclaimed the conventional image of the harsh father and caring mother against a family reality where he had failed to live up to the masculine breadwinner role. Hong-chang admitted that he tried to shore up his place as the authoritative patriarch by reinforcing his wife's traditional domestic role:

HC: To be honest, I hate to punish these two like that, but I lose my temper sometimes. . . . That's really the only way I can change how they look at me.

LAN: Are you saying that you want to establish a father's authority in front of your children?

HC: Yes. I want them to understand that their mother has a soft and caring role and their father has a strong role. I don't ask for much, but one thing I demand is control. What does this power mean? It means that in the future, the kids would never dare disrespect their elders.

LAN: Do you think that your children see you as having power right now?

HC: Their mother is always shouting at me in front of them, and it's become something they are used to. . . . No matter what, boys never fear their mothers, but they always fear their fathers. This is the way things are and the way they should be. I don't make the rules. From the beginning of time, it has always been like this.

The division of parenting labor in most Taiwanese working-class households still largely resembles traditional patriarchal norms. When I asked working-class fathers about their participation in childrearing, many answered matter-of-factly, "My job is to make money to put food on the table!" By contrast to the hegemonic ideal of cosmopolitan masculinity that we saw in Chapter 2, working-class fathers like Hong-chang experience precariousness in the globalized economy as emasculation.

Minjeong Kim applies the term *compensated masculinity* to describe that South Korean husbands of foreign wives stage gendered performance in daily marriage acts to compensate for their social subordination; they brag about their virility, breadwinning, and even cosmopolitan flair ("bringing globalization to rural towns").[30] In Hong-chang's case, he attempts to reassert his dignity and compensate for his emasculation by enforcing authority upon their children and control over their wives. He mobilizes the traditional script of filial piety to justify the need for patriarchal authority and to disguise his frustration at the loss of paternal legitimacy. Yet his actions only intensify his inner anxieties and his conflicts with his wife and sons.

Cross-Class Pathway Consumption

Although the working-class parents we met earlier avoid reproducing a painful childhood filled with academic frustration, many others view education as a critical pathway for the next generation to escape stagnant mobility. These working-class parents are remarkably similar to the middle class in their emphasis on children's education, but their strategies of pathway consumption are rather distinct. I use the term *cross-class pathway consumption* to describe that working-class families spend to place children in cross-class contexts, including after-school programs and schooling districts, that they perceive beneficial to their children's trajectory of class mobility.[31] They also rely on cross-class networks, including teachers and college-educated relatives, to navigate their children's education beyond the constraint of the family reality.

In particular, immigrant mothers living in the city are likely to pursue pathway consumption to fulfill their dreams for their children. Although they initially hoped to achieve socioeconomic mobility by marrying Taiwanese husbands, many ultimately face troubled marriages, social discrimination, and economic difficulty. Their children's future is their source of hope for a happy end to a dark journey of dislocation and resettlement. However, the strategies of cross-class pathway consumption often incur unintended consequences upon the mother and the children.

Seeking Cross-Class Resources

Li-min Tseng is a construction worker; year after year of working in the harsh sun has made his skin dark and rough. At the age of forty, he married a Taiwanese wife, Ya-fan, an assembly worker in an electronics factory. After the factory moved its production to China, she began working alongside her husband at the construction site. They tried to get pregnant for years but in vain. When Ya-fan turned thirty-nine years old, they used assisted reproduction and welcomed twin boys into their family.

When returning home at night covered in dirt and sweat, Li-min feels worthwhile upon seeing the two smiley faces. Sitting next to his father, one of the boys innocently responds, "Daddy works hard to make money so we can happily play computer games." In a proud tone, Li-min describes his work: "I do everything. I can pretty much build a whole house." However, unlike the middle-class fathers in Chapter 2, Li-min is reluctant to pass on his occupational skills to his sons, despite the relatively decent wages. He depicts the construction site: "Wind, sun, rain, cold, you name it. It's very dangerous. . . . I've seen people falling from the scaffolding several times. They lie on the ground like a crushed watermelon." He is firm in his desire for his sons to attend college. "I'd like them to do office work, typing on the computers or something."

Ya-fan shares a similar aspiration for the children's futures. When I asked her what will happen if her children would like to pursue their father's line of work, she replied firmly: "No way! If they do construction work, I'm just going to send them to their aunt's company to run some errands." Feeling incapable of offering educational guidance, she sends her two sons to cram school. Before midterm and final grades are posted, Ya-fan often calls the teacher anxiously to inquire about her sons' grades. When their grades regress because of careless mistakes, she doesn't hesitate to practice "tough love" to discipline them.

Like many working-class families in this study, Ya-fan's benchmark for measuring educational quality is based on the amount of homework assigned. When choosing after-school programs for their children, they generally prefer activities with educational value like English, math, and computer lessons. This orientation indicates not only their financial constraints but also their class-specific dispositions and concerns. The working class embodies a habitus that prioritizes the necessary and pragmatic as a result of their accumulated exposure to scarce resources.[32] They view talents as something children are born with rather than something one can acquire through cultivation. Exploring "personal interests" through trying out a variety of talent lessons is a class privilege they cannot afford. One working-class father explains:

> Some families have the money, so they send them [the kids] to all these music or art lessons. They look at what their kids are interested in and let them go [develop] in that direction. We can't do that. You have to pay tuition every semester, and if they don't learn anything, your money's gone! All those extra classes become a waste of money!

In addition, the lack of information and cultural resources also contributes to the sole focus of academic training among the working class. They do not identify with the goal of holistic education that is central to Taiwan's educational reform. Few have heard of the college admission reforms to consider "invisible skills" that cannot be measured with academic tests. They also lack the cultural literacy to evaluate the purpose and content of extracurricular activities. For example, when Ya-fan's son brought home a pamphlet for the street-dance club at school, she was confused: "What is 'street dance'? Dancing on the street?"

Working-class parents like Ya-fan mobilize cross-class social connections to expand the life horizon of their children. Although Ya-fan only completed junior high school, her younger sister, the twins' aunt, has a university degree and runs a business together with her husband. Since they have no children of their own, they generously assisted Ya-fan with the twins' education. The aunt offers advice and money for their after-school programs, English classes, and swimming lessons. On weekends, the boys love to go to the nearby night market with their parents to enjoy street food and goldfish scooping. When the aunt comes to visit every other month, she takes the kids to amusement parks and buys them with expensive items such as a computer, cellphone, and Game Boy. With financial backing from their aunt, the boys are able to enjoy some of the luxuries of middle-class childhoods. Ya-fan even shares a vague aspiration for her children to explore a globalized future: "If possible, I want the kids to go abroad for university. Like their aunt says, you can't do anything big with a Taiwanese degree."

Another more common security strategy for working-class families is to build *guanxi* (personal networks) with schoolteachers. When the twins' teacher was hospitalized with an illness, many of the students' mothers, including Ya-fan, took time to visit her at the hospital. These mothers hope that by building a close relationship with the teacher, the teacher would pay better attention to their children or at least be of assistance when the children are in need. Yan, the Chinese immigrant we met earlier, similarly builds up personal relations with a teacher at cram school, who is kind enough to offer free tutoring lessons for Abu. These parent-teacher conversations even include details not directly related to the children's schoolwork such as the children's behavior problems and parents' marital conflicts at home.

Many working-class parents in Taiwan view teachers as a source of cross-class social capital and they strive to personalize the relationship. This situation is distinct from American working-class parents in Lareau's book, who develop a contentious or alienating relationship with teachers because they distrust or feel excluded by the institutions.[33] The difference is partly explained by Taiwan's relatively mild class segregation in neighborhood and school. An international survey of social capital also confirms that Taiwanese, compared to people in other East Asian countries, have more access to variegated social networks; even those at the lower end of the social class spectrum are likely to make acquaintance with high-status professionals, such as teachers, lawyers, and professors.[34] Cross-class personal interactions offer potential resources for the disadvantaged families, but they can also trigger psychological insecurity among those who travel across the class border.

Martyr Mother and Exposed Childhood

Arong is one of the few children at Central School who lives in a working-class family. His mother, Ling Zhang, is a thirty-year-old immigrant and a former military nurse from Hunan Province in South Central China. Ling's aunt, already a marriage immigrant to Taiwan, introduced Ling to a car mechanic ten years her senior. Her parents hoped that the union would bring Ling to a life of economic mobility, but upon arrival in Taiwan, she confronted the stigma and distrust attaching to "Chinese brides." Her in-laws objected to her opening a savings account or finding a paid job because they suspected that she might steal from the family or have an affair. "They think that if you come from China, you're going to steal all the family money," Ling said with a sigh. She continued:

> My husband is an honest, quiet person. When people tell him bad things, he believes them. . . . His brother said, "Your wife is so young and wants to work outside. She's going to run off with someone! Look how pretty she is. Do you see how friendly she talks on the phone?" And then my husband starts getting worried. Whenever I came home late, we had a fight.

Ling's husband frequently blamed her for conflicts in the family. Once he put his hands around her neck as he chastised her, angrily yelling: "You never listen to a word I say!" The couple separated after six years, but they have not divorced. Ling agreed not to seek alimony from her husband, and she raises their son on her own. Ling's mother moved from Hunan to help out, working as a cleaning lady during the day and selling fruit at a stall at night. Ling works as an assistant for a wealthy family. For an annual salary less than 15,000 USD, she chauffeurs the family around and runs errands, which she shamefully admits is "no different from being a servant."

Despite her modest income and single-parent status, Ling refuses to compromise on her son's education. She rents a rooftop add-on apartment in the central area of Taipei City, even though a bigger apartment near Riverside School would cost two-thirds as much. Choosing a quality school through physical relocation (moving) or virtual relocation (registering the child in a friend or relative's household) is a common strategy of pathway consumption for working-class parents. Although public school funding in Taiwan is not related to property taxes like in the US, parents can identify "star schools," with better teachers, richer resources, and more effective administrators. Many are willing to pay a significant premium for apartments located in the catchment areas of these quality schools. To regulate increasing competition over admission to star schools, in 1993, Taipei City began requiring parents or grandparents to present an ownership certificate in the school district. Rental tenants were excluded until 2006, but even now, they must have rented in the area for three years to attend the local school.[35]

In addition to enrolling her son in one of star schools, Ling also schedules after-school tutoring, as well as writing, English, and math class, with fees totaling to one-third of the household income. Every time I met her, she showed me the books she recently purchased at the bookstore, usually Chinese classics like *Romance of the Three Kingdoms* or biographies of world leaders. Ling emphasizes: "We don't have much else at home except for books. I let him watch some movies but they are usually educational."

Immigrant mothers view outsourcing education to cram school as instrumentally necessary for children's learning; it is also an important symbolic practice that helps them reclaim the legitimacy as "good mothers" or even "martyr mothers." By prioritizing her son's education over her own consumer needs, Ling highlights her sacrifice and defends herself against the gold-digger image associated with "foreign brides." Ling explains:

All the money I make is for his education. Nobody can tell that my son is from a single-parent home. . . . Why do I spend so much money [on supplementary education]? It's because I can't help him with his homework. What we learned at school [in China] is completely different from what they teach in Taiwan. I understand it, but I can't explain it to him. Our textbooks are different. . . . So I have to spend money, no matter what, so he can get the help he needs. . . . His classmates are all from wealthy families, and they think that we foreigners would never spend money on our kids' education. I could save my money or buy other things, but to me, those material things are not important. What's important is his future so he can do better than me.

To cover the cost of pathway consumption, working-class parents must spend more time at work or take on multiple jobs. Because of her long work hours, Ling almost never participates in school events. Single parents like her, who struggle to balance work and family, are susceptible to criticism from the school and the state. Arong occasionally stays home alone, and he once wrote about this in his school journal. The teacher called Ling to come to school for a meeting and told her, "You cannot leave your child at home alone until he is twelve years old." This information was actually incorrect; by law, a parent may leave a child older than six alone in a relatively safe environment.[36] But Ling responded meekly, humbly handing over the authority over to the teacher. She said to the teacher: "As long as you can control him, you can do anything you like. Even if you hit him, I'll allow it. Anything that works."

In addition, working-class children who enroll in a middle-class schooling district are simultaneously placed in a landscape of consumption where they perceive their childhood realities as starkly different from their peers. The strategy of cross-class pathway consumption may produce an unintended consequence of "exposed childhood"[37]—to borrow from Allison Pugh—in which being exposed to a context with wealthy students as the majority, working-class children become more aware of their lack of material possessions and are forced to acquire intimate knowledge about class inequality.

Arong's entire class at Central School went to the Yingge Ceramics Museum on a field trip. It is very unlikely that Riverside School would take a similar field trip because the tickets are relatively expensive, as is the transportation (a hired coach bus is needed to get to the remote location). After lunch, almost every child went to buy an ice pop, which cost significantly more than a regular ice pop because the stick was made of beautiful ceramic. As his fellow students licked their delicious treats, Arong rifled through his backpack, mumbling that he could not find his money, although it is possible that he had none because his mother does not usually give him an allowance. He eventually stopped his search and started drawing an image of ice pop in his notebook with a dejected expression on his face. I tapped his back and asked, "How about I treat you?" He happily closed his notebook, chose a pineapple flavor, and joined his classmates.

Transnational Links to Global South: Burden or Asset?

In Taiwan, immigrant mothers' cultural heritage and transnational connections were not considered valuable assets to pass on to the next generation until very recently. They were generally discouraged from talking to their children in their native tongue. Their in-laws worried that the children might speak Chinese with an accent, and they did not see the need to acquire Southeast Asian language skills.

Some immigrant mothers send their children to their countries of origin for a period of time, mostly before the child enters kindergarten or elementary school, because the mother is occupied by paid employment or unpaid care work. For example, when Hong-chang's parents were still alive and seriously ill, caregiving responsibilities fell on Yan's shoulders. For several years until her parents-in-law passed away, Yan had to send her two sons to Canton to be raised by their grandparents. In Taiwan, such transnational transfer of childcare is hardly considered a positive experience for children. Even Yan herself considers this journey counter-productive. She quickly attributes the negative characteristics of her sons to the outcome of "being spoiled rotten" in China.

In fact, many native-born Taiwanese parents similarly leave their children in the countryside under the care of grandparents so they can focus on work or business in the city. This practice was even more common in the 1980s and 1990s, but it still happens now. However, transnational transfer of childcare concerns the public much more because it implies the failure of the paternal state to properly cultivate "new Taiwanese children" into subjects of ethnonationalism. Similar childcare arrangements by Chinese mothers receive even more criticism among the Taiwanese public because of the political tension across Taiwan's Strait.[38]

Immigrant mothers are vulnerable to social blame that criticizes their childrearing styles as being backward or uncivilized. Their alleged lack of modern parental competency endangers not only the development of their own children but also the quality of national population as a whole. A few clinical studies published in the early 2000s indicated that immigrant mothers had newborn babies weighed less than the national average. Despite their small samples, these studies attracted serious attention from public health experts and the general public.[39] Siti, an Indonesian immigrant mother whose son received treatment for a minor developmental delay, was subjected to the "incapable mother" stereotype as she went about the daily work of caring for her son:

> We were waiting at the school while my son talked to the therapist. There was a woman in the kitchen and she asked us what we were doing and we told her that our son was doing an evaluation. She turned to my husband and said, "Let me tell you, you married the wrong woman. You should have married a Taiwanese.

These foreigners don't know how to teach children, no wonder your child is developing too slowly."

Taiwan's government views family education as a critical vehicle for immigrant mothers' cultural and social integration. The National Immigration Agency regularly holds education seminars for newly arrived Chinese and Southeast Asian immigrant spouses. To reduce the divorce rate among transnational couples, which is higher than the divorce rate for local unions,[40] the seminars attempt to create family harmony by enhancing communication skills and marital intimacy.[41] Some parental education workshops for immigrant mothers focus on parent-child relations. I observed one of these workshops, comprising sixteen free seminars. Each seminar lasted about two hours, and the workshop met twice a week. Seventeen people signed up for the workshop, but only about eight to ten showed up at each seminar. Most were Chinese women in their thirties or forties; many brought their small children to class, and the women joyfully took turns comforting crying babies.

The instructors were college professors in nursing or child education, who offer similar curricula to Taiwanese parents or students who are earning their childcare licenses. The seminars covered a wide range of topics, including care for babies' safety, diet, and nutrition; routines and exercise habits for children; children's cognitive and emotional development; and tools of communication and punishment. Most instructors gave lectures accompanied by PowerPoint slides and short video clips. They interacted with participants through questions and occasionally held activities to facilitate group discussion. The pedagogy of the workshop is designed not to disrupt a cultural discomfort about disclosing family issues to outsiders, even including professionals. Most Taiwanese are more comfortable learning about family relations through lectures and activities where they do not have to disclose their domestic conflicts.[42]

The Ministry of Education expanded the scope of family education in 2013 to include "multicultural education" with the aim of helping family members to understand and respect cultural differences. Accordingly, two sessions of the workshop I observed focused on "multicultural childrearing," but they simply overviewed myriad childrearing styles around the globe. The instructor referred to popular writing about global parenting and discussed various customs and practices in the US, Germany, Japan, France, and Israel. She said relatively little about China or Southeast Asia, with a tendency to essentialize these countries' customs in a reductive manner.[43]

I held a focus-group discussion with eight immigrant mothers who attended the workshop. They found the seminars informative, but many also thought that the skills and knowledge conveyed, with their implicit normative assumptions, were too distant from their family's reality. Some instructors encouraged the mothers to stay home until the child turns three years old—an alleged critical period of cognitive development. This instruction reinforces what Sara Friedman calls the "dependency model" of Taiwan's marital immigration regime, defined by "the ideal model of the national family built around a masculinized citizen-breadwinner and feminized immigrant-homemaker."[44] Yet many immigrant mothers have to work outside the home, either for economic independence or because their husbands are not competitive on the job market.

The instructors suggested that parents try to reason with children and use new methods of punishment, such as removal of privileges, instead of corporal punishment. Yet these methods are difficult to execute for immigrant mothers who are equipped with limited local language skills. They were also unwilling to challenge husbands or mothers-in-law who prefer harsh discipline given their marginal status and weak bargaining power in the family. Nevertheless, the state's pressure to follow a "modern" style of childrearing falls on the shoulder of mothers. Parental education like this separates the knowledge and techniques of childrearing from immigrants' cultural contexts and family realities.

"New Second Generation"

Two decades have passed since the early waves of marriage migrants entered Taiwan. Nongovernmental organizations that advocate immigrant rights have mushroomed. State policies have gradually shifted away from a linear view of assimilation and toward the mutual exchange of multiculturalism.[45] An Indonesian mother, Siti, noticed a similar shift in the attitude of her Taiwanese husband, a policeman. At first, the husband said, "There is no use for [the children learning Indonesian] because we live in Taiwan and not in Indonesia." But recently, he changed his mind. Siti told me:

> Now my husband keeps telling me to teach my son Indonesian so my son can go to Southeast Asia to make money. . . . Some people told him about a kid whose mother is from Indonesia, and he went to Indonesia to work as an adult. Because he can speak both Indonesian and Chinese, he makes a lot of money. [After hearing that story], my husband told me I should teach our son Indonesian.

The social perception of immigrant mothers' cultural differences has shifted from a threat to the ethnic homogeneity of the population to an asset that should be passed to the next generation of mobile workers. Such transnational cultural capital, or we may call it "Southern cultural capital," not only can help a mixed child to broaden his or her job prospects in the future but may also benefit the Taiwanese nation in its quest for new capital outlets in the global economy. Several highly ranked government officials, including the director of the Bureau of Vocational Training, commented to the press that the children of immigrant mothers are "the best human capital for Taiwan to deploy the Southeast Asian Market."[46] Politicians use the familial metaphor of "in-laws" to describe Southeast Asia and encourage the mixed children to familiarize themselves with their mothers' native languages. Even the official document from the Ministry of Education use the subtitle "In-Law Diplomacy" to elaborate the goals of empowering the children of new immigrants as a way to smooth Taiwanese diplomatic relations with Southeast Asia.[47]

The previous label of "new Taiwanese children" is replaced with the "new second generation" (*xin er dai*), which not only gives the younger generation an identity as a group but also positively affirms their immigrant background and multicultural heritage. Both central and local governments have poured in institutional resources to help them cultivate linguistic skills and cultural knowledge related to their mothers' homelands. The Ministry of Education offers grants for them to visit their maternal grandparents during summer vacations as well as fellowships to study in Southeast Asia. Local governments hold summer camps for the new second generation to spend time in Southeast Asia, including visits and internships at Taiwanese-owned factories to "experience international workplaces."[48]

These market-driven changing perceptions of immigrant culture exemplify what scholars call "neoliberal multiculturalism," where neoliberalism provides a new strategy of governance that recognizes cultural diversity and endorses intercultural exchanges.[49] In addition, the agenda of national development shadows Taiwan's state-led project of multiculturalism. Mixed-race children are expected not only to become "cosmopolitan market actor[s] who can compete effectively across state boundaries,"[50] but they also serve as culturally adaptable warriors who can help the nation diversify its markets at the frontier of global capitalism.

When the Democratic Progress Party, the current ruling party in Taiwan, offered a summer fellowship to support children of marital immigrants to visit Southeast Asia, the grant recipients were called "root seekers," a term that implies an essentialized view of cultural heritage. The government and political agents wrongly assume that the new second generation will have a "natural" affinity with culture and language associated with their mothers' homelands. In fact, the majority of the second generation cannot speak their mothers' native languages due to the previous social stigma attached to Southeast Asian immigrants.

The combination of multiculturalism with neoliberal economic policies creates opportunities for immigrant mothers to covert their cultural heritages and transnational ties into ethnic capital for their children. However, the new policy may also create unintended negative effects, such as social labeling or ghettoization in the career path of the second generation. One daughter of an immigrant mother offered a poignant commentary on this policy turn: "I feel tired of hearing people describing us as the promising second generation. It seems that we are only supposed to go to Thailand or Vietnam. What if I want to go to Spain? We don't want to be segregated from the others."[51]

With Taiwan's New Southbound Policy, immigrant mothers recently acquire better opportunities to turn their cultural and social connections with Southeast Asia into an ethnic capital for their children. However, when the policy agenda is driven by a profit-centered instrumental goal and reifies ethnic culture as packaged products, multiculturalism falls into political sloganeering and state paternalism, losing its essential aims of achieving intercultural understanding and empowering immigrants in their struggle for cultural recognition.

Conclusion

Globalization casts dark shadows and some shining light on the family lives of working-class Taiwanese. Unlike the middle class, who were able to take advantage of Taiwan's economic ascendance to secure intergenerational and transnational mobility, many parents in this chapter suffer from stagnant mobility and economic precariousness. While global economy shatters working-class men's job security and breadwinning masculinity, transnational brokerage facilitates their cross-border marriages. This new form of global family stirs social anxiety and incurs stigmatization of immigrant motherhood, but, under particular institutional circumstances, immigrant mothers are able to convert their differences into an ethnic capital for their children.

Although limited personal interaction exists between parents across class divides, their childrearing strategies and life chances are structurally connected, indicating the relational nature of class inequality. Working-class parents experience intensified feelings of frustration and helplessness when the globalized discourses of childrearing become the norms for state-sponsored campaigns and school's requirement for parental participation. In the social field that constitutes symbolic struggle over the goals and means of childrearing, the less resourceful parents manage to mobilize cross-class resources to secure their children's future but they lack sufficient cultural capital to establish the symbolic legitimacy of their strategies.

Many working-class parents lean toward a childrearing style that allows children to grow naturally and avoids placing much academic pressure. Chapter 2 also identified the growing trend of orchestrating natural growth among middle-class parents in Taiwan. Although both groups of parents seemingly prefer a "free-range childhood," the middle-class children at Garden School engage in free play within an enclosed area bounded by parents' careful orchestration. Working-class parents, by contrast, loosely organize children's activities because they have few resources of money or time. Highly educated parents are capable of activating their cultural capital and mobilizing social influence to change institutional rules, including relaxing the legal regulations on alternative education and reforming college admissions to their children's advantage. By contrast, working-class families face social criticism about their children's natural growth as a lack of parental attention.

Some working-class parents, especially immigrant mothers, share middle-class parents' aspiration for their children's competitiveness, but they use different means to achieve this goal. Unlike middle-class mothers who are intimately involved in their children's learning, parents with lower education levels must rely on the cross-class resources of teachers, tutors, and cram school. While middle-class parents increasingly embrace holistic cultivation and global pathway consumption, working-class parents rely on local educational resources with a narrow focus on academic learning. They tend to favor standardized examinations over individualized applications as a class-blind mechanism to college admission.

Working-class parents strive to protect security and dignity for their children, but their security strategies sometimes create results otherwise. Some parents reinforce harsh discipline to claim their legitimacy as responsible parents, but such an endeavor is equal to child abuse or maltreatment in the eyes of institutional authorities. The strategies of cross-class pathway consumption do not necessarily produce the intended result, either. Parents have to pay the price of working multiple shifts and losing time to spend with children. Children who attend schools with a middle-class majority are forced to encounter class inequality on a daily basis. Moreover, as college admissions and professional recruitment increasingly focus on applicants' communication abilities and well-rounded character, the narrow focus on academic subjects may place working-class children at disadvantage when competing with middle-class children in the new games of social mobility.

4 Immigrant Middle Class

Raising Confident Children

THE US MEDIA HAS CALLED IT THE "new white flight": white parents shy away from school districts with a high concentration of new Asian immigrants to avoid intense competition and academic pressure.[1] In December 2015, the *New York Times* reported on heated tensions among parents at a high-achieving school in New Jersey, an area that has received an influx of East and South Asian immigrants in recent decades.[2] White parents, fearing that their children will be outmatched, blamed Asian immigrants for an obsession with academic success at the cost of children's emotional health. While the school proposed limiting homework, tests, and advanced programs, Asian parents criticized these measures as "dumbing down" American education; they worried about the greater consequence for Asian children, who would be evaluated against a higher bar in college admissions.

The popular discourses tend to interpret such "ethnic divides" as inherent cultural differences in educational ideas and parenting practice. Sociological studies, by contrast, demonstrate how structure reshapes culture, particularly how the contexts of immigrant incorporation and the racialized structures of opportunity affect parents' concerns and strategies of childrearing. Jennifer Lee and Min Zhou, for instance, argue that so-called Asian values are actually class-based mind-sets that highly educated immigrants reproduce in the new country because they are considered useful for second-generation mobility in the context of institutional racism.[3]

This chapter builds on these insights to further examine the security strategies of professional immigrant parents, who worry about not only racial inequality in the US but also insecurities in the new global economy. To delve into the contested process of cultural negotiation in everyday family life, this chapter investigates immigrant parents' emotional conundrums and strategic negotiation, and explores the kinds of challenges, choices, and conflicts that emerge in engineering a bicultural identity for their American-born children.

Unlike Lee and Zhou, who view the Asian "success frame" as a singular framework, I emphasize that professional Chinese immigrant parents are not a monolithic group. They negotiate cultural differences and ethnic boundaries in different ways, and their divergent security strategies are analyzed here as a spectrum: Parents at one end of the spectrum wish to achieve "competitive assimilation" by orchestrating their children's development of US-based social skills and cultural confidence. Parents at the other end of the spectrum manage to turn their immigrant background and cultural difference into an ethnic cultural capital that can facilitate their children's social and transnational mobility.

Blocked Mobility and Lost Confidence

How immigrant parents understand their experience of mobility shapes their perception of desired security and potential risks in their children's future. Middle-class immigrants from Taiwan share a narrative of "three-generation mobility." The grandparent generation, most of whom attained an education lower than high school, began the family's upward mobile trajectory through microentrepreneurship and invested their hard-earned assets in their children's overseas education. The parent generation achieved transnational mobility but feels relatively marginalized in the new country, thus expecting the child generation to achieve full-fledged success and integration in the US.

Immigrants from China apply a similar narrative of three-generation mobility, one that was more forcefully shaped by national development. The grandparent generation, especially those who grew up during the Cultural Revolution, suffered from a shortage of material resources and educational opportunities in communist China. The parent generation experienced the great transformation of China's "opening up" and gained access to increased freedom to pursue various opportunities, including raising children overseas.

Despite growing up in different social settings, both Taiwanese and Chinese immigrants achieved class and spatial mobility far beyond what their parents' generation was able to achieve. Most parents in this chapter hold advanced degrees from American institutions and work in professional occupations. They earn a decent salary and own single-family houses in suburbs known for quality schools. Yet many of them, fathers in particular, also feel frustrated by their blocked mobility at work despite their educational achievements and respectable performance.

I met Joseph Liao, a handsome-looking man in his midforties, at a holiday celebration that his wife, Annie, arranged for Taiwanese friends in their beautiful suburban home. After their daughter's piano performance had received great applause, I chatted with Joseph about his life in the US. Holding a PhD in physics, he works at a prestigious company and earns a salary of more than 120,000 USD, yet he is not satisfied with his career and feels socially isolated at work. Over a bowl of heartwarming noodle soup, he told me:

> Americans prefer those who not only get work done but fit in socially. Immigrants are disadvantaged in every way. Our generation is doomed; our English is not good enough. When they use difficult vocabularies, we cannot understand. We eat different kinds of food, so they don't invite you to lunch. They talk about things like politics and songs they listened to when they grew up. You don't understand; you just can't catch up with them.

I asked Joseph if during his twenty years of US residence, he ever thought of moving back to Taiwan. He answered with some regret: "Several times! We were almost back, but we simply couldn't do it." He looked over at Annie, who was busy hosting. "Women here do not want to go back. Even if they do not have to live with in-laws in Taiwan, they still have to deal with many personal relationships over there." Annie acquired a master's degree in the US but quit her job as an engineer after their second child was born. At Annie's persistence, Joseph declined a few invitations to work for start-up companies in Taiwan during the 1990s, when the country's high-tech industry was taking off. As he watched many of his classmates who decided to return become successful entrepreneurs in Taiwan, Joseph wondered whether he made the right decision to stay. But he felt some comfort and validation about his choice when learning that these return migrants were now sending their children to the US to attend school.

Consistent with Carolyn Chen's research on Taiwanese immigrants,[4] I find that professional immigrant men are more likely than women and nonprofessionals to express their frustration with downward or blocked mobility at American workplaces. As they work to sustain their middle-class livelihood, they must contend with increasingly common layoffs in a flexible economy shadowed by global competition and financial crisis. Immigrants lack membership in corporate "old-boy networks," which makes them more vulnerable to economic downturns. One Taiwanese father was unemployed for almost six months after being laid off from his job as an engineer. He searched for jobs through his immigrant networks but received little help. His wife said to me, "Then I realized that immigrants like us have little *guanxi* [social networks] here and how vulnerable we actually are."

Professional male immigrants share a common narrative of "lost confidence" that describes their sense of failure to achieve the success and security they have aspired in the US. This narrative has a significant effect on immigrant fatherhood. Xiping and her husband both acquired a PhD in the US and work as a computer engineer. She describes herself as a relaxed mother while portraying her husband as a "wolf dad" who takes an authoritarian and disciplinary attitude toward their only daughter:[5]

> I don't quite understand why he became so aggressive [about the daughter's education]. Anyhow, he was a very ambitious, very competitive person (in China), but here, he has become . . . [*pause*] you know. I think he is more laid back at work than I am. He puts all his aspiration upon our daughter. I think this is a classic case, and he is willing to invest his time.

In their home country, professional men like Xiping's husband achieved a status approaching the local norms of hegemonic masculinity based on their career success and transnational mobility.[6] However, in the US, they suffer from not only the language and cultural barriers but also the racialized hierarchies of masculinities. US ideals of manhood primarily reflect the ways of being of white, middle-class, heterosexual men, encompassing qualities like aggression, toughness, athleticism, and competitiveness. In contrast, Asian men are associated with a racialized form of "marginalized masculinity" in which they are discursively emasculated as quiet, passive, and malleable.[7] Even in the high-tech industry, which celebrates a new "nerd masculinity" based on "aggressive displays of technical self-confidence" rather than looks and athletic ability,[8] Asians are underrepresented in leadership ranks—they occupy 27 percent of professionals but only 14 percent of executives in Silicon Valley.[9]

Xiping's husband presents a classic case of what I call "domesticated fatherhood," a pattern widely seen among professional immigrants who experience blocked mobility in the US, or at least perceive their experience as such. Their career setbacks in American workplaces motivate them to invest more energy in childrearing and give them more time to balance work and family. A few fathers mentioned that, after failing to get promotion or recognition at work, they reoriented their life goals toward family life. They want to make sure that their children will grow up equipped with the necessary tools and achieve the success they could not attain.

Compared to their counterparts in Taiwan and China, immigrant fathers are more involved in their children's education, especially in dual-earner households. Yet these "domesticated fathers" do not necessarily take on a significant share of hands-on childcare. Instead, they set the principles for securing their children's futures while the mother remains the primary caregiver in most households. Many mothers, particularly those from Taiwan, quit their jobs after having children.[10] Immigrant women gain a sense of freedom from living far from their in-laws, but they also shoulder more mothering work in the US—kin support for childcare is scarce, and market outsourcing, such as hiring nannies, is expensive. As described by Chien-Juh Gu, immigrant mothers struggle with "emotional transnationalism" because they have to redefine the meanings of home and work by shifting back and forth between the homeland and the new country to search for behavioral and moral guidance.[11]

Asian Quotas and Bamboo Ceiling

While the children of immigrants escape the overly competitive education systems in China or Taiwan, they face a different, sometimes even fiercer, competition in the US system. According to Jerome Karabel, in the 1920s, elite universities like Harvard, Yale, and Princeton introduced new admission criteria emphasizing athletic and extracurricular achievements in order to exclude the increasing number of Jewish applicants.[12] Today, colleges' emphasis on holistic development still disfavors families that lack sufficient local cultural knowledge and social networks to cultivate their children. Immigrant parents are baffled by the weight of individualized consideration in the college admissions process.[13] They find the rules of the game foreign and opaque in comparison to the Asian system of national entrance exams as a standardized measurement of merit.

In immigrant metropolises such as Los Angeles and New York, Chinese immigrants are more likely to form ethnic enclaves or ethnoburbs; Asian children, as the dominant majority at school, may even benefit from the stereotype that associates Asianness with academic success.[14] By contrast, middle-class Chinese and Taiwanese immigrants in Boston reside in majority-white suburbs and their children feel greater pressure to integrate like whites at school. These parents found it harder to instill an ethnic identity while also fostering class mobility for their children, as the theory of segmented assimilation presumes. Meanwhile, they fear that their children may not be able to compete locally and globally if they become more like white Americans.

In particular, immigrant parents are concerned about a hidden racial bias in college admissions. Recruitment policies that emphasize diversity and affirmative action appear to benefit other minority groups such as African Americans, Latinos, and Native Americans. Meanwhile, an abundance of highly qualified Asian applicants makes college admissions particularly competitive for Asians, who must fight for limited slots. Although colleges do not operate under strict racial quotas, evidence shows that Asian students are disadvantaged by college admission policies. While the Asian college-aged population in the US doubled between 1992 and 2011, Harvard's Asian enrollment shrunk from 20.6 percent in 1993 to around 16.5 percent for most of the 2000s; this pattern is also present in other Ivy League universities.[15] Thomas Espenshade and Alexandria Radford analyzed data from National Study of College Experience and found that Asian Americans must score 140 points higher on average than whites on the math and verbal portions of the SAT in order to have the same chances of admission. At highly competitive private schools, only 16 percent of Asian students are admitted, compared to 26 percent for white students with similar academic records, 37 percent for Hispanics, and 51 percent for blacks.[16] In addition, because Asians are a much smaller population than whites, blacks, and Hispanics, race-conscious admission results in a much starker disadvantage for Asian applicants than for whites.

The job market is another field that stirs insecurity among immigrant parents, who fear that their US-raised children will confront a "bamboo ceiling"—an invisible barrier that keeps them from rising to upper-level positions involving managerial and supervisory duties. Despite Asian Americans' high educational achievement, they are underrepresented in upper management positions. Asians make up 5.5 percent of the US population and 15–20 percent of Ivy League students, but only 0.3 percent of corporate officers, less than 1 percent of corporate board members, and about 2 percent of college presidents.[17]

Immigrant parents' anxiety is exacerbated by the insecurities inherent in the new global economy. As mentioned in Chapter 1, an increasing number of Chinese children who grew up in North America have "returned" to their ancestral homeland. They hope to escape economic depression or racial inequality in North America by taking advantage of their bicultural background to seek job niches in thriving Asian markets. For example, Mr. Su came to the US to pursue a PhD in the 1980s. He gave up an academic career and became a local public servant so that he could spend time with his children. His son attended a liberal arts college and completed a master's degree in fine arts. During the recession, the son experienced years of underemployment before eventually moving to Taiwan to secure a career in the fast-growing industry of animation. Mr. Su's daughter obtained a job in New York City thanks to the Chinese language skills she acquired after attending an exchange program in Taiwan.

Despite sharing a similar trajectory of blocked mobility in the US, professional middle-class immigrants employ distinct narratives to make sense of their experience. Some view their frustrated career paths as a product of institutional racism, whereas others attribute their career setbacks to their personal shortcoming in cultural skills and social networks. The various reflexive understandings of their migration experience shape their divergent views of second-generation incorporation and lead to their distinct strategies of securing their children's futures.

Orchestrating Competitive Assimilation

Immigrant parents in this section lean toward a security strategy that I call "orchestrating competitive assimilation." These parents employ a narrative of "parental transformation," or even "parental conversion," to describe their agency in facilitating their children to achieve cultural assimilation. I follow Richard Alba and Victor Nee to view "assimilation" as bridging cultural distance and ethnic boundaries.[18] These parents hope to achieve an American version of happy childhood by diluting the Chinese tradition of authoritarian parenting. And they rely on extracurricular activities to construct a *context* for their children to acquire a "well-rounded" character as a critical capacity to compete in the mainstream America.

Bridging Cultural Distance

John Wang is a forty-eight-year-old engineer who left Taiwan for the US in the mid-1980s to pursue a master's degree in computer science. His wife, Jane, also works as an engineer, and they are raising three children in an affluent suburb north of Boston. John is eloquent and outgoing with co-ethnics, especially when speaking Chinese, but he finds it stressful to socialize with his American coworkers, who like to grab a beer after work and chat about sports. John prefers to go home early to cook dinner for his family. His *kong bao* chicken is famous among friends and relatives.

John attributes his loss of confidence in the US to his ineptitude in tasks valued in American work culture, such as socializing with colleagues and clients, making impressive presentations, and being a charismatic leader. He does not have the cultural competence that comes from growing up in the US, but he still holds some "immigrant optimism" for the future of his US-born children. His children speak English without an accent and have more exposure to American pop culture, thus erasing some of the most visible markers of cultural difference.

Like most parents in his generation who grew up in Taiwan, John and Jane focused only on schoolwork and were exposed to few extracurricular activities as children. They are pleased that the US provides widened opportunities for children to develop personal interests, but as adult immigrants, they have little time to cultivate their own hobbies. Unlike his friends who established their business in Taiwan and thus earned the class privilege of luxury time, John was uprooted by immigration and felt the constant pressure to fight against the current of downward mobility:

> I see most Americans have at least one hobby, either music, arts, crafts, or even sports. Our generation in Taiwan, we grew up differently. Some of my friends who stay in Taiwan end up doing pretty well financially and now they can start to enjoy their lives and create some hobbies. But immigrants like us have to go through one thing after another and do not have the chance to. We came to the US, back to zero, and we had to slave away to make it.

Chinese immigrants I interviewed mostly use the term *Americans* to refer exclusively to middle-class, white Americans. John was no exception. Modeling after the middle-class American paradigm of concerted cultivation, he orchestrates his children's holistic development by guiding and channeling their interests and activities. He sets clear guidelines for his children regarding which activities are "culturally appropriate": all his children must participate in one sports activity, one Chinese-related activity, and one musical activity. John emphasizes that he does not "force" his children to learn anything, he simply "encourages" them to do so, and he always "allows them to choose." He also volunteers with his children's Scout troops and soccer teams to encourage them to stay involved.

These parents' careful orchestration of children's nonacademic interests provides a path to cultural assimilation, but it also serves another purpose: to compensate for their own childhoods. Growing up in the same generation as the Taiwanese parents in the previous chapters, many immigrant parents recall high-pressure environments in which their parents sometimes resorted to yelling and spanking to enforce academic success.

I visited Ian Lin, his wife, Lily, and their three young sons at their cozy home, a modest attached townhouse in a suburb south of Boston. We had homemade pizzas for dinner. The boys were having fun with adding toppings by themselves. Lily explained to me, "Because of the kids, we mostly eat American food at home now." Ian, a thirty-eight-year-old engineer, and Lily, two years younger, both converted to Christianity while attending high school in Taiwan; their non-Christian parents considered private Christian schools a better place for academic training and moral discipline. Ian's schooling experiences inculcated his desire for US immigration. He met some families in Taiwan's Christian community and was impressed that their children grew up in a bicultural environment. He managed to find a job to sponsor his green-card application after completing his master's degree in the US. Lily quit her career as an elementary school teacher in Taiwan and became a full-time homemaker after moving to Boston.

On a single salary of around 75,000 USD, the Lins needed support from their parents in Taiwan to buy a house in the US, and they could not afford the more expensive real estate in northern suburbs where most Taiwanese immigrants reside. Ian is keenly aware that his classmates achieved a higher income and greater career success in Taiwan, but he is content with his family-work balance in the US. Ian arrives home around 4:30 pm every day; his friends who are engineers in Taiwan stay at work until 8:00 or 9:00 pm. Ian hugged his younger son and softly said, "They enjoy something I don't, while I enjoy something they don't."

Ian and Lily praise American schools for respecting students' individual development and pace of learning. Lily appreciates the sleep-hour sheet the teacher asks parents to fill out: "We never got enough sleep while growing up in Taiwan!" On one occasion, I accompanied them to a parent-teacher meeting at their eldest son's school, where they made sure to address their primary concerns with his verbal communication skills and personal relations with American classmates. Outside school, Ian and Lily prioritize their sons' soccer practice over Chinese-language school. When I ask about their expectation for the three boys, they respond, "To become good husbands and good fathers." This answer deviates from the dominant "success frame" among Asian immigrants who tend to push their children to get into a "good university" and secure a "good job."[19]

Immigrant parents who orchestrate children's assimilation do not try to erase their culture of origin but attempt to narrow their social distance from the white majority. Chinese culture is preserved like a garnish and carefully placed at the corner of the multicultural salad bowl. John is actively involved in the Taiwanese immigrant community and wants his children to acknowledge their Chinese heritage, but he also does not want them to develop such a strong Chinese identity that Americans might discriminate against them. He said, "We can introduce Chinese culture, but we cannot be too dominant, because you don't want people to feel a little bit offended."

Alternatively, some parents highlight the common values they share with Americans to indicate shrinkage of the cultural gap. Ian describes the American families he knows as being "almost the same" as Taiwanese families regarding the strong bonds across generations. They also connect their Christian faith, including the American version of family values, with the Confucian traditions of family duty and indebtedness.[20]

Interestingly, several mothers I interviewed, including Lily, learned about the American style of permissive parenting through reading books, parenting magazines, and blogs written in Chinese by coethnic mothers in Taiwan, China, the US, and other countries. One mother listens to internet radio programs from Taiwan that offer advice about child-centered parenting and finds it perfectly useful in the US. These cultural venues not only introduce Westerncentric ideas of global childrearing to parents in Taiwan and China but also help the Chinese diaspora to negotiate cultural differences and ethnic traditions as they raise children on foreign soil. In other words, these parents' journey of acculturation is not a linear process of immigrant adaptation; instead, it is embedded in the transnational circuits of culture, values, and resources.

Brave New Parenthood

Dr. Chang is a dentist who has an easygoing attitude and a great sense of humor. He moved from Taiwan to the US in the 1980s to pursue postgraduate studies. His wife has been a full-time homemaker and the couple raised two sons who are now college graduates. When the children were young, Dr. Chang emulated his father's strict parenting style, including corporal punishment and patriarchal authority. After one event where Dr. Chang hit his son, one of the son's American friends told him: "You don't have to listen to him. Call me if your father [does] this to you again." But Dr. Chang disregarded this threat. At that time, he was critical of American parenting styles: "I used to think that Americans treat their children like pets because they coddle them so much."

Transnational family ties often become a source of pressure for immigrant parents despite raising children thousands of miles away from their own parents. Dr. Chang's father held strong aspirations for the future generations of his family; he strongly objected to his grandson Sam's decision to attend a liberal arts college (the older grandson attended Harvard) and to major in psychology. Dr. Chang recalls:

> During those years, my father often called [from Taiwan] and asked me: "Did Sam transfer to a different school? What did he choose as his major?" Oh, I was the sandwiched generation who had to appease the old and comfort the young. . . . My father kept telling me that Sam's major could not help him to find a job. He blamed me for being an irresponsible father.

Despite facing pressure from the previous generation, Dr. Chang deliberately transformed his parenting after Sam wrote him a letter during high school, in which Sam described his father as "like a monster" who "never tried to communicate or reason." Shocked by his son's negative perception, Dr. Chang was determined to change:

> Then I asked myself—why did we leave Taiwan? Because everyone said you could come to the US to chase your dreams and achieve whatever you want to. Now that we are in the US, we should create the happiest future possible. If you are just doing the same things you did in Taiwan like sending your children to endless *buxibans* [cram school], forcing them to be the top of the class, and punishing them harshly, you might as well just go back to Taiwan. That way, we parents don't have to suffer so much and the children won't have to see how happy American children are. . . . So I decided, since I am here, I am going to Americanize. I changed 360 degrees.

Immigrant parents like Dr. Chang initially subscribe to the authoritarian parenting style they experienced in their own childhood. Yet at various points during the settlement process, their contact with American parenting scripts or resistance from their US-raised children pressures them to reflect on their cultural upbringing and to "denaturalize" the habitus they acquired from their parents or national origin. For instance, immigrant Chinese parents mostly prefer individual sports, such as tennis and swimming, for their children. They consider team sports time consuming, and practice schedules often conflict with weekend Chinese-language classes. Some parents also dread the burden of socializing with American parents on the athletic field. Dr. Chang, however, encouraged his sons to play ice hockey when they wanted to learn. He not only values sports activities because athletic excellence is a significant factor in US college admissions decisions.[21] He also views group sports as a critical path to American socialization and a way to avoid the geeky stereotypes associated with Chinese people:

> You need to let them feel like they are American, so they don't feel different from the others. Even though they might not look the same, but they can feel like "whatever you do, we can do too, and maybe do it even better." The stereotype of Chinese people is they are really studious but don't work well in a group, right? They just go home and play their violin or piano. . . . So when you play sports, you need to be in a group. Of course you can play tennis by yourself and swimming is good for your health, too. But team sports are very important.

Parents who orchestrate competitive assimilation deliberately encourage children's involvement in team sports because they see it as an important avenue to acquire interracial social skills and establish cultural confidence. Honyin Zhen, a forty-one-year-old mother from Beijing who speaks with a gentle voice, shares a similar narrative of parental transformation and preference for extracurricular activities. She and her husband both received scholarships to attend graduate school in the US and now work in the pharmaceutical industry. Honyin told me that more than once, they have considered moving back to China to take advantage of the opportunities in the rising economy. But they decided to stay in the US because they believed that an American education would provide a better environment for their only daughter, Jasmine.

Like most Chinese immigrants, Honyin sent Jasmine to piano lessons and Chinese-language school at a very young age. The family emulated some of their immigrant friends and forced Jasmine to speak Chinese by saying that they would not respond to her when she spoke English. But Jasmine was a seven-year-old with an "adamant disposition" (as Honyin put it), and she resisted by simply refusing to talk. Honyin eventually gave up on these parenting strategies because she preferred to maintain a good relationship with her daughter.

Despite facing criticism from other Chinese mothers for "not trying hard enough," Honyin gradually took a critical view of Confucian traditions. "The Chinese emphasize too much on so-called filial piety," she said disapprovingly. She worries that children growing up in a Chinese home might become afraid to express themselves or lose the ability to make autonomous decisions. She teaches herself to "act like American parents," especially by expressing affection toward

Jasmine through verbal communication and body language. She was proud when Jasmine wrote on her homework, "Mom gave me a lot of hugs!" Although her husband is unable to transform his manner of affective expression, Honyin tries to "translate" cultural difference in the ways of communication and helps Jasmine to understand his devotion to the provider role as a form of father's love.

After quitting Chinese-language school, Jasmine joined a synchronized skating team at her own request. Honyin approves of figure skating because few Chinese children participate in this sports activity, so the family could avoid competition with coethnic peers. She praises the skating team for helping her daughter become "confident and independent." After Jasmine's elementary school cut the all-girls choir program, Jasmine and her friends brought a petition to the school principal. The principal eventually agreed to keep the program because the girls convinced a number of fellow students to support their petition. When Honyin asked Jasmine if she was afraid to speak to the principal, Jasmine replied: "It's like talking to the coach on the skating team. You just speak." The mother gladly said:

> I really feel like she grew up and can deal with a lot of things now. She is very in-dependent and confident. She is very good at interacting with people her age or people who are older, even my friends think that she is very good at socializing with others. . . . So I feel like these activities are very important in developing a person's character. They help children to build confidence and teach them how to deal with different people and different situations.

Honyin identifies several benefits to participating in team sports that im-migrant parents otherwise struggle to provide. First, children learn to improve their social skills by working with people from different backgrounds, ages, and skill levels. Second, young skaters learn to communicate directly with adults through their contact with coaches. Annett Lareau similarly identified the fact that American middle-class parents teach their children to reason with institu-tional gatekeepers and to bargain for their own interests.[22] Immigrant parents often lack the language skills and cultural competency to teach similar lessons, but they can "outsource" this training by sending their children to participate in activities like team sports.

However, both parents and children may feel frustrated when their pur-suit of competitive assimilation encounters the barricade of American racism. Moreover, these parents frequently face anxiety and self-doubt when they send children to activities and cultural arenas they are not familiar with.

With a sigh, Honyin told me of the difficulty she faces as a volunteer for Jasmine's skating team: "This is where I really feel the difference as a Chinese immigrant in the US." Although her English is reasonably fluent, she finds it challenging to communicate with the coach, the competition committee, the event organizer, and the skating club, especially when the topics are not related to her professional expertise or personal experience. She feels she lacks the cultural capital and local knowledge to help the team manager, who is in charge of the skaters' costumes, hair, and makeup. Honyin shook her head in frustration:

> Our tastes are not the same as theirs, and we just don't have as many resources. There are a lot of things we don't know, such as where to buy the costumes. I only know the big department stores, but the skating costumes are only sold at special stores, and I just don't know where they are. Besides, if you select colors or styles that the children don't like, you will definitely hear about it from the kids [*sigh*]. So really, Chinese parents are just not capable of doing these jobs.

Immigrant parents also feel hesitant to enroll their children in team sports because of the widely held perception that Asians do not excel at sports, both because of their perceived physical limitations and because of racial discrimination. I conducted fieldwork around the time when "Linsanity" caught the American attention, so the celebrated Taiwanese American basketball player, Jeremy Lin, often came up during interviews. Despite Lin's later success, his pre-NBA experiences strengthened Chinese parents' belief that Asian players' confronted blocked opportunities on the athletic field. Lin received no athletic scholarship offers from colleges, and during Ivy League games, he endured racial taunts from fans who told him, "Go back to China" and "The orchestra is on the other side of campus."[23]

Immigrant parents who place their children in team sports may unwittingly put their children in direct contact with Americans' racial and ethnic prejudice. Asian athletes are more likely to be bullied because they violate racial stereotypes of Asians as "quiet," "non-athletic" and "short and wears glasses."[24] For example, Sam, Dr. Chang's younger son, frequently heard racial slurs from opposing players when he played ice hockey. Sam described these taunts to his father with staged calmness: "I am used to it. I just pretend I did not hear it. If you fight back, the conflict gets even worse."

Dr. Chang felt heartbroken upon realizing that exposing his children to the dominant majority incurred the "hidden injuries of race." Keith Osajima uses this concept to describe a psychological condition of internalized oppression in which Asian Americans "feel inferior or different because they have come to believe the dominant society's message that they are different or do not belong."[25] Dr. Chang tried to turn these unfortunate encounters into learning opportunities for his sons. He provided an optimistic outlook on the second generation's hyphenated identity and the eventual outcome of incorporation: "I told them, 'Your heritage is Chinese, but you were born in America and you are American by US law.' Even Americans, they might be Italian or British. But they were born in the US and after a while, everyone calls them American too." Still, the father sounded dispirited as he concluded, "But the main thing is you have to protect them from those peoples' words so they won't be hurt too much."

The "Transitional": Juggling Autonomy and Authority

Only a few middle-class immigrants in this study clearly indicate their intention to "Americanize" their childrearing style and to democratize intergenerational relations at home. Far more parents are positioned in the middle of the spectrum, and I refer to these parents as "transitionals." They value children's autonomy and acculturation as the foundation for building cultural confidence in the US, yet they are inclined to uphold parental authority. As such, they unwittingly develop a style of helicopter parenting when zealously preparing their children for the competitive path to American elite schools and jobs.

Raymond Chen is a fifty-year-old IT engineer of Taiwanese origin who is lean and energetic. Together, he and his wife, also an engineer with a master's degree in the US, earn a household income of more than 200,000 USD. Yet Raymond feels dispirited by his stagnant career. Although his software innovation contributed greatly to the company revenues, he was not offered a managerial position. Afterward, he decided to shift his devotion to the cultivation of his children, a twelve-year-old son and an eight-year-old daughter, as his primary "project."

Immigrant parents are keenly aware of their shortage of US-based interpersonal skills and social capital that they can pass on to their children. Raymond repeatedly states that children must "depend on themselves" by establishing local networks and helping their siblings. He views elite education as a way to counterbalance this limitation of immigrant parenting:

> RAYMOND: I think that they must rely on themselves. Parents can only help them get to a certain place. When he gets older, he must go to a really good college because truthfully, only elite colleges have good networking.

LAN: So when you say good college you mean like Ivy League?

RAYMOND: Yes, Ivy League. I think he can make it. You don't necessarily learn more at an elite school, but the point is that the resources are better. You need to build your own networks because your parents can't help you with that. . . . I can't even help myself. In the US, networking is everything.

Raymond hopes to prepare his children for admission to elite universities, where students can develop similar hobbies, interests, and lifestyles, regardless of their background.[26] Elite colleges also pave the road to elite jobs because recruiters in high-paying corporate sectors tend to emphasize social "fit" and to prefer candidates who "look and play like them."[27] Raymond pays close attention to his children's social lives. When his son Kevin was smaller, Raymond drove to school and waited until recess to observe whether Kevin was playing with the other non-Chinese children. Raymond explained:

I keep telling him that he must make a new friend every day and talk to different people. . . . I don't care what he learns at school, I ask him whether he did anything fun at school and whom he played with. . . . I always emphasize to him, "Presentation is very important and Daddy cannot teach you, so when you have the opportunity at school, you must make sure you learn from the others."

Raymond is very proud of Kevin, who not only achieves high grades but also has mastered fencing. Recognizing that Americans link sports with the development of leadership and resiliency, he encouraged his son to pursue athletic activities instead of playing a music instrument, a typical "Asian activity." Yet he worried that Asian children were at a physical disadvantage against white athletes and thought that if Kevin participated in a more mainstream sport like baseball or soccer, he might lose confidence as Raymond had at work. His solution was to find a less "competitive" sport.

Raymond learned about fencing when browsing an elite university's athletics website. He quickly identified the potential value of this sport for his son's future college admission. Raymond studied fencing carefully and helped Kevin practice even though he had never played or even watched the sport. With his father's supervision and support, Kevin grew into a talented fencer. Raymond takes great pride in watching his son gain tremendous confidence: "He is really good at fencing, and it's given him a lot of confidence. You can see how he's completely changed as a person. . . . He thinks of himself as super cool. People always come shake his hands. They respect him."

Kevin's athletic achievement and social confidence have cost the family a small fortune. In 2012, Raymond paid for a weekly private fencing lesson (40 USD per 40-minute lesson) and a twice-a-week group lesson (120 USD per month). A set of fencing equipment cost over a thousand dollars. Fencing was also time consuming—Raymond had to drive back and forth for weekly practice, lessons, and competitions. Notably, the father deliberately exposed these financial details to his children so they would recognize and appreciate their parents' efforts.

Immigrant parents like Raymond aspire to cultivate self-reliance in their children, but in practice, they act like helicopter parents who carefully guide their children into new territories. When I asked Raymond who made the decisions about the priority of extracurricular activities, he answered without hesitation:

RAYMOND: They're all my calls because parents understand their kids the best.
LAN: When you were growing up in Taiwan, did your parents play such a role?
RAYMOND: I was on my own. . . . But it's different here. Time is different. The invisible competition is huge. . . . I have to coach him. You should not fight a war that you cannot win. Many things in life cannot be started over. So parents have to do research. You have to open your eyes to watch your kids. I have understood my children so well. I told him yesterday: "Do you think you are great, you are smart? I don't think so. It's because you are growing up in a good environment, and Daddy is helping you."

According to Lareau, middle-class American parents usually avoid mentioning the financial burden that children's many extracurricular activities incur on the family budget, and children tend to develop a sense of entitlement, taking their parents' efforts for granted.[28] By contrast, many immigrant Chinese parents tell their children about the financial costs of their activities to highlight the parents' nurturing efforts rather than the children's natural talent. They convey not a sense of entitlement but a sense of indebtedness toward the extended family, which, according to Hyeyoung Kang and Reed Larson, refers to "a person's recognition of his or her immigrant parents' child-centered immigration aspiration and their sacrifice for the sake of children."[29] This cultural framework does not simply reproduce the Confucius value of filial piety but is rooted in the family's immigration experience—immigration intensifies parents' feelings of insecurity and costs of sacrifice for their children, leading to their hands-on intervention to secure their children's futures in the new country. Paradoxically, immigrant parents' strong aspiration for children's assimilation and integration in the US unwittingly reinforces parental authority and reaffirms Chinese cultural tradition.

Cultivating Ethnic Cultural Capital

Parents who orchestrate competitive assimilation hold an optimistic view about their children's inclusion in American mainstream society and are willing to transform their parenting to fit white middle-class conventions. The majority of Chinese immigrants in this study think otherwise—they are pessimistic about their settlement experiences and about their children's entrance into the US racial hierarchy. They believe that their children, despite being born and raised in the US, will still face a future shadowed by the stigma of being an immigrant as well as by institutional racism.

I observed a parental seminar held at a Chinese-language school for suburban immigrant families mostly from the PRC. The instructor, an immigrant father with a PhD in education from a US university, urged parents to transform their old Chinese ways of childrearing. Not all parents agreed; one mother with the nickname "Tiger Mom" was particularly zealous in debating him. The instructor told the audience: "We Chinese don't know how to communicate. We have to change the ways we talk and fix the problem." She interrupted in agitation: "This is a social defect! Not a personal defect! This society is full of racial discrimination, don't you know that?" The instructor emphasized the importance of socializing in American workplaces and advised, "Never eat your lunch alone." The mother strongly disagreed: "You don't understand the politics in the lab! Sometimes we avoid communication to avoid mistakes. This is a strategy of survival, a mechanism of self-protection! You are way too naïve about American society!"

Parents who orchestrate competitive assimilation criticize fellow immigrants with strict parenting style as archaic. In turn, parents like the mother above criticize immigrants with a permissive parenting style as ignoring the brutal reality of American racism. Although most of my informants disapprove of the extreme "tiger mom" style, many also see their white neighbors as too lax or lenient with their children. They question the value of indulging children with excessive praise, viewing "free-ranged parenting" and its uncertain consequences as a racial privilege that immigrant families cannot afford.

I use the phrase "cultivating ethnic cultural capital" to describe the security strategy adopted by parents who manage to cultivate the values, language, culture, lifestyle, networks, and resources associated with their immigrant background to facilitate their children's pursuit of success and mobility.[30] I do not use the term *ethnic cultural capital* to refer to a parcel of values and customs that newcomers bring directly from their homeland; Umat Erel has aptly described this view as a "rucksack approach" that reifies ethnically bounded culture.[31] Instead, ethnic cultural capital involves a dynamics process of cultural negotiation in which immigrant parents selectively mobilize their cultural heritages and sometimes mix and match it with values and practices in the new country.

The security strategy of cultivating ethnic cultural capital can be seen as a parallel to what scholars call the "minority culture of mobility."[32] For instance, Jody Vallejo found that second-generation, middle-class Mexicans look to successful coethnics, instead of native-born whites, as their role models; for them, assimilating as a minority is a more secure pathway to upward mobility in the context of racial discrimination and group disadvantage.[33] Many middle-class Chinese immigrants in my study similarly recognize that there are multiple pathways into the American middle class, and they further assert that their ethnic cultural resources and social networks facilitate not only social mobility in the US but also geographic mobility in the global economy. They seek transnational references—class peers in the home country—to define the benchmark of security and use a global framework to validate their ethnic difference as transnational cultural capital.

You Must Be "Twice as Good"

Cathy Wu and her husband, John, are both software engineers in their forties with two children, aged twelve and eight. They have a comfortable home in a white-majority neighborhood, but their social lives in the US center on the Taiwanese immigrant community. Every Sunday afternoon while their children attend Chinese-language class, Cathy and John gather with other parents in the school cafeteria, chatting about their children's education and recent news from Taiwan. After the school activities end, Cathy's family likes to join other immigrant families for a heartwarming dinner at an authentic Chinese restaurant.

John, who practices Chinese martial arts, is harshly critical of the American admiration of professional athletes. He perceives these athletes as lacking loyalty when they move to different professional teams. Unlike parents who attribute their career setbacks to the shortage of cultural skills, John does not consider socializing as an essential part of their job or as a "required" duty. He says, "It's just small talk. After working for so many years, I don't need to talk to people like 'Did you see the game last night?' People need to respect that."

Cathy and John prefer to keep their interactions with colleagues within the professional realm, and they believe that no one can deny their ability so long as they put in good work and show their merit. Yet they still recognize the structural constraints they face as immigrants. They argue that they earned their career recognition by working "twice as hard" and being "twice as good." Cathy says:

> CATHY: Some people say that you can't get promoted at work because you are not good enough. But if you are that good, they will promote you. How good is "good enough"? If you are just *as good* as the local, they will certainly *not* promote you. For us immigrants, when you're in a foreign country, you must be twice as good if you want to be recognized. This is just the truth and I can't complain about it.
>
> LAN: This is for the first generation. How about the second generation?
>
> CATHY: The same!
>
> LAN: Even when they were born in the US?
>
> CATHY: The same. People can't tell if you are the first or second generation. They only look at your face. [My children] might not have to be twice as good, maybe one and half times. They will definitely go through things like this in the future.

The narratives of Cathy and John seem contradictory. On the one hand, they believe in the principles of meritocracy and individual efforts, and as such their cultural difference can be neutralized in the workplace. On the other hand, they view the divide between the white majority and racial minorities as a bright line that even their US-born children cannot easily cross. These contradictory narratives lead them to take an individualized solution to the structural problem of racial inequality: the only way for their children to overcome the barriers of institutional racism is to become "twice as good" and outperform white student with merit and skills.

Immigrant parents tend to encourage their children to pursue professions like law, science, medicine, and engineering that are premised on meritocratic factors of educational achievement, credentials, and "hard" skills. They disfavor careers like business that focus on "soft" skills such as socializing with clients and excellent rhetorical and leadership skills.[34] Their desire for job stability partly reflects a humble immigrant attitude. Having faced uncertainty during their cross-border journey, immigrant parents desire greater security, if not outstanding success, for the next generation.

Instead of bridging ethnic boundaries, these parents attempt to positively affirm their cultural difference. Cathy and John's son once brought an Asian seaweed snack to kindergarten but did not eat it because his classmates laughed at its "funny" smell. John then offered his son the reward of one dollar if he dared to eat the snack at school. Ever since the children were small, Cathy and John worked to cultivate a bicultural identity (as "Chinese-speaking Americans") by exposing them to a rich diversity of Chinese books and cultural items. They did so not just to preserve their ethnic heritage but also to prepare the children for cultural conflicts looming in the future. Their son is now a teenager, and Cathy views his feeling of "not fitting in" as a realistic, healthy attitude:

> If we wait until the identity conflict to happen and then deal with it, it will be too late. So ever since he was little, we've taught him, "You are different from other people. You are *Chongwenren* (Chinese-speaking people). Yes, you are American but you are of Chinese-speaking origin." . . . We've instilled this ideology in his head ever since he was very young, so now he is less troubled and he even says, "I don't think I can fit in." He is already different from others, and he doesn't have to fit in.

Parents who steer away from assimilation also hope to combat the negative influence of American culture, such as consumer materialism, radical individualism, and excessive freedom.[35] Cathy and John are highly critical of the American overemphasis on children's "fun" and middle-class children's entitled nature as a consequence. Cathy explained why they stopped throwing birthday parties for their children:

> CATHY: American children are very entitled and they think that everything
>   is supposed to be fun. We teach our kids that they must work hard, work
>   for the results. . . . Our kids understand that everything costs money. They
>   should not be wasteful.
> LAN: Do they earn money by doing housework?
> CATHY: I don't get money by doing housework, why should they? [*Laugh*]
>   When we do laundry, the children have to fold their own clothes. Everyone
>   contributes, whether it be shoveling snow or raking leaves. Working hard
>   is a given, [and] you shouldn't expect a bonus prize for doing something
>   you are supposed to do. Americans are so entitled because their children

know that they would receive thirty or sixty dollars on their birthday or whatever.

Cathy praises the values of frugality and hardworking as part of a selective framework drawing on Chinese cultural traditions to guide her children away from American materialism. Lareau describes a "sense of entitlement" as an embodiment of privileged class habitus and an outcome of American middle-class parenting, but Cathy simply sees it as a cultural force of moral corruption. The parents' detachment from mainstream American culture takes a toll on their children's social lives. Cathy and John's son does not like group sports and their daughter does not go on play dates or care much for the trends followed by other girls at school, such as playing with American Girl dolls.

Although the family discourages their children from holding birthday parties or play dates with their American peers, they intentionally encourage their children to socialize with other second-generation immigrants or even to make friends in Taiwan. Cathy and John's son is an avid Chinese yo-yo player. Cathy encourages him to search online for information about yo-yo clubs and events in Taiwan they can visit when they return during vacations. Cathy considers ethnic peer networks as critical for her children to reaffirm their ties to the ancestral homeland:

> It's very important for children to have the opportunity to meet people who look like them, speak the same language as them, but have different lifestyles and viewpoints. . . . If children have friends in Taiwan and they can grow together and have the chance to meet during vacations, they wouldn't feel so distant to Taiwan, right?

In sum, Chinese immigrant parents who reject competitive assimilation see academic excellence and professional skills as the more secure pathway to status and confidence in the US. Painting American popular culture in dark shades, they turn to the homeland for promising cultural resources and social connections to brighten up their children's future.

Reclaiming Cultural Traits

Ling Zhao is a forty-two-year-old woman with short hair and sharp eyes. After receiving a PhD in biomedical science from a leading Chinese university, Ling decided to pursue a postdoctoral research position in the US. Her husband, then a senior manager at a major company in Beijing, was at first unwilling to accompany her. They eventually found jobs and settled in Boston, but Ling described their situation as a path of downward mobility—their current salaries and positions did not match their education and skills. To provide an affordable quality education for their two sons, the Zhao family purchased a small older house in one of the most expensive suburbs in the Boston area. They continue to shop at bargain stores and drive a decades-old used vehicle.

Discipline and diligence are two critical attributes that Ling tries to instill in her children. Tony's daily life follows a strict schedule; TV and video-game time is strictly monitored. Tony's grandmother, a retired school principal in China who lives with the family in the US for about six months of every year, gives Tony daily homework to strengthen his Chinese vocabulary and math skills. Tony complains to me, "It takes 15 minutes for me to finish the homework from American school, but I need to spend one or two hours to finish grandma's homework!" The parents use children in China as a reference group for Tony to raise the standards for his academic performance. Ling explains: "When we are studying at home, we often tell him how diligent Chinese children are, how much more they have learned (than American children), so he becomes scared of that."

Ling believes that parents have a responsibility to help their children to maximize their potential and minimize the loss of confidence—children's interests may be fleeting, so parents must intervene to guide children away from distractions and toward excellence. She criticizes those Chinese parents who superficially emulate American parenting and let their children experiment with any activity they choose, especially athletic ones:

> My job is to identify Tony's strengths. I don't think he has any athletic talent. He loves to play soccer, but every time I see him play, he never gets the ball. Once I took him to play basketball; he tried so many times, and he couldn't score. At first, we just encouraged him because he was smaller than most of the other kids. But later we saw some kids who were smaller than him could score, and he asked us why in frustration. My husband immediately decided that we should quit basketball. He said, "You don't have to be the best, but you absolutely can't be the worst. If you're the worst, you lose confidence." Tony's confidence is more important than anything else.

Immigrant parents who are sensitive about the structural disadvantage faced by ethnic and racial minorities try to protect their children from a failure that may incur a loss of confidence. Meanwhile, Ling sees American parents as overly indulgent with praise; instead, she believes that children should be rewarded instead for their resilience and efforts and parents should provide their children with honest evaluations of their talents. For instance, Tony once told his mother that he wanted to be a violinist, and Ling responded with a straightforward advice that his musical talent was limited. Yet she continues to send Tony to violin lessons on a weekly basis and orchestra group practice every other week. Like most of my informants who invest in musical education, she does not want her children to become professional musicians but instead sees the routine practice of music as a good way to instill discipline and focus.

Ling's narratives present a contradictory combination of mindsets. On the one hand, it confirms the theory of cultural psychologists that Chinese parents tend to hold an "effort mind-set," believing that performance can be improved by increased effort, in contrast to American parents who place more weight on children's innate ability as a determinant of performance.[36] On the other hand, to protect her son from shredding confidence, she also falls back on a "fixed mind-set," in which she focuses exclusively on outcome rather than process, potentially depriving her children of learning opportunities to tackle new challenges and deal with the fear of failure.

Chinese immigrant parents view musical education as an essential strategy to secure their children's futures for a multitude of reasons. They widely believe that winning musical competitions can help their children gain entrance into selective high schools and colleges. Middle-class immigrants, in particular, invest a great deal of money in musical education and pressure their children to take music exams or enter music competitions, which turn learning into measurable accomplishments.[37] Musical excellence signifies well-rounded development, which helps Chinese students combat the negative stereotype that they are rote learners. Music can also bolster Asian children's confidence. A Chinese mother interviewed by Wei-Ting Lu described her preference for music activities over sports: "Although my children can't play baseball as well as their classmates, they can say to themselves, 'I can play music. It is fine that I can't play baseball. I still have my piano.'"[38]

Immigrant parents like Ling reclaim the effort mindset as an intangible cultural resource and potential ethnic cultural capital. Grace Wang interviewed Asian parents whose children attend professional music schools and found a similar rhetoric: these parents do not perceive so-called Asian traits such as hard work, persistence, and self sacrifice as "a natural part of one's identity" but as "qualities to be learned and repeated practiced."[39] Their strategies of cultural negotiation involve various ways of cultural hybridization and capital conversion: they cultivate these cultural traits through Western classical music training and translate them into musical achievement and, hopefully, academic advantage in the future.

Reverse Cultural Mobility: US Education Is Not Enough

Immigrant parents often justify their personal sacrifices by citing their children's educational opportunities in the US. Yet professional Chinese immigrants feel increasingly ambivalent about American education. Although many appreciate the emphasis on individuality, creativity, and well-roundedness, they are also concerned about the light homework load and underdeveloped curriculum. One Taiwanese mother said: "I like the curriculum of public schools and it is very different from what I learned growing up. But [*pause*] I just think the standards are too low."

Many immigrant parents perceive American schoolwork as "too easy" in comparison to Taiwan or China, especially in the subjects of math and science. Their unease with the workload is exacerbated by their concerns with the racialized opportunity structure. They worry that their children will not be able to surpass the "Asian quota" in college admissions if they learn only from the American curriculum. The "normal" American educational standards might be all right for white students, but Asian students must outperform whites and compete with one other.

Some parents are also worried that the lower expectation of American education leads to a negative impact on children's work ethics. Annie, a mother with a master's degree in engineering, described why she must supplement school education to stimulate her children:

> The American math curriculum is too slow, too simple. If you have a smart kid but you don't give them anything new to challenge them, they start to get bored, lose interest, and become very careless. Carelessness can become a habit, and that is the most dangerous. When children get used to being careless, they stop paying attention and these bad habits will just get worse and worse.

Immigrant parents with similar concerns seek additional education or home tutoring for their children. After-school programs with foreign origins, such as the Japanese program Kumon and the Russian School of Mathematics, are widely popular among Chinese immigrants.[40] Some parents import learning kits for math and science from Taiwan or China because they prefer the challenge and repetitive practice in the Asian curriculum. If children cannot read Chinese well, their parents order English-language versions of the materials published in Singapore. Chinese immigrant parents appreciate the encouraging style of American teachers, but they also worry that children will be spoiled by a lack of discipline and excessive compliments. When hiring instructors or trainers, parents prefer immigrants—if they cannot find Chinese, they hire Russians or Indians.

These families pursue cultural mobility in a reverse direction from their path of transnational migration—they mobilize learning materials, teaching methods and educational opportunities through transnational circuits of information, commodities, and people with their countries of origin. Some of the second-generation teenagers attend cram school during the summer in Taiwan to improve their SAT scores. Some take advantage of tutoring and college counseling businesses started by Taiwanese and Chinese immigrants who attended prestigious American graduate schools.

The learning of Chinese language and culture is another common practice of reverse cultural mobility. Although the earlier generation of Chinese immigrants were inclined to keep their children from speaking Chinese to avoid speaking English with an accent, immigrants who arrived in the mid-1980s and beyond try to cultivate some Chinese fluency so their children can communicate with grandparents and other relatives back home. The Boston area is home to several Chinese languages schools that use space in local public schools to offer weekend classes in conversational Mandarin, Chinese writing and composition, and Chinese customs and history. These Chinese-language schools also function as nodes connecting geographically dispersed suburban Chinese families to a virtual ethnic community.

For the recent generation of immigrant parents, the familiarity of Chinese language and culture may help their children to combat racial discrimination in the US by cultivating Chineseness as a form of ethnic cultural capital in a cosmopolitan world.[41] A Chinese teacher at the language school told me that an increasing number of Chinese American parents, who are mostly second generation and grew up speaking little Chinese, are determined to raise their children speaking their heritage language. These parents regret their own lack of Chinese fluency and recognize its increasing instrumental value with the rise of China's position in the global economy. They also acknowledge that Asian Americans can never entirely escape the label of "foreigner," no matter how many generations of a family have resided in the US. The teacher told me:

"Americans think they [the second generation] are weird for not knowing 'their language.' It doesn't matter if you want to identify yourself as Chinese or not, everybody else sees you that way."

Chinese language as a form of ethnic cultural capital receives increased cross-ethnic recognition and institutional validation in recent decades. Chinese-language programs have become increasingly popular among upper- and middle-class non-Chinese parents; some even hire au pairs from China or send their children to Mandarin-language immersion schools. This cultural trend makes it easier for immigrant parents to encourage their children to learn Chinese. Mainstream US college-preparatory standardized tests such as the SAT II and the AP now validate Chinese fluency, helping students convert Chinese language skills into an institutionalized form of cultural capital (credentials) for an academic future.

The instrumental value of the Chinese language can bolster ethnic pride among the children of Chinese immigrants, and cultural identification increases their incentive to learn the language. The teachers at the Chinese school encourage parents to expose their children to Chinese culture, such as eating Chinese food or attending Chinese festivals. Some parents also enroll their children in workshops that teach Chinese cultural practices such as martial arts, Chinese yo-yo, and lion dance, which children then perform at school and community events.

Previous studies on Asian Americans have found that ethnic cultural enrichment programs can help the second generation to cope with their marginalized status as racialized minorities.[42] One mother in this study decided to enroll her teenaged son in a Chinese cultural workshop after he was verbally abused by white schoolmates; she hopes to bolster his self-image through positive confirmation of his ethnic identity. These ethnic institutions provide peer networks for children to share feelings about growing up with bicultural conflicts and offer an alternative space to nurture an ethnic identity that children might otherwise reject due to pressure to assimilate.[43]

Resourceful families send their children to summer school in Taiwan or China as a more effective way of cultivating ethnic cultural capital. Several institutions in Taiwan offer Chinese-learning summer programs that target second-generation children. Some parents also hope to instill ethnic values such as respecting teachers and parents when children attend Chinese-language lessons. Victor is an investment banker with a lucrative career, which includes previous posts in Hong Kong and Shanghai. His parents emigrated from

Taiwan to the US when he was young, and he is grateful to his parents for their insistence on speaking Chinese at home. Now, he and his wife bring their two children back to Taiwan to attend private school every summer. For two months, the family stays in a luxurious hotel apartment because none of their immediate kin resides in Taiwan anymore. The cost of lodging and tuition, excluding airfare for four, amount to 14,000 USD each summer. Nevertheless, Victor thinks the money is well spent because only immersion will allow his children to carry on the cultural heritage of their homeland. Victor and his wife emphasize culture as the reason for these pricey summer trips, but they also admit that Chinese-language skills have an important instrumental value in today's global economy.

The Paradox of Ethnic Cultural Capital

Immigrant parents try to inculcate ethnic cultural capital in their children based on tangible and intangible resources. Tangible resources include supplementary education, home tutoring with transnational curricula, Chinese-language schools, and other ethnic cultural enrichment programs. Additionally, these parents try to reclaim cultural values that either contrast to American parenting styles or blend with Western culture; they also actively establish transnational ties and ethnic networks.

Yet the security strategy of cultivating ethnic cultural capital often ends in paradox. Immigrant parents seek to escape the intensive academic pressure of their home countries, but their concern about an Asian quota in US college admissions drives them to reproduce the Chinese educational culture. Parents' pervasive intervention to US-born children may lead to tensions across generations or the strategy may simply fail to work.

Take the example of learning Chinese. Although many immigrant parents hope to preserve the language in their children, there is no guarantee that their children will achieve bilingual fluency. Compared to other immigrant groups, second-generation Chinese are actually less able to retain the ethnic language.[44] Those who grow up in predominantly white neighborhoods often converse with parents in English while their parents speak to them in Chinese. Without access to a sizable Chinese-speaking ethnic community like those in California or New York that offer opportunities for everyday conversation, these children are less likely to achieve fluency.

For many children, Chinese-language school represents an archaic place that conflicts with American life, especially because it usually takes place on weekends. The dropout rate at Chinese-language school rises along with the age of children, as teenagers develop stronger opinions about their free time or struggle to balance Chinese school with other extracurricular activities. Children also complain about the Chinese classroom being characterized by rote learning, repetitive practicing, and frequent exams. The teachers at Chinese-language school are usually immigrant volunteers without official teaching certificates or experience. Many run the classroom on the basis of their memory of attending school in Taiwan decades earlier, even though the pedagogy and teaching styles in contemporary Taiwan have become much more flexible and lively. In other words, ethnic culture is often subject to ahistorical essentialization or nostalgic construction in the immigrant community, while many of these cultural practices are constantly transformed in their countries of origin.[45]

The cultivation of children's language skills largely falls on the shoulders of immigrant mothers. One Taiwanese mother told me that when the Chinese-school teacher scolded her son for poor grades, she felt that "she was actually blaming me for being a bad mother." On another occasion, two Chinese mothers were discussing a friend's daughter who dropped out of Chinese school. One commented: "It's the mother's fault. She should have helped her daughter prepare the homework so the kid would not have lost her interest in learning." As Chapter 2 showed, middle-class mothers are burdened with an increasing load of emotional work to secure their children's academic success and class privilege. Immigrant mothers feel extra pressure from the community or extended household to attain the cultivation of Chinese language and culture as a means of ethnic socialization as well as a minority strategy of class mobility.

Even for those children who do attain Chinese proficiency, their cultural resources are not readily converted into capital in the ethnocentric field of American education. Non–Chinese Americans often assume that children of immigrants, with their Chinese looks and ancestral origins, naturally speak Chinese fluently. College admissions officers may treat Chinese-language ability as an inherited trait rather than a "hard-earned" skill.[46] Parents' focus on academic subjects and selective extracurricular activities, such as the "Asian instruments" of piano and violin, reinforces stereotypes that Chinese children do not pursue personal interests and lack "individuality" or "creativity," which work to their disadvantage in the college application process.

The ethnic culture and transnational identity that parents instill in their US-born children help maintain kin networks across borders and to preserve return migration as a future option. In particular, China's growing prominence on the global stage bolsters children's cultural pride, especially among those with parents from the PRC.[47] Ling Zhao's son Tony, who was born in the US but visits China almost every summer, speaks perfectly fluent Chinese and is very proud of his Chinese background. Ling said: "We always tell him that, in twenty years, China will be the strongest country in the world. It is indeed the trend, perhaps less than twenty years."

Yet children feel conflicted when they are pressured to identify themselves in a singular frame. Ling, currently a green-card holder, is close to fulfilling her residency requirement for naturalization. Tony is so committed to Chinese patriotism that he discourages his mother from becoming a US citizen. Ling says, "He warns me, 'Mom, never get an American citizenship, otherwise your connections with China will be cut, will be loose.'" Ling feels ambivalent about her son's liminal identity: "I am not sure if this is good or bad. . . . Sometimes I think this is perhaps his fate, he was conceived in China, but he was born here."

Although my research focuses on parental practice and cannot assess the long-term impact on those parents' children, other studies reveal that the strategy of ethnic cultural capital entails ambivalent consequences for Asian Americans in the long run. While these parents pressure their children to acquire immigrant toughness as an advantage in the pathway to social mobility, their validation of ethnic traits may lead to the paradox of racial otherization. As Angie Chung has documented in her book, second-generation Asian Americans widely suffer from ethnic stigmatization and are thus excluded from "full social citizenship in the American racial imaginary." Although the myth of the model minority family praises Asian immigrant parents and their children for their cultural exceptionalism, it also ridicules their "excessive parenting, oppressive hierarchies and emotional pragmatism in a monolithic Asian culture."[48]

Conclusion

Despite their achievement of professional status in the new country, middle-class immigrants encounter blocked mobility in American workplaces and worry about their children's future in the shadow of institutional racism. Straddling two cultural worlds and geographic lands, immigrant parents navigate multiple meanings of confidence and success in their arrangement of extracurricular activities and supplementary education for the second generation. As Ming-Cheng Lo and Emerald Nguyen have cautioned, cultural blending is not as smooth a process as the theory of segmented assimilation optimistically presumes.[49] Instead, it is a contentious process that often exacerbates frustration and conflicts among immigrant families.

Parents who lean toward the strategy of orchestrating competitive assimilation see their blocked mobility mainly as a consequence of their individual shortcomings. They view social skills and cultural competency as necessary components for their children to survive or compete in American society. These immigrant parents seek immigration to the US as a spatial break from Taiwan's cultural traditions and educational practice. Their intention is similar to middle-class Taiwanese parents who embrace new cultural scripts or Western education as a way to create generational rupture.

Parents toward the other end of the spectrum mobilize tangible and intangible resources associated with their cultural origins and transnational connections to benefit their children. They attribute their blocked mobility to structural discrimination against immigrants and racial minorities, and they worry about the harms this discrimination will continue to inflict on their US-born children. They seek coethnics in the US or in their home countries, instead of native-born whites, as their reference groups for success.

The ideal types presented here provide an analytical frame to capture the difference in childrearing styles, but we cannot lose sight of similarities between the groups as well as the potential for shifts in parenting strategy across the life course. Although parents who orchestrate children's assimilation seem optimistic about the possibility to bridge cultural differences, they too express concerns about exposing children to racial prejudice and defeating their confidence. Parents who cultivate ethnic cultural capital are critical of institutional racism, but some of them blame diversity policy—not white privilege—for the disadvantaged status of Asian Americans in college admissions, reproducing an individualized solution and even animosity toward other minority groups. Finally, children are not passive recipients but active agents in negotiating intergenerational dynamics. As several examples in this chapter have manifested, children initiate voices and actions to transform their immigrant parents, or their life events like racist bullying at school turn their parents to calibrate their childrearing strategies.

Like middle-class parents in Taiwan, professional immigrants similarly use market consumption and transnational connections to offer concerted cultivation to the next generation. Despite their shared ethnic origin, these two groups of parents use distinct strategies of cultural mobility to cope with different opportunity structures. Their distinct approaches to global security projects nevertheless lead to the unintended consequences of cultural essentialization. On the one hand, middle-class Taiwanese parents seek Western ideas of childrearing to broaden their children's opportunities to pursue a globalized future, but their security strategies often idealize and glorify Western education, overlooking its friction and rupture with local institutions. On the other hand, professional immigrants who feel ambivalent about American education turn to their home countries for learning and teaching materials; their strategies to secure their children's futures in the context of racial inequality may idealize and reify their cultural heritage and create tension and conflicts across generations.

5 Immigrant Working Class
Reframing Family Dynamics

A DOZEN IMMIGRANT PARENTS in their thirties or forties, mostly mothers and some fathers, attended the first seminar of the parental education workshop held by a nonprofit in Boston's Chinatown. The instructor, an immigrant woman from Hong Kong, asked the attendants what they most wanted to learn. The parents eagerly responded: "Discipline! How do we get our children to listen to us and not talk back?"

The instructor suggested that the issue of "identity affirmation" was more important than discipline. Citing research by an Ivy League professor, the instructor asked the attendants in Mandarin: "Guess which type of immigrants are the most successful in the US? First-generation, one and a half, or the second generation?" Most had no answer; a few guessed the second generation. When the instructor revealed that first-generation immigrants were usually the most successful, the class looked surprised. They shook their heads: "How can each generation do worse than the previous [generation]?!" One of the parents speculated on the cause: "American education is too free and children become lazy!" Another nodded: "American children are too happy, no homework! You can even walk around freely in class!"

Immigrant parents with working-class jobs in the US face far more financial constraints and cultural challenges than their middle-class counterparts. Despite their concerns about "too much freedom" in American schools and society, they are generally hopeful about their children's prospects of attending college and achieving social mobility. What troubles them most is intergenerational relations at home—they have lost parental authority in the new country and the old ways of discipline are not legal or valid for their US-born children.

This chapter examines how working-class immigrants raise their children in response to their conflicting experience of mobility and shifting family dynamics. Although they are seemingly achieving the "American dream" in the eyes of friends and relatives back home, they generally suffer downward mobility because of the lack of recognition for their human and cultural capital in the new country. The US state's intervention, including low-income welfare programs and parental education, may empower socially disadvantaged immigrants in their daily battle for survival, but it can also conflict with their family realities and weaken their upward mobility.

These parents creatively use various strategies of cultural and transnational mobility to cope with their loss of authority at home and to maintain their particular version of family security. Some try to project an "American" outlook on their family lives by either interpreting the reversed dynamics of parent-child relations as an indicator of cultural assimilation or attending parenting seminars to learn about American knowledge and techniques of childrearing. The others seek resources from immigrant communities or transnational kin networks to sustain the cultural practices of education, care, and discipline.

Downward Mobility and Welfare Entrapment

Unlike middle-class professionals who mostly immigrated through employment, lower-class immigrants came to the US largely through family reunification. This study defines immigrants' class position according to their occupations in the US.[1] Of the 17 working-class informants (4 men and 13 women), 9 immigrated through sponsorship by parents or siblings and 7 women reunited with their husbands. In addition, one woman from Taiwan immigrated through the "green-card lottery."

Immigrant men with limited education and English proficiency are mostly confined to job opportunities in the ethnic economy. They work in the blue-collar or low-skilled service sectors as waiters, cooks, butchers, locksmiths, carpenters, and construction laborers performing house renovations. Many started working immediately after their arrival to the US; they have had no time to improve their English skills and are trapped in an "occupational ghetto."[2] They work long hours, returning home late and spending little time with their children. Their practice of fatherhood remains traditional, mainly performing the paternal role as breadwinners.

The patterns of labor-market incorporation for working-class immigrant women in this study are a bit different. In addition to employment in the ethnic economy, many women work as beauticians, elderly caretakers, child caretakers, hotel custodial staff, and other service workers with non-Chinese clientele. To maintain eligibility for low-income welfare subsidies and to accommodate their children's needs, several mothers work short hours or stay home with children. Eight out of 17 mothers in the sample were full-time homemakers at the time of our interview. They were able to join NGO-sponsored activities and to attend English classes; some also attended training classes for childcare or elder care conducted in English. The divergent gendered pathways of social integration allow immigrant women to acquire more English skills and cultural knowledge for social adaptation than their husbands.

Most working-class immigrants, men and women alike, suffer from some degree of downward mobility in the US because they lack language skills, social ties, and institutionally recognized degrees or qualifications.[3] Their status slide is significant compared to their previously comfortable conditions back home; remember that immigrants tend not to come from the lowest strata of poverty because resources are needed to make the journey.

Although downward mobility in the new country curtails their social status, self-esteem, and quality of life, lower-income newcomers are entitled to social protection from the US welfare state. Twelve out of 17 working-class immigrant families in this study receive some forms of means-tested benefits, such as subsidized health care, public housing, and preschool programs. Government support also relieves some of the financial burdens of generational transfer for lower-class immigrants, who under Chinese tradition are duty-bound to both care for aging parents and support their children through college.[4]

Owing to their limited knowledge about the American education system and their entitlement to welfare benefits, working-class immigrants are more optimistic about their children's futures than the anxiety-ridden middle class.[5] None of the working-class parents in this study expressed worries about the competition of college admission or the so-called Asian quota. They are generally confident about the prospect for their children to receive postsecondary education, given the prevalence of community colleges in the US. They are not concerned about the costs of college tuitions since their children are most likely to receive some financial aid due to their limited household incomes.

However, many of these benefits disappear once the family income exceeds a certain amount. Therefore, immigrant parents feel trapped in the low-income status by their dependence on subsidized welfare programs. To circumvent this problem, some families develop flexible strategies. For example, some file for divorce and keep the property under the name of only one spouse; others take informal jobs with unreported income to maintain eligibility. This section shows that working-class immigrants' experience of downward mobility, and the consequence of shredded confidence and curtailed social exposure, has a profound influence on their capacity and attitude in childrearing.

"There's No Bridge to Cross the River"

I met Shenli Yu at an educational event held by a Chinatown NGO at Boston's Museum of Fine Arts. The volunteers were a little embarrassed to tell me that most immigrant parents were not interested in these cultural events. Only one father had signed up. Shenli, a short man with glasses and slightly balding, rushed in late, just after finishing his shift making sushi in a supermarket. With a self-deprecating laugh, he pointed at his white shirt with golden buttons and told me: "I used to wear the same outfit working as a public officer in China; now, I am making sushi in America!"

In Canton Province of southern China, Shenli worked as a public servant, but his Chinese college degree was not recognized in the US. Since he immigrated to the US ten years ago, he could find work only at supermarkets and fast-food restaurants. At the museum, Shenli eagerly eyed the various pamphlets at the information desk, asking whether any museum activities were available for his three young daughters, all of whom love to draw. But the brochures and tours were in English, making them difficult for him to understand. Shenli said to me apologetically, "We are too busy working here in the US to catch up with any culture."

A week after the museum tour, I visited Shenli's family in their old apartment building on the outskirts of Boston. He initially suggested that we meet at Burger King because "the apartment is too messy and crowded." The unit, about one hundred square meters in size, included three bedrooms and a living room that was converted into a fourth bedroom. It was packed to accommodate multiple households—Shenli's family of five lives there, as does his elder sister, her two teenaged children, and her husband, who was a doctor in China but now works at a Chinese restaurant in Boston. Next week, another sister and her family of three will come to the US and stay in the living room until they find their own apartment. Shenli's wife proudly told me that her husband found and repaired most of the furniture in the apartment. The only decorative object I could see was a wedding photo of theirs from China.

Shenli's is a typical immigrant tale of downward mobility, and he feels further trapped by the US means-tested welfare system. During our interview, he repeatedly described this feeling using the analogy of a river: "My dream is to have a bridge to cross the river. If you have a bridge, you can go step by step across to the other side. Some people can just jump or fly to the other side, but I don't have that kind of ability. If I take one wrong step, I will fall into the river."

The river represents barriers to mobility for working-class immigrants. So long as Shenli is limited to jobs with few benefits and little prospect of promotion, he is "stuck at one side of the river." He hopes to obtain a second university degree in the US that will provide a starting point to that elusive "bridge" toward cultural integration and social mobility. Yet this bridge was hard to reach for Shenli, who was burdened with the economic responsibility of providing for a large family.

Low-income welfare benefits become a double-edged sword for Shenli's family. If he took "one wrong step" by earning more money or starting a small business, the family might lose health insurance coverage and "fall into the river" of having no social safety nets. To maintain his access to welfare, Shenli decided to give up his plan to earn a second degree and also his aspirations for upward mobility. With a heavy sigh, he said with a wry smile: "We've decided to accept our status as a low-income family. We just put our hopes on our children."

Although his own American dream has shattered, Shenli advises his friends and relatives to stay in the US for their children's education. He is still ambivalent about his children's future because he feels incompetent as a parent in the US:

> But really, even though you are hopeful, you are not sure about it. You don't know how things will really end up for them because you can't offer much to them. All you can do is drop them off at school and pick them up. If you had more of a cultured background in China, you could probably raise them in the Chinese way. But we just don't get the American way.

Shenli's mother-in-law, around eighty years old and still healthy, lives nearby in a subsidized apartment for the elderly. She comes over to take care of all the grandchildren during the day. Such arrangement of childcare is common among working-class Chinese immigrants. However, Shenli does not view their cultural heritage as much of a source of ethnic capital as many middle-class immigrants do. He describes his "background culture" like luggage that "we brought with us but not useful here." He says: "Chinese culture is useless. Since you cannot use it to make a living, you might as well get rid of it! Just let it go and start over." By contrast, he views American culture as a "foreground culture." The second generation must embrace this culture, but the first generation is unequipped to guide them in this journey.

"Don't Teach Your Children Because You'll Just Confuse Them"

Wendy Li and her husband came to the US under the sponsorship of her in-laws, who immigrated in the 1980s. Both were high school graduates and entrepreneurs in the city of Guangzhou and had experienced success during China's period of economic ascent. But after they rapidly expanded their businesses and made some bad investments, their laundry and restaurant failed. Feeling "unsure of what to do with our lives," they decided to move to the US in 2006, along with their three-year-old son, when Wendy was thirty-eight years old.

A petite woman with a stern voice, Wendy recalls the time after their arrival with tears in her eyes. They slept on her in-laws' couch for months. Her husband quickly joined many of his fellow Chinese immigrants as a construction worker on housing renovation projects, even though he had never worked on his own home in China. Wendy stayed home for two years to care for her sons—the second one was born after their arrival—while taking free English classes in Chinatown. She took part-time jobs cleaning houses and caring for elderly Americans until her younger son started kindergarten.

Wendy tried to prepare herself for the hardship in the new country, but she was shocked by the decline in her material standard of living and her loss of personal supports and social connections. She feels confined by her lack of language skills and cultural knowledge in the psychological cage that she calls an "immigrant mentality":

> Our understanding of American society is very surface level. . . . There are many places we cannot go because our English is not good and we cannot fit in mainstream society. It's not that other people reject you, but that you are afraid to go. Do you understand? You feel like you will embarrass yourself in those places. You are afraid that you don't know what to do, so you don't fit into their world. In all my years here, I have only been to the movies once. And why did I go that one time? It was Chinese New Year and they were showing a Chinese movie. . . . The truth is, I want to go all the time but I am afraid that I won't understand a thing and will just sit there like an idiot, you know?

Wendy blames her and her husband's economic failure on their limited education. She is determined to give their children a better education: "If you have no knowledge, then you have no taste, no investment strategy, and no information." Yet, she also believes that it is necessary for her to withdraw from teaching her sons, ages nine and six, so that they can learn properly in the US:

> Sometimes I feel sorry for my sons. They ask me many questions, but I don't know how to answer at all. We live in the US, and American culture is very different from Chinese culture. I advise my friends, "If it's something you don't know, don't try to teach them because you will just confuse them." If you teach children something wrong, they won't know how to fend for themselves in the US. What if they encounter a problem and think, "but my parents told me so"? They cannot adjust and will develop similar immigrant insecurities to the ones we have.

Immigrants like Wendy believe that responsible parenting means backing off from the educator role. One father described this even more directly: "Teaching nothing is better than teaching the wrong thing." Instead of taking the duty of education upon themselves, these parents assume the mission of finding the right places and people to educate their children. As we will see later in this chapter, they rely on the ethnic economy to provide children's pathway consumption. Wendy says: "No matter how hard it is, I will get my sons to study whatever subject. Even if it [cram school] is expensive and I have to work very hard, I am going to send them."

Lost Authority and State Intervention

Working-class immigrants suffer from a loss of parental authority at home for two major reasons. First, transnational relocation, followed by the consequence of downward mobility, constrains their ability to raise children in the new country. Many feel defeated that they could not supervise their children's homework, read teachers' notes, or advise their children on college applications. Some even have to rely on children to assist with language translation or cultural interpretation. In addition, the US-born or US-grown children are often one of the major sources to challenge their parents' cultural competency. One mother who spoke limited English described the problem of helping her son with homework from his elementary school: "To be honest, I often ask Google Translate to help us when there is vocabulary I don't understand. My son says, 'Mom, why are you so stupid?'"

Second, working-class immigrant parents feel baffled by the new cultural repertoire of childrearing in the new country. In Bourdieu's words, they simply have no "feel for the game,"[6] or they do not have time to acquire or execute a new parenting style. Parents find it increasingly difficult to communicate with teenage children who resist speaking Chinese. American youth culture, which is strikingly different from the youth culture in China or Taiwan, renders immigrant parents further concerned about children's discipline and behavior.

In particular, immigrant parents feel powerless by the deprivation of the traditional tool of corporal punishment. Previous studies have reported that many immigrants hold back from spanking their children in the US because they are afraid of institutional consequences for child abuse.[7] Similar to the West Indian immigrants in Mary Waters and Jennifer Sykes's study, working-class Chinese immigrants see corporal punishment as part of their culture and feel that "the American state is making them abandon a practice they believe to be the best way to raise their children."[8] In fact, the US only recently labeled corporal punishment as inappropriate. In the late 1960s, over 90 percent of Americans expected parents to spank a child when necessary; this approval declined only recently, and most significantly among the white middle class.[9]

Some middle-class immigrants in this study also had a similar experience of being reported by schools for punishing their children. For example, Mandy Liao is a full-time homemaker and her husband is a PhD-educated engineer. When their son was at elementary school, the father once took his hand and hit it with a hanger, and this act raised concern from his teacher. Mandy described their encounter with the school principal as a humiliating experience that belittled their cultural background and parental competency:

> We were so upset. We had to promise [to the principal] that something like that would never happen again. It was like giving my son a get-out-of-jail-free card, you know? I don't agree with corporal punishment but I don't think they have the right to completely take it away. . . . Especially with a young principal like that, he was maybe like thirty years old. Being lectured by someone like that, my husband was really angry. He didn't have any personal experience with what he was talking about and he dared to label us "child abuse." . . . There was definitely a bias [against immigrants]. Most certainly there was. . . . We know how to raise our children and we would never do anything to hurt them. Their decisions like that actually hurt the kids even more.

The following two stories show that working-class immigrant parents, who have even less cultural confidence than their middle-class counterparts at the encounter with American institutional authorities, experience a more substantial decline of parental authority vis-à-vis their American-born children. The government-sponsored programs, such as free English classes, welfare sub-sidy, and parenting seminars, can empower immigrant parents in their pursuit of social adaptation and cultural mobility. Yet state intervention in regard to corporal punishment can also shatter the authority and security of immigrant parents.

"How Can I Be a Mother if My Child Threatens Me?"

Sue Deng, a mother of two in her late forties, was an outspoken participant in the parental workshop. She migrated to the US in 1996 under her sister's sponsorship. Soon after her arrival, she married her husband, who had also em-igrated from Canton. Sue finished high school in China and worked in Guang-zhou in a small company that exported clothes. She was unable to continue this line of business in the US because of her limited English and lack of social ties.

Sue's husband, Biao, works as a waiter in a Chinese restaurant for longer hours (from 10 a.m. to 10 p.m.). Biao regrets his decision to immigrate: "We are only surviving, not living a life!" With only one day off a week, Biao earns a monthly wage, including tips, of slightly over 2,000 USD. The job does not pro-vide health insurance, so Sue stays home full-time to keep the family income low enough to receive subsidized health insurance.

Sue is worried about her two daughters, eleven and nine years old. They used to attend a traditional public elementary school in Quincy, but Sue re-cently transferred the younger one to a charter school. Sue complained that the teachers at her daughter's previous school were irresponsible and assigned too little homework: "I don't like the education system here because they don't give the kids any pressure." The cultural gap also prevents her from appreciating American teachers' upbeat and encouraging style. Instead, Sue felt like she was being lied to by her daughter's teacher:

> Every time the teacher saw me, she told me, "She's excellent! She's the top one of the class!" I am a very honest person, so I don't like it when people fake-talk to me. One summer I put my daughter into this summer program and everyone just kept telling me how smart she is.

Sue tries to push her daughters to learn beyond their assignments at school. She asks them to write Chinese compositions on the weekends and enrolls them in academic tutoring and weekly Chinese lessons.[10] This packed sched-ule stirs conflict between mother and daughters, especially the younger one, Bridget, who has a stubborn personality. When Sue pressures Bridget to study harder, Bridget answers with brutal honesty: "What's your problem? You are crazy! Every Saturday and Sunday you tell me to do homework, and everyone else is out there playing. You have a problem!"

Bridget sees her immigrant parents as an embarrassment and tries to keep them from coming to school. Sue said: "She doesn't want us to pick her up from school and she doesn't want her classmates to see us because it is awkward. She's afraid I will tell the teacher to give them more homework. All her classmates say to her, 'Is your mom crazy? Why does she give you so much homework?'"

Bridget rebels against her parents by questioning their cultural competency and labeling them as *Chongwenren* (Chinese-language persons). When Sue asks to check Bridget's homework, Bridget replies: "You are not an *Ingwenren* (English-language person), you don't understand," "Your way is not the way the teacher says!" "Their [the classmates'] dads understand English so they can help, that's why those kids are smarter. But you two don't know English, especially Dad. He doesn't even bother to learn so he understands nothing!" Bridget's use of *Chongwenren* to undermine her parents' cultural competence and authority at home stands in stark contrast to the function the term served for Cathy Wu in Chapter 4. For middle-class immigrants, the term *Chongwenren* instead establishes a shared cultural identity and family bonds across generations.

The American style of childrearing is confusing to Sue; it seems like simply letting go. In despair, she asked the instructor at the parenting workshop, "I see all these American children skiing in the winter or playing in the lake, but they get so dirty and their parents just let them play around. Is this really the American style?"

Sue also feels conflicted about the use of spanking as a form of discipline. Each week, the instructor started the seminar by asking us to recall memorable events that happened at home in the previous week. Sue often responded by expressing regret that she had hit her daughter, although she emphasized her selective approach to corporal punishment:

[My parents'] generation was all about hitting. My dad would hit me in the head with ivory chopsticks. I'm not sure if the ivory chopsticks represented some sort of authority he had. I have continued this in our home, but I do it selectively. For example, a couple of days ago, my youngest was still watching TV at 11 p.m. and wouldn't go to bed. So I asked her, "Do you want me to hit you, your older sister to hit you, or will you hit yourself?" She said her sister, so I told my older daughter to hit her since I want my eldest to develop a sense of authority. I always hit the left hand because they need to write with their right hands, and I use a flat board so it doesn't leave a mark. I know it's bad to hit children, but I can't help it. Their father always raises his voice, [saying], "I'm about to hit [you]," but he never actually does it. He doesn't want to be the bad guy.

Sue views corporal punishment as a symbolic tool of parental authority, and she creatively modifies the disciplinary practice to match her family dynamics, offering her rebellious younger daughter some "choice" and extending some parental authority to her older daughter, also a US-born child. The eldest child is assigned the role of mediator because her husband is too busy at work. But Sue's strategy does not always work because Bridget is able to challenge her mother by threatening with the intervention of state authorities:

Once I told her I was ready to hit her and I was going to get a stick, [and] she headed straight to the telephone! So I said to her, "OK, you call them. I am going to take a shower first. When I finish, you should be all packed up. I'll take a shower because there is no hot water at the police department. After that you can go with black people, black ladies, and I can go with the police." I came out of the shower and my older daughter, trying to protect her sister, said to me, "Mom, she wasn't calling the police. She was just calling a class-mate about homework." Then I said with a sigh, "How can I be a mother if she threatens me?"

Immigrant parents live in fear that the child welfare system will take away their children if corporal punishment is reported. Their children are aware of their rights and sometimes threaten to contact the police if they are physically punished or even sharply scolded. In response to Bridget's threat to call the police, Sue reminded her daughter that the dire consequence would be a sever-ance of family ties, leaving Bridget alone with "black ladies" (i.e., foster par-ents). Sue's family lives in a subsidized public housing project with a significant racial minority population. One reason that Sue transferred Bridget to a charter school was to avoid the largely African American population at the traditional public school. Sue's decision drew on racist stereotypes about African Ameri-cans and practical worries about the possibility of downward assimilation, by which the second generation is assimilated into the American underclass in urban ghettos.[11] Both concerns increase her conflicted feelings about the use of corporal punishment and her frustration at failing to control and protect her children.

"Women Need to Be Disciplined, or They Will Misbehave"

The threat of state intrusion for corporal punishment can also become a tool for family members to enforce abuse against those who are vulnerable in the kin networks. The story of Hong Liang is a case in point. In 1996, when she was a registered nurse in Guangzhou, she met her husband, Zheng Han, who returned from the US to find a wife. They married in 1998, but the processing of her green-card application slowed down in the post-9/11 era. She finally reunited with Zheng in 2005, when their son was almost seven years old.

Zheng's family runs a Chinese restaurant in Boston's Chinatown. Hong hoped to attend English courses to improve her life chances in the US, but Zheng and his mother strongly objected. Despite their disapproval, Hong decided to attend the English classes. Her endeavor to learn English and acquire US citizenship was interpreted by the husbands' family as violating the submissive role of a daughter-in-law and transgressing the moral boundary of modest femininity:

> My mother-in-law yelled at my husband, "Why would you let a woman go to school? We have been here for twenty years and never went to school! Why do women need to study?" I was pregnant [with their second child] at the time, and she made me cook breakfast, lunch, and dinner every day for ten plus people. They want me to work [in Chinese restaurants]. I was very unhappy back then. Every time I went home after [English] class, I felt like going back to prison [sobbing]. They did not let me out. Sometimes I went out to talk to someone for just a minute; they were so cautious as if they were afraid I might run away. . . . They don't like me learning and they probably just want me to be a dumb servant at home. They don't like it when I have ideas because then they cannot control me.

Hong's mother-in-law maneuvered US state intervention into corporal punishment to undermine Hong's custodial power over her children. The mother-in-law had a Chinese lawyer write a letter to the child welfare system reporting that Hong hit her son with a stick. The agents interviewed Hong and visited the son's school to investigate whether he had any emotional problems. Hong was shaken by this event. The teacher at the public school, also a Chinese immigrant, sympathized with Hong's struggle at home. Instead of urging Hong to give up corporal punishment, the teacher advised her to hide her disciplinary practices from the surveillance of public authorities. Hong said:

I was so stupid. I used to believe that your friends and family would never hurt you. After the investigation, I had a meeting with the teacher. She told me that she was on my side and nothing would happen to me this time, but I need to be careful. She taught me a trick. Next time I want to punish my son, I should take him to the bathroom and turn on the faucet so no one will hear. And use a ping-pong paddle! That way there would be no mark.

Hong's marriage eventually dissolved following the outbreak of marital violence. One day she got home after the English classes and found her six-month-old baby crying out loud because the father had not fed him. The mother-in-law viewed childcare as Hong's duty, telling Zheng: "His damn mother is home. Just give her the child. Stop holding him." Hong talked back to her in a rage. Then she ran to the kitchen to make congee for her hungry son, angrily making a lot of noise with the pots and pans. Zheng came in and yelled at her, "What right do you have to be angry?" His mother in the living room added fuel to the fire: "Women need to be disciplined. If you don't hit them, they will misbehave." Then he hit Hong's arms. A different day he yelled at her: "Did you marry me for another purpose? How come you took the citizenship test after being here for only five years?" She rebelliously answered, "Yeah, so what?" and he grabbed a knife to threaten her.

After another assault by her husband, Hong applied for a restraining order. She eventually divorced her husband and received her American citizenship in 2010. For immigrant mothers like Hong, the loss of parental authority is entangled with their marginal status as an immigrant daughter-in-law. Immigrant mothers occupy an ambiguous location in the everyday acts of cultural negotiation. On the one hand, they are burdened with the pressure from the extended family and immigrant community to reproduce gender order and inculcate ethnic culture in the next generation. On the other hand, they view cultural adaptation as an essential motherly practice. They desire to attain language skills and cultural competency in the US and embrace their children's freedom and a permissive style of parenting in line with American norms.

Narrating Assimilation

For immigrant parents like Sue Deng, children's entitlement and autonomy in the US imply a dangerous kind of freedom. This freedom can lead to a weak work ethic, a lack of respect for elders, and straying from the family's values under bad peer influence. Yet other working-class immigrants embrace the narrative of children's freedom as an essential feature of the "American family," and they manage to reframe the changing parent-child dynamics as a progress toward cultural assimilation.

In her study of Asian American college students, Karen Pyke argues that the "normal American family," an image constructed largely in relation to white, middle-class heterosexuals, serves as both interpretive framework and moral dogma to shape the consciousness of all it excludes or marginalizes. Asian American children use this template to contrast with their "Asian family" and view the differences as shortcomings or deviance.[12] Immigrant parents also use their image of the American family as emotionally expressive, open, lenient, individualistic, and self-centered, in contrast to the Asian family, which they view as emotionally distant, authoritarian, and strict but committed to the family collective.

For instance, Yutang Su, a forty-five-year-old homemaker whose husband works in a Chinese restaurant described her relationship with her two teenaged daughters:

> We are more like sisters, not like parents and children. We are open, not very serious. We are equal. [Children] can point out whatever is wrong. . . . My daughters sometimes educate us [smiling]: "Mom, this is the tradition of you Chinese. It's too old-fashioned for us. It's not good. I am smart. You don't have to worry." . . . If it was up to us, we would like to educate them the Chinese way. We did try, but it didn't really work. Because American children are totally different from Chinese children. . . . American education is all about freedom.

Yutang's perception of American parenting may sound reductive or even naïve. It reflects her limited encounter with the American mainstream, especially the helicopter parenting style in suburban middle-class life. The narrative also indicates a common immigrant aspiration for cultural assimilation. Especially in the context of an interview with a college professor who may be viewed as an extension of expert authority, less-educated informants may feel compelled to iterate an Americanized, seemingly "politically correct" model of parenting, that is, to replace the vertical hierarchy of the traditional Chinese family with a horizontal, "friendlike" relationship with their American children.

More important, working-class immigrants prefer a hands-off approach to parenting because it suits the constrained reality where they are short on time, cultural resources, and kin assistance. The rhetoric of permissive parenting as a dominant repertoire of childrearing in the US provides a culturally acceptable framework for these parents to reposition the shifting parent-child dynamics.

They manage to justify their hands-off parenting by associating it with positive changes, including children's independence and the consolidation of family bonds.

Fanfan Luo is a thirty-three-year-old homemaker and mother of two young children. She immigrated to the US through her marriage to the husband, who resides in Boston with his parents and works as a cook in a Chinese restaurant. Fanfan started sending her son to preschool as early as one year old. This is not a common practice among Chinese immigrants with older women relatives in the US who can help with childcare. But Fanfan prefers paid, out-of-home childcare to the unpaid service provided by her mother-in-law because the former seems more in line with American culture:

> I wanted him to start integrating into society at a very young age. He needs to learn how to work with people but also how to be independent. I don't want him just to play at home all day. . . . My husband and I are both immigrants. Our English is terrible, so they need to learn to help themselves in the future. I want them to learn to become independent now so whatever happens in the future, they can handle it on their own. I don't even try to help him with anything. I don't understand English, I don't understand American culture, so I can't fit into this society. My hope is that they can do much better than us.

Fanfan recognizes her and her husband's limited ability to parent in the US, which gives them no other choice but to allow her son "to develop by himself." She also criticizes parents and grandparents in China for overindulging their only child and turning him or her into a "little emperor" who lacks self-sufficiency. By contrast, the American emphasis on children's freedom seems to promise the positive outcome of children's independence and autonomy, which are essential survival kits for the children of immigrants.

The existing literature has documented that immigrant parents who lack English fluency rely on their children for language translation and cultural interpretation; children act as "brokers" by facilitating their immigrant parents' access to institutional resources and opportunities in the new country.[13] For instance, Shu-fen Chen, a Taiwanese mother who is attending an evening class to become a certified childcare worker, needs to ask her eight-year-old daughter to translate some of her own school work. She feels embarrassed by this role reversal and worries about placing too great a burden on her daughter. As Lisa Park has described, the "brokering" role casts a negative shadow on children of immigrants because they are forced into a "premature adulthood."[14]

However, some immigrant parents develop a positive outlook on the reversed intergenerational dynamics. Ping Xia, a Chinese mother with children of similar age, interprets this role reversal differently. Ping is aware of her thick accent and wants her daughter to speak American English like a native speaker. She is pleased when her nine-year-old daughter corrects her pronunciation:

> Before, I taught her. Now, she teaches me. Since my English isn't so good, now that she is older, when I read something, I always ask her what it means and she will explain to me. . . . It's still the same [as in China]. When I don't know something, I can rely on them, and when they don't know something, I must teach them.

Marjorie Faulstich Orellana reminds us of the complex consequences of "translating childhood." The children of immigrants may see the duty to translate as a burden or even a means of parental surveillance, but they can also feel empowered by this service because it indicates their contribution to the family.[15] Ping worries that children raised in the US will become selfish and that their family bonds will erode. In her eyes, children's work as cultural brokers for parents indicates a relationship of interdependence and helps consolidate family bonds. According to the traditional script of Chinese families, love is expressed through instrumental help and support rather than through verbal expression and open displays of affection as in US culture.[16] By translating or explaining documents to parents, the children of immigrants act not only as recipients but also as providers of care and support. These new cross-generation dynamics affirm parents and children's joint commitment to the family collective, shaping what Angie Chung calls "reciprocated empathy" among the second generation: the children "develop a greater sense of empathy for the vulnerable status of their parents and their discrimination from the dominant society."[17]

We're Not "the Normal Asian American Family"

Working-class immigrants use the cultural frame of "the normal American family" to positively interpret their hands-off style of childrearing. Yet the narratives of assimilation obscure these families' constrained reality and undermines a predicament widely faced by working-class immigrants and their children—they are often compared with "the normal Asian American family," that is, professional immigrants in the wealthy suburbs and their children with academic prowess.

Lisa Huang is a tall forty-six-year-old woman with long, curly hair that is dyed chestnut brown. She owns a modest beauty salon in Quincy, a suburb south of Boston with a large working-class Asian population. Lisa has two daughters from her first marriage in Taiwan and one younger son with her current husband, John, a first-generation Taiwanese American. During our interview held in the salon, the seven-year-old son returned from school. He fixed himself a snack and quietly played on the computer. Lisa's eldest daughter, Susan, stopped by the salon after class at a local community college. With curiosity, she asked me about the topic of my research. After I explained, she commented, "Parenting? But there's no parenting at all in our family."

Lisa grew up with working-class parents in southern Taiwan. She began working right after high school and had a short-lived marriage with a soldier in her twenties. Around the age of thirty-four, Lisa met John, eight years her junior, who was taking a vacation in Taiwan. After visiting John in the US, Lisa was determined to seek a future in *meiguo*, the Chinese term for the United States, which has the literal meaning of "beautiful country." She believed that an American upbringing would promise her children a life of safety and happiness.

During the first few years after their arrival, Lisa and her daughter lived in the basement of the Chinese restaurant run by John's family. John's parents initially objected to this marriage until Lisa gave birth to a son. Susan, then fifteen years old, worked at the restaurant to help win the in-laws' approval. Lisa's family eventually moved out her in-laws' house. She found a job as an assistant in a salon in Chinatown and brought her son, then three years old, with her to work every day. Lisa recalls hectic winter mornings rushing to the subway along snow-covered streets, clutching the hand of her crying toddler. Sometimes she had to leave the children at home by themselves or ask the older daughters to watch their baby brother. Afraid of being reported to the child welfare system, Lisa asked the children never to bring any friends home.

After Lisa passed her licensing exam to become a hairdresser, she rented a chair in a barbershop run by an Italian American and started her own practice. She slowly improved her English conversation skills and learned to use the computer for bookkeeping. With some help from her sister in Taiwan, she eventually purchased a house and opened her own salon. Although many of her friends have congratulated her for achieving her version of the American dream, Lisa regrets her failures as a mother, especially compared to middle-class Asian immigrants who have more time and resources to invest in child-drearing. Lisa says:

Most Asian immigrants in the US are very highly educated. They know how to raise their children. But nobody helped me. I don't know how to read or speak English, and I can't help my children. Like her [Susan], she came here and life was very difficult because I had no power to help her. She couldn't make friends, she had no confidence, so she had to see a psychiatrist for many years.

Turning to Susan, I asked whether her mother threw birthday parties or allowed her to have sleepovers as a teenager. She choked back a laugh: "You probably watch too much TV. . . . Even my American classmates are not like that." She cuts off any further questions along these lines, saying, "My family is not that *mei*!"

Susan sees through the intersection of ethnic culture and class privilege behind the glorified fiction of the "normal American family." She notes that even her classmates from non-Asian, working-class families do not live up to the idealized image. She uses the Chinese word *mei* as a double entendre. First, the family does not enjoy a typical *meiguo* (American) lifestyle. Susan jokingly says, "My mom did not bake a cake for my birthday, but she steamed some buns." Second, she uses the word *mei* to communicate that her life growing up could not be described as "beautiful" or "wonderful."

Children of working-class immigrants also feel pressured to be compared against middle-class coethnic children. Asian Americans' assumed academic prowess shapes how people of other racial and ethnic groups interact with them, especially in school. Susan recalls her encounter with the high school counselor:

> The moment I walked in, she [the counselor] listed all of the Ivy Leagues, and then asked me which one [I wanted to attend]. I said none [of them]. Then she said to me, "Why are you asking me for help? You are Asian, you should be smart." There was a lot of pressure because I felt like I was stupid and I needed to be as smart as the other Asians.

Previous studies have found that Asian Americans who do not attend four-year colleges generally feel a sense of alienation and failure.[18] These feelings not only come from their parents' expectations, but they are also inflicted by the powerful model minority stereotype. The public perception about Asian American achievement may create a "stereotype promise" for some Asian youth during their encounters with educators,[19] but it is far more likely that working-class immigrants and their children feel pressured to be evaluated against the norm of "the middle-class Asian American family." The coethnic reference group makes them feel inadequate or incompetent as parents and students.

Parenting Education: Building Therapeutic Selfhood

To move beyond a narrative strategy, some immigrant parents actively pursue new knowledge and skills in line with the US repertoire of childrearing. Public schools and NGOs have offered parenting seminars to help immigrants, especially the less educated, to get familiar with American education and childrearing. For instance, the Parent University program launched in 2009 by the Boston Public Schools Office of Family and Student Engagement holds panels on immigrant parenting conducted in non-English languages, including Chinese, during its regular learning conferences.[20]

An NGO in Boston's Chinatown regularly offers free parenting seminars. I attended one of such workshop in 2012, and together with ten to twelve other participants, we met for three hours each week over twelve sessions. Parenting programs usually teach topics such as how to communicate with children, conflict resolution and problem-solving strategies, assertive parenting, and adolescents' development. These programs are usually derived from Western theories with little consideration for cultural differences.[21] This section shows that parental education, which tends to advocate cultural scripts that are both culture-specific and middle-class-centric, do not necessarily empower disadvantaged immigrants but rather conflict with their family realities.

An ethos of reflexive thinking dominated the parental workshop. The instructor asked people to bring a meaningful item to one seminar and to draw a picture in another. These assignments were intended as stimuli for participants to reflect on their childhood and evaluate its influence on their parenting. In another seminar, the instructor asked people to write a letter to their parents and read it out loud to the group. Some parents, mostly mothers, complained that their own parents were authoritarian and emotionally distant. For instance, Ying Chang, a thirty-five-year-old homemaker and mother said:

> My parents' biggest problem is that they don't know how to communicate, and it's still a problem today. They think whatever they choose for me is the right thing. . . . I don't want to be like my parents, so I always communicate with my children. I ask for their opinions and I let them make their own decisions. But my parents don't agree with me. They keep telling me, "It doesn't work like that! How can you listen to your daughter?"

Chinese parents' protective actions sometimes extend into intrusion into or surveillance of their children's lives. Even after children enter adulthood, some still feel trapped in a "prolonged childhood," where their parents assign them childlike roles and responsibilities.[22] In the same seminar, Jenny Lo, a mother of two who emigrated with her parents at the age of nineteen, tearfully read her letter to her parents. While she used soft communication instead of harsh discipline to correct her children's misbehavior, her husband and parents-in-law questioned her Americanized approach. She views the domestic disputes in the area of childrearing as a cultural war: "I am not just fighting against my family. I am fighting against an entire generation of Chinese people; I feel very powerless and sad."

American parenting seminars generally assume a therapeutic model of self-hood, which is a dominant cultural framework across the class spectrum in neo-liberal America. According to Jennifer Silva, the therapeutic model of selfhood "posits an inner-directed self preoccupied with its own emotional and psychic development. This self is individually negotiated and continually reinvented."[23] The "therapeutic narrative" takes a few steps to achieve self-transformation:[24]

> First, it compels one to identify pathological thoughts and behaviors; second, to locate the hidden source of these pathologies within one's past; third, to give voice to one's story of suffering in communication with others; and finally, to triumph over one's past by bringing into being an emancipated and independent self.

Parents at the Chinatown workshop described their intentions in the rhetoric of willed self-change: "I wish to learn about the difference between Western and Chinese culture and change my old bad habits," and "My life goal is to better educate my children and to change my incorrect ways of childrearing." By taking a reflexive view on their childhoods in China, the immigrant participants were compelled to identify unexamined problems with Chinese parenting in their upbringing and explain how those problems affect their current thoughts and behaviors. By placing their unhappy childhood stories on public display, Chinese immigrant parents were supposed to not only "triumph over the past" by building a liberated self but also alter their children's futures by learning new methods of emotional management and expression. In this way, parenting classes did not simply teach practices; they also encouraged parents to constantly recalibrate their cultural selfhood.

At the workshop, immigrant parents were encouraged to practice new techniques of discipline and punishment, such as communication, withdrawing privileges, and time-outs. They also learned about American emotional scripts, or "feeling rules,"[25] which emphasize emotional expressiveness and affective sentimentality. Similar to the middle class in Taiwan, working-class immigrant parents in the US become more affectionate with their children in general. Although most working-class immigrant cannot speak English fluently, they use select English words to "translate" their emotions to children. Ying, the mother who complained about her own emotionally distant parents, worked to rid herself of the "tiger mom" parenting style, which she saw as ill-suited to American childrearing:

> We still speak Chinese at home but we use words in a more Western way. There is more display of affection here. Kids here will say, "Mommy, I missed you all day" and when you are wrong, you must apologize to them. The relationship here is more equal. We can't order them around like a tiger mom who beats her kids. That is not useful here.

Notably, some practices taught in the seminars, such as setting goals, making plans, and keeping a schedule, are more in line with a middle-class lifestyle. In one seminar, the instructor said that Americans emphasized the principles of standardization, measurement, efficiency, and streamlined processes. Everyone looked puzzled, and she asked if these terms were too abstract. She then explained using the example of potty training. She handed out a sample schedule for parents, encouraging them to use it when teaching their children. She suggested that parents schedule a timetable for their children's after-school activities. Most participants found the idea of rationalizing family life strange and could not imagine using timetables that assume a child-centered family life and do not match parents' inflexible work schedules.

Many of the seminars started with group meditation. The instructor used lines such as "Imagine you are in a place that makes you feel very comfortable" and "Imagine that some miracle happens and you achieve your ideal life." The instructor often ended with the suggestion that parents should not focus exclusively on their children ("Love yourself more!") but should "pamper" themselves by engaging in leisure activities or through consuming items. These rituals were intended to soothe parental anxiety, but most Chinese participants who grew up with collectivist values were alienated by the individualistic tone of "privatizing happiness" and did not understand its relevance to childrearing.[26]

After the meditation, participants were asked to share their imagined comfortable spaces and ideal lives. Instead of concocting fantasies, most imagined something rather realistic. One mother said, "I imagine myself in a quiet room all by myself, then my children came in, the end." The ideal life another mother had in mind involved a vacation back to China with her sister to visit a beautiful lake near their hometown. Their humble wishes reflect what Bourdieu describes as the working-class habitus—a taste for the necessary and pragmatic[27]—and they indicate an ability to adapt to unpredictable life circumstances learned on their rugged paths of immigration. As Sue's husband says, "We are just surviving, not living a life here."

"Nothing Very Useful, Actually"

Only a few fathers participated in the Chinatown workshop. One of them is Yao Chen, a forty-five-year-old college graduate and former engineer in China, who immigrated to the US only two years previous under his sister's sponsorship. His wife, a high school graduate, quickly found a job as a caregiver for older adults. In his job search, Yao was determined not to enter the "occupational ghetto" of Chinese restaurants: "Once you work in a Chinese restaurant, there is no way out!" He currently teaches Chinese lessons to children at the Chinatown community center, but this job provides only a few paid hours per week. In spite of its humble earnings, this job allows him to pick up his two children from elementary school and to spend more time with them than he did in China. Yao's new focus in life is similar to that of "domesticated" middle-class fathers: "Some people think it's important to make money. For me, educating children is the priority now. The goal is to change my ways of parenting within a short time."

After the last seminar of the Chinatown workshop, Yao and I met for lunch. Similar to the other participants, Yao grew up with strict parents who used corporal punishment from time to time. But he questions whether the workshop's psychologized self-reflection exercises exaggerate the damage caused by spanking. He suggests that spanking may be more or less hurtful for children in particular contexts:

> After I came to this meeting, I realized that a lot of people had been heavily influenced by their parents. My mom used to hit me, but I don't think I was hurt that much. I have always been a happy, upbeat person. When I was hit, I never felt that bad. I keep thinking about what kind of influence corporal punishment has on kids. Maybe it's a cultural context thing. It's the norm in China, but in the US, it's illegal, so kids will compare. I try my hardest not to spank them.

Yao's perspective echoes the cultural psychologists who argue that cultural frameworks shape individuals' subjective life experiences. In a series of studies conducted in the 1980s, Ronald Rohner and Sandra Pettengill compared how Korean and Korean American children perceived their parents' childrearing practices. In Korea, where family ideology emphasized parental responsibility for children's behavior and welfare, children associated parental control with love and concern, and saw a lack of control as a sign of neglect. By contrast, under the influence of American family ideology, the children of Korean immigrants living in the US viewed their parents' strictness as a lack of warmth.[28]

Yao tries to avoid spanking and the harm it might cause under the US rubric of childrearing. He also alters his behavior and his method of emotional expression to match American scripts. He says: "I've changed too! I've become more sensitive with the children. In Chinese culture, children just listen to their parents and there is no communication. Here, you have to take the time to explain or bargain with them, 'Why don't you do this?' 'Is this OK?' We use much less demanding language here."

At the workshop, Yao brought up a scenario in which his two boys were fighting over a toy and Yao intervened by spanking his older son. The instructor told Yao that instead of spanking, he should have communicated with his son. She suggested using the common American strategy of a time-out, for the boys to calm down individually in an isolated spot without any toys or stimulation; during this time-out, parents should watch the child but avoid direct eye contact.

When I asked Yao what he found most useful in the workshop, he paused for a few minutes and embarrassedly responded: "I am not sure. Nothing very useful for us, actually." Yao lives with his sister's family, so four adults and four children share a three-bedroom apartment. He complains that the technique of time-outs is unsuitable to this setting: "[The instructor] said you need to find a place or corner that is empty, with no stuff to distract the child. How could I find a place like that? There is stuff everywhere."

Yao is not alone in finding the skills or methods learned at the workshop impracticable. To use elaborate communication instead of commands to interact with children, parents need sufficient time and language skills. Some methods also assume the existence of domestic privacy in a nuclear household and are therefore mismatched to their home settings. The curriculum focuses on individual parents as the agents of childrearing, but working-class immigrants widely share living space with extended family members or rely on grandparents for childcare. It is especially challenging for women who immigrated through marriage and have little bargaining power in the husband's family. American parental education tends to psychologize and individualize parents' life experiences, isolating the knowledge and techniques of childrearing from immigrants' cultural contexts and family realities.

Sustaining Ethnic Practice

For those immigrant parents who find the narratives of assimilation empty and the techniques of American childrearing alienating, their strategies to secure their children's futures shift to rather different directions—they turn to immigrant communities and transnational kin networks to continue and modify the cultural practices of education, care and discipline. Min Zhou and other scholars have argued that Asian immigrant communities offer supplementary education to help the children of immigrants to cope with parental constraints and attain academic success. These programs also shield the second generation, especially economically disadvantaged youth, from negative influences and reinforce educational agendas with ethnic cultural values.[29]

Many working-class parents in this study adopt security strategies along this line of argument. For instance, Wendy Li uses the resources in Chinatown to provide her children with affordable supplementary education and enrichment programs. She spends 400 USD per month on math and English tutoring for her son and also sends him to free or low-cost nonacademic activities. Ballet and Western music, in the form of affordable group lessons, are two popular options for extracurricular activities in Chinatown. The academies that provide these classes are bridge institutions that provide practical knowledge for immigrant families to navigate their children's applications to elite public schools and community orchestras.[30]

Shenli Yu similarly uses academic and nonacademic programs in Chinatown for his three daughters. They attend lessons in piano, choir, and drawing. In addition, he zealously seeks opportunities to make the acquaintance of "people with better *suzhi* [quality]." Although they are not religious, Shenli's family attends a Chinese-speaking Christian church on a regular basis. He praises the members of the church for their "kindness" in helping newcomers, and he uses the church activities as an opportunity to interact with professional immigrants who can provide up-to-date information on the children's education. Religious organizations, including Christian churches and Buddhist temples, are also important venues for lower-class parents to accumulate ethnic social capital across class divides and soothe their anxiety about the loss of cultural confidence and parental authority.[31]

Furthermore, working-class Chinese immigrants' dependence on the ethnic economy for educational and social support is actually similar to the strategy of cross-class pathway consumption among working-class Taiwanese in Chapter 3—only immigrant parents are more willing to spend money on extra-curricular activities and talent lessons in addition to academic drill and tutoring. The cross-Pacific comparison shows that working-class immigrant parents reproduce a similar cultural practice in the new country but modify the goals and acts of pathway consumption to adapt to the opportunity structure in the US. Ethnic institutions in Chinatown, including both for-profit and nonprofit ones, provide a range of enrichment programs to match the norm of holistic education for US college admissions.

"Satellite Children" and Transnational Discipline

The elevated status of the Chinese language as a transnational cultural capital also helps working-class immigrants like Wendy to gain some confidence in the Chinese repertoire of childrearing. She completed a training program in child-care and began working in a center near Chinatown. This Mandarin-speaking day care near downtown Boston has attracted a clientele of non–Chinese American professionals who want their children to grow up with some Chinese proficiency. Wendy manages to mix American and Chinese repertoires of childrearing at work: "We respect children, have fun time, but we also have Chinese culture. . . . If the parents value children's education, sometimes they like to be a bit more 'dragon,' not too loose." According to Wendy, an American father originally complained about her interaction style with his child with special needs as "being too harsh." A year later, the father witnessed the child's improvement, telling Wendy, in broken Chinese, to show his gratitude: "Wendy, you are a good teacher!"

Some working-class immigrants further use transnational kin networks to arrange care and discipline for their children. Unlike middle-class immigrants who send children back home for the purpose of transnational education, working-class immigrants incorporate transnational kin networks into their childrearing for more practical reasons. Their journey of transnational mobility, however, is hardly viewed as a positive exposure to multicultural and multilingual environments. Instead, it attracts social criticism in the United States, in a way similar to what happens to Taiwanese children of immigrant mothers in Chapter 3.

The psychologist Yvonne Bohr has used the term *satellite babies* to describe a common trend among Chinese immigrants in which parents sent their children back to China for a period of time under the care of extended kin.[32] Forty percent of the working-class families in this study (7 out of 17 families) sent their children back to China for a period of time, mostly before the children attended elementary school. According to recent data collected by a research team in Boston's Chinatown with immigrant parents whose children age from birth to 10 years old, approximately 20 percent of the sample reported having separated from their children in China for at least six months or having considered it.[33]

Although the practice of transnational transfer of childcare appears to occur across socioeconomic levels, working-class immigrants who experience more economic pressure, job schedule inflexibility, and limited childcare options are more likely to make the family decision to separate.[34] The proportion is expected to be higher among undocumented immigrants who are burdened with debts and have weak family ties in the US. In a qualitative study conducted in New York City, over 70 percent of the undocumented Chinese mothers recruited to the study from public hospitals sent their infants to China by the age of six months.[35]

Some immigrant parents send children back to China for more positive reasons, such as the grandparents' desire to spend more time with grandchildren, parents' desire for their children to preserve cultural and linguistic heritage, and some new parents' considerations of their own parents as more experienced in infant care.[36] Nevertheless, US media coverage has raised social alarms about potential harm in such transnational separation, including disrupted infant and early childhood attachments and children's confused cultural identities. For instance, the documentary *The Confusing Lives of Chinese-American "Satellite Babies"* by Jenny Schweitzer uses a sentimental tone to describe "the trauma that these children experience after being shuttled between two worlds. More often than not, they feel like they don't belong anywhere."[37]

In fact, Chinese society has traditionally endorsed three-generation childcare; it is still a common practice in China and Taiwan for parents who work in the city to send children back to the care of grandparents in rural areas or another city.[38] The phenomenon of so-called satellite children should be viewed as a transnational extension of this custom, although the consequence of family separation is more complicated when three-generation childcare straddles greater geographic distances and distinct cultural and linguistic settings.[39] One should bear in mind that Western mental health and attachment theory are not universal models but cultural-specific paradigms. Evidence is lacking to be able to conclude that the short-term displacement of mother-child attachment harms other facets of a child's development.[40] We need culture-sensitive frameworks that reveal how transnational families manage to parent from afar,[41] as well as contextualized understandings of why immigrant parents seek transnational care in relation to their predicaments in the US.

Some immigrant parents also send their school-aged children back to China for a period to correct children's misbehavior, practicing a security strategy that I call "transnational discipline." They rely on kin networks in China to enforce discipline and instill Chinese moral values against the allegedly corrupting forces of American youth culture. Transnational discipline also provides a solution for immigrant parents who struggle with a loss of authority at home and a sense of powerlessness in US society.

Scholars have found a similar pattern among Mexican, Yemeni, and Central American immigrants who send their children back home, especially when reaching adolescence, to get them "straightened out" and avoid problems.[42] Cati Coe also finds that Ghanaian immigrants in the US send their children to be cared by grandparents or foster parents in Ghana for similar reasons: they feel more anxious as raising children in the US because the tool of corporal punishment is outlawed and their reputation is intensively monitored in the immigrant community. Alongside a "dystopian view of families in the US," immigrant parents develop a nostalgic image of Ghana's harsh parenting based on the memory of their childhoods.[43]

Jin Li is handsome, with the gray hair of a fifty-three-year-old, but he is a sullen man with sad eyes, especially when talking about his life in the US. Jin immigrated at the age of twenty-nine after selling his travel agency business in Guilin, a city in Guangxi Province known for its beautiful landscape. His attempt to open a Chinese restaurant in Boston failed after a few years. Now he stays home to take care of his three children, between the ages of five and seventeen, while his wife works as a hotel housekeeper. They own two small apartments, living in one and renting the other for additional income.

Jin has a high school diploma and speaks little English. When I asked if he had ever taken English classes in the US, he shook his head: "I don't want to learn anymore. I am too old. I've never fit into this society, and I no longer want to. . . . We stay here only because of our children." He considers his act of immigration as a mistake, but he has little choice to return because most of his immediate family, including his parents and siblings, also relocated here.

Jin is critical of the US, including the welfare state, which he thinks indulges the poor, and the American school system, which he believes gives children excessive freedom. He is frustrated by raising children here, where corporal punishment is excluded as a legitimate tool of punishing children. When I asked how he punished his son when necessary, he paused for a few seconds before saying:

> Well . . . most of the time we just yell at him. If you spank him, he will just go to school tomorrow and tell the teacher you abused him. In China, it's normal for parents to spank their children for discipline. You can't do that here. . . . The kids here don't know what is right or wrong; they just know what makes them happy, and you have to let them do it. Americans like everyone to be happy. That is superficial. I try to explain to them [his children] that Chinese people are not like that. We are stern and strict, but it is for your own good. It matures you.

Jin sent his two older children back to China for periods of their childhood. Between the ages of one and three, his older daughter (now twelve years old) lived in China under the care of her grandparents because Jin and his wife were busy with the Chinese restaurant. When the son (now seventeen years old) was eight, he was sent to China for a year because he was "too naughty" and had "no awareness of Chinese values." Jin blamed American culture for his son's misbehavior and used transnational discipline to infusing moral virtues:

> I couldn't teach him, so we just sent him back. . . . He just wanted to play and did not listen to you. He did whatever he wanted and would not listen at all. Maybe that's just the ways it is here—to be free and self-centered. But in China, it is not like that. In China, you listen to the teacher and the teacher tells you to obey your parents. It is not like that here. Here, people think you are abusing your child. How can you teach them anything?

At the beginning of his trip to China, Jin's son felt miserable, but Jin says he now appreciates the effects of this trip: "He says that it was good for him to go back for a year because his math is so much better than everyone else's." In addition to their son's academic progress, the parents feel that his year in China helped bridge the cultural distance across generations. Jin feels strongly that transnational discipline had a positive effect on his son: "He learned more about Chinese culture so he can communicate better with us now."

Hong, a nurse and survivor of domestic violence, live in a subsidized apartment near Chinatown with her two sons, six and twelve years old at the time of our interview. Hong does not have immediate family members in the US, and her prior encounter with the child welfare system increased her distrust of the US institutional authorities. These factors push her to seek transnational discipline as a solution to the conundrum of childrearing. A few years ago, her elder son was diagnosed with attention deficit hyperactivity disorder and was taking medication for the condition. He frequently got into trouble at school and was threatened with suspension in the sixth grade. Hong felt helpless: "He became a completely different person. I didn't know what to do anymore because I had tried everything. I thought he was hopeless and the school was going to give up on him."

In despair, Hong called her family in China. Her brother-in-law had a friend who read fortunes and looked at her son's date of birth. Hong recalls the fortune-teller's words:

> This boy is tall and skinny. He is very filial to his parents, but this past year he has started to behave very poorly. But he is very smart. If you can teach him, he will become a good person. But if you do not teach him well, he will become very bad—not just bad but devious. This child needs to go through a ritual. He needs to honor and follow Confucius. If he has the opportunity, he must go to Confucius's village in Shandong and sweep his tomb.

Hong could not afford a trip to Shandong Province in northeastern China, the birthplace of Confucius, but she did send her son back to her brother-in-law for a summer in Canton, where he underwent a spiritual ritual. The fortune-teller identified filial piety as an innate characteristic of Hong's son and portrayed the US environment as filled with social evils. The transnational ritual of paying homage to Confucius symbolizes the reinforcement of Chinese cultural values for the children of immigrants. A picture of Confucius still hangs in Hong's Boston apartment to remind her son of his transnational moral guardian. Effective or not, this technique of cultural reinforcement offers some reassurance to working-class immigrant parents who must walk a tightrope of cultural negotiation in the US.

Conclusion

Social class matters in shaping family lives, but unequal childhoods configure differently across national contexts. Working-class groups in Taiwan and the US both face shredded confidence and consider themselves incapable of teaching their children. However, immigrant parents experience the additional pressure of declining status at home. The boundary between adults and children, which is relatively rigid in working-class families when children are young,[44] is blurred in immigrant homes. Children are pressured to enter "premature adulthood" by helping parents with language translation and cultural interpretation, advocating for their parents in institutions, and even contributing financially to the family economy. In addition, the threat to report parents to the state authority when corporal punishment is involved is more eminent in the US, making parents hesitant to reinforce discipline to sustain their authority.

As a context-specific security strategy, working-class immigrants attempt to "Americanize" intergenerational relations. They emphasize positive gains associated with the loss of parental authority—whether the increase of cultural assimilation or the tightening of family bonds. Their seemingly optimistic narratives mirror their struggles to adapt to social marginalization and the new family dynamics. By contrast, middle-class immigrants are more skeptical of the American dream because their exposure to mainstream society allows them to have intimate experience with racial discrimination and blocked mobility.[45]

Immigrant parents across the class spectrum rely on pathway consumption to offer their children learning contexts to match the US model of holistic education. Yet their arrangements of extracurricular activities diverge because of their class-based ability to access resources locally and transnationally. Professional immigrants send their children to white-majority suburban schools and hire private tutors for extra lessons, while the working class depend on the ethnic economy to provide group lessons that are more affordable and yet of much less variety.

The middle-class strategies of transnational education and ethnic cultural capital are less plausible for working-class immigrants. Frequent visits to Asia cost money, and parents need time off work for vacations. Those who transfer childcare to transnational kin do not attempt to inculcate multicultural advantage in their children, mostly because they lack childcare resource or parental authority in the US.

The patchwork of parental experiences reveals the relational nature of class inequality. Working-class immigrant families are forced to be compared against the Asia American stereotype of the model minority. The security strategies of middle-class immigrants unwittingly intensify emotional stress for their working-class counterparts, who struggle to overcome the barriers related to not only their minority status but also their class disadvantage in the path to social integration.

Conclusion

In Search of Security

RAISING GLOBAL FAMILIES EXAMINES how ethnic Chinese parents on either side of the Pacific navigate transnational and cultural mobilities to arrange children's education, care, and discipline. Parenting is a well-studied mechanism of class reproduction, and childrearing is widely understood as a practice of delivering cultural values. Bridging these two sets of literature, this book conducts multisited research to investigate family life at the intersection of cultural transformation and persisting inequalities. Parents who experience either compressed social changes or geographic relocation feel an augmented sense of uncertainty and ambivalence, but they also become more reflexive about their class experiences and more cognizant of the cultural boundaries and structural constraints within which they raise children. Social class, however, constrains their abilities to select, hybridize, and reconstitute a range of cultural repertoires in response to particular insecurities they identify in local and transnational contexts.

The security strategies of raising global children are not only prevalent among middle-class families in Asia; they also have spread among North American and European parents who fear "the squeezing out of the middle class" as a result of the expansion of offshore outsourcing and the decline of local economies.[1] Popular books pressure ambitious parents to "raise children to be at home in the world" by acquiring new tools and knowledge to discover the wisdom of "parenting without borders."[2] Children are encouraged to attend bilingual education or study abroad for a period to cultivate "transnational cultural capital."[3] With China becoming a global superpower, the demand for Chinese immersion schools and Mandarin-speaking nannies or au pairs is rising among American elite families.[4] Even Donald Trump's granddaughter is learning Mandarin from her Chinese nanny.

Recent political events, including the "Brexit" referendum for the United Kingdom to leave the European Union and Donald Trump's victory in the US presidential election, demonstrated growing concerns and divided opinions regarding the pros and cons of globalization. For those who are able and would like to pursue transnational mobility, especially the wealthy and highly educated, open borders create a flat world that celebrates mobility and connectivity. Yet for those whose work and fate are tied to local economy, free trade and immigration indicate a threat to their economic security, breeding the desire to resurrect border controls to insulate competition and uncertainty that their children will face in the future.

In the introduction to this book, I proposed the framework of transnational relational analysis and the concept of global security strategies to illuminate how class inequality mediates parents' access to transnational and cultural mobility and shapes their relations to each other locally and transnationally. Here, in the concluding chapter, I situate the four groups of parents in a transnational geography of social inequality, identify between- and within-class differences in their strategies of childrearing, and discuss the theoretical and practical implications of this research.

Global Security Strategies Across the Pacific

Scholars who study the connection between childrearing and class reproduction face a common dilemma: How do we talk about class categories without reifying them or losing sight of nuanced differences within class groups? The multisited research in this book reveals a variety of parenting approaches that are not easily reducible to social class or ethnic culture. Parents' reflexive thinking mediates the influence of social structure, resulting in not only between-class but also within-class differences in their strategies of childrearing. Parents creatively mix and match cultural scripts, between the global and the local and between the home and host countries, to make sense of their particular class experience and to adapt to the constraining opportunity structure. Table 1 summarizes the findings presented in the previous chapters.

Taiwanese parents who have achieved a middle-class status lament their own loss of childhood in a poorer, authoritarian Taiwan. They hope to bring their children greater happiness and autonomy by breaking with the traditions

Table 1 Global security strategies across the Pacific

	Taiwanese middle class	*Taiwanese working class*	*Immigrant middle class*	*Immigrant working class*
Parents' class experience	Intergenerational mobility	Stagnant mobility	Blocked mobility	Downward mobility
Narrative of parenting	Lost childhood	Lost legitimacy	Lost confidence	Lost authority
Institutional structure	Education reform; schooling choices	Education reform; state monitor of family risks	Asian quotas; "bamboo ceiling"	Welfare entrapment; state intervention upon corporal punishment
Security strategies	Cultivating global competitiveness; orchestrating natural growth	Reinforcing harsh discipline; seeking cross-class resources	Cultivating ethnic cultural capital; orchestrating competitive assimilation	"Americanizing" intergenerational relations; sustaining ethnic practice

of authoritarian parenting and rote learning. The reform of college admission and schooling systems with a new emphasis on holistic competition allows parents to seek new childrearing scripts and educational curriculums. Many try to raise globally competitive children by choosing elite schools and cultivating Western cultural capital, while some orchestrate their children's natural growth by seeking a Western model of alternative education as a form of cultural mobility.

Professional immigrant parents share a similar narrative of lost childhood, but they also feel a decline in cultural confidence when their immigration leads to a common experience of blocked mobility in American workplaces. Their aspiration for the next generation to achieve full-fledged success in the United States is dampened by their anxiety about the racialized opportunity structure for Asian Americans—the so-called Asian quota or bamboo ceiling. Some parents try to orchestrate their children's holistic development as a means of competitive assimilation, while others idealize and validate their cultural heritage, hoping that the ethnic culture capital can help their children to excel in a context of racial inequality.

Although middle-class parents develop distinct security strategies to cope with different opportunity structures in Taiwan and the United States, they share similar class privileges and both look beyond national borders for their children's capital accumulation. Equipped with the necessary economic power and cultural sensibility, these parents pursue transnational or cultural mobility to offer concerted cultivation to the next generation. While middle-class

Taiwanese parents strive for spatial mobility and cultural connections to the global North, immigrant parents in the United States seek reverse cultural mobility to establish linguistic, cultural, and social ties with their countries of origins.

Working-class parents in Taiwan and working-class Chinese immigrants in the United States confront a disadvantaged status. Both groups suffer from limited access to global resources, and their styles of childrearing are seen as outdated or culturally unfit by power holders such as bureaucrats, teachers, and social workers. With shredded confidence, parents in both groups opt to outsource the job of education to schoolteachers and cram schools. Their pursuit of transnational mobility through cross-border marriage, transnational transfer of childcare, and transnational discipline indicates their constrained options due to class disadvantage rather than privileged access to global pathways.

However, these two groups of parents cope with their social disadvantage by developing different methods of cultural negotiation in their childrearing practices. Working-class Taiwanese suffer from a decline in parental legitimacy under state monitoring that problematizes their style of accomplishing children's natural growth. Many turn to the tradition of harsh discipline to reassert their parental authority. In particular, fathers who suffer from economic insecurity strive to sustain patriarchal authority to disguise their frustration at the shattering of breadwinning masculinity.

Working-class immigrants in the United States experience the additional pressure of declining status at home when their children are pressured to enter "premature adulthood" by helping parents with language translation and cultural interpretation, advocating for their parents in institutions, and even contributing labor to family business. In contrast to their class peers in the country of origin, working-class immigrant parents pick up the American rhetoric of "permissive" parenting as a means of cultural assimilation and reframe the changing intergenerational dynamics to emphasize positive gains associated with the loss of authority.

I urge future researchers to investigate the intersection of social class and ethnic culture in diverse contexts of globalization and transnationalism. By doing so, we are able to destabilize the essentialist representations of ethnic and class groups and to see how culture repertoires travel and transform in response to global hybridization and local circumstances. We should neither assume the trajectories of cultural mobility and spatial mobility as singular or linear directions. In today's world, where people and ideas move around in multiple directions, we need more complex and dynamic models of social class to comprehend their various ways of cultural negotiation and symbolic struggle.

Interconnections of Mobilities and Immobilities

Bringing in the insights of migration scholars to shed new light on the study of parenting and class reproduction, I propose the transnational relational analysis to attend to the constitutive and interactive nature of social class on a global scale. The four groups of parents across the Pacific have limited personal interaction—they live in separate neighborhoods and even different continents, and their children attend different schools and move on to various career trajectories—but their life chances are structurally connected. The previous chapters uncovered structural interconnections along various dimensions.

First, the class-specific global security strategies indicate parents' unequal positions in the power geometry of globalization. Parents' experiences of mobility and immobility generate their "sense of reality" regarding what constitutes critical opportunities or potential risks in their children's future. The professional-managerial class, whose career paths are intricately tied to globalized production, are sensitive to increasing competition and heightened uncertainty in the global labor market and thus prioritize the cultivation of Western cultural capital and holistic development as a pathway for their children to achieve global mobility. By contrast, the working class and even the local middle class, which includes public servants and small business owners, tend to prioritize academic performance to extracurricular activities in the allocation of educational resources, and they prefer standardized exams to individual applications for college admission to secure their children's opportunities in the local regime.

The juxtaposition of the various global security strategies shows a stratification of transnational mobility—some mobilities and connections generate cultural capital, whereas others are considered far less productive. While cross-border couples in Taiwan have the potential to develop rich transnational connections with the Global South, the state and school hardly recognize their spatial and cultural mobilities as valuable cultural resources because of the global nation-state hierarchy. To survive long working hours and the lack of affordable day care in the United States, working-class immigrants send their children back to China for a relief of childcare. Educational experts in the United States tend to associate the transnational childhood of these "satellite children" with negative consequences such as the disruption of parent-child attachment and the confusion of cultural identity.

Second, social institutions, especially the state and school, function as important nodes in the emotional landscape of class inequality that connects middle-class and working-class parents living in the same country. The hypermobility of some families across spatial and cultural arenas comes at the expense of other families who are trapped locally, by intensifying the latter's emotional stress or limiting their life opportunities. In Taiwan, with the advocacy of middle-class parents' organizations, school curricula and national policies increasingly treat intensive parenting and child-centered family life as the "normal" approach to childrearing. Parents with insufficient economic and cultural capital suffer from a decline in parental legitimacy when they cannot live up to the middle-class norm of participating in school activities and children's holistic education. Working-class children are also at disadvantage when competing with middle-class children in the new games of college admission that give extra credits to extracurricular achievements and global exposures.

In the US, middle-class children's academic prowess is produced through careful orchestration by their immigrant parents, reinforcing the "model minority" image. Such stereotypes, widely held by educators, can pressure or even punish working-class Asian Americans who cannot afford similar cultivation or who do not meet a high bar of attainment. Working-class immigrant parents and their children are evaluated against middle-class Asian American families, and this coethnic reference group makes them feel like inadequate students or incompetent parents.

Finally, parents across class and geographic divides are situated in a transnational social field, in which they compare, connect, and compete with one another while exchanging ideas, circulating resources, and modifying practices in raising their children. The middle class, in particular, is inclined to seek transnational references—class peers around the globe—to define their meaning of security and to imagine their children's future. The newly rich Taiwanese seek membership in the global middle class by consuming childrearing and educational styles they perceive as fitting a Western ideal. Meanwhile, immigrant parents feel largely satisfied with their suburban American lives by comparing the US version of happy childhood with pressured middle-class childhood in Asia. However, the decline of the US economy shatters their confidence in the American dream and the rise of Asia stirs their anxieties about the new global order. Some look to the Asian middle class as a reference group in their selection of educational strategies and attempt to set a higher bar for their children's academic performance.

The transnational relational analysis raises critical questions for the studies of migration and globalization to investigate the interconnections of spatial mobility, cultural mobility, and social mobility: What sorts of physical and cultural mobility are possible and for whom? How are those who seem immobile actually linked to the mobility of the others? Who or what controls the mobility of some people and obstructs the mobility of others? How can some mobilities be easily converted into capital and power while others cannot? In what circumstances does transnational mobility lead to spatial or cultural entrapment as institutionalized power relations constrain rights, choices, and life chances?[5]

Why Security Strategies Magnify Parenting Insecurities

Parents strive to keep their children safe in a world that is interconnected and rapidly becoming more risky and unpredictable. Their global security strategies of childrearing, however, often lead to unintended consequences and paradoxically magnify anxieties among families across the social class spectrum. The widespread parental insecurities, along with the cultural rhetoric of neoliberalism, not only burden individual parents but also increase intangible social costs.

The dominant parenting discourses in Taiwan have shifted from the traditional emphasis on parental authority and child discipline to the rhetoric of granting *choice* and *autonomy* for both parents and children. Against the backdrop of Taiwan's democratization, middle-class parents advocated the deregulation of the highly centralized education system and strived to exercise their civil right to choose schools and educational styles for their children. They also encourage their children to develop individuality and autonomy—personal traits that were suppressed in martial-law Taiwan but now indicate the pathway to cosmopolitan identity and global mobility.

The rhetoric of "neoliberal mothering" or "neoliberal parenting"—that is, mothers or parents who view their capacity and practice of childrearing as based on individual choice and effort[6]—is becoming increasingly prevalent among the middle-class Taiwanese. Parents who are anxious about global competition in their children's future alter the liberal narrative of raising children as autonomous individuals by mixing it up with the instrumentalist goals of producing self-governing, entrepreneurial subjects who are culturally wired for the flexible accumulation of global capital.[7] Even among parents who deliberately reject competitiveness and embrace the rhythm of natural growth, neoliberalism casts a shadow over their alternative practice of childrearing. These mothers see themselves as the "managers of risk and good choice-makers" to protect their homes and children from commercialism and other social toxins.[8]

However, in reality, most parents, including the resourceful ones, find the new ideal of parental competency difficult to attain. Dual-earner parents struggle with long working hours and have limited time to carry out the new script of intensive parenting. Fathers who intend to achieve the new paternal role end up spending most of their time at work in order to cover the cost of raising global children. Parents also worry about cultural contradictions across multiple spheres: despite their celebration of children's freedom and autonomy at home, many schools and workplaces still privileges obedience and hierarchy. The frictions between global scripts and local institutions continue to impose pressure on parents and create paradoxical pathways. Although middle-class parents resent their lost childhood or authoritarian upbringing, many unwittingly repeat the controlling style through micromanaging children's lives. Despite embracing the ideal of happy childhood, some parents fixate on children's "natural growth" and make the orchestration of children's development rather "unnatural."

The security strategies of professional Chinese immigrants also lead to ambivalent consequences because they have to navigate multiple cultural repertoires in an environment of racial stratification. Those who place their children in Americanized extracurricular activities, such as team sports, unwittingly put their children in direct contact with racial and ethnic prejudice. Yet the alternative strategy of validating ethnic traits may also lead to the paradox of racial othering for the second generation. Immigrant parents seek to escape the intensive academic pressure of their home countries, but their concern about American racism drives them to reproduce the Chinese educational culture.

Whether they embrace competitive assimilation or multiethnic upbringing, professional immigrant parents display a similar neoliberal rhetoric that turns structural barriers into personal challenges. Although many attribute their blocked mobility to institutional racism, they still believe that the only way for their children to surmount "Asian quota" discrimination in college admissions is to become "twice as good" and outperform white students. As many writers have pointed out, the myths of "honorary whites" and the "model minority" uphold the social illusion of the American dream and blame other minorities for their individual or group-based cultural failures.[9] This not only makes it harder for Asian immigrants to identify with other racial groups who face similar barriers but also obscures socioeconomic gaps *within* Asian immigrants and Asian Americans.

This neoliberal rhetoric prevents middle-class parents from seeing through the constituting power structure, including Western hegemony and institutional racism. It also obscures the fact that their "choices" are facilitated by the significant resources of time, culture, and money associated with their class privilege. For those parents with limited resources to exercise similar choices, their structural predicaments are reduced to personal failures in the accomplishment of parental competency. This reinforces what Val Gills calls the individualization of inequality: "Rather than addressing the root problem of inequality, the moral choices of the privileged are normalized to warrant the regulation of the disadvantaged."[10]

For working-class parents in both Taiwan and the US, their security strategies create results otherwise because they are trapped in a double bind: they are compelled to follow a cultural script of childrearing that overlooks their family reality or cultural background, whereas their failure to meet such ideal—by either poorly replicating or simply rejecting it—proves the lack of competence or efforts in the eyes of power authority. For those who reinforce harsh discipline to claim their legitimacy as responsible parents, their disciplinary practice amounts to child abuse or maltreatment by the definition of social workers and state bureaucrats. For immigrants who endeavor to acquire American techniques of childrearing, they feel alienated from the parenting curriculum that carries class and ethnocentric biases. Yet, when they feel they have no choice but to seek transnational help, their strategies of childcare face criticism from the receiving society.

The widespread parental insecurities increase social costs on many fronts. The fertility rate in Taiwan continues to decrease despite the government's efforts to boost reproduction. Similar demographic crisis is happening in other East Asian societies, including Hong Kong, Singapore, and South Korea. People, especially women, withdraw from parenthood and even marriage because they live in a compressed condition of modernity characterized by a partial transformation of patriarchal culture, the tension between modernity and tradition in intergenerational relations, and global-local frictions across multiple institutions and spheres.[11]

Immigrant parents' intensive involvement in children's education is also likely to inflict emotional stress on the second generation, who straddle two cultural worlds between Chinese homes and American peers. National surveys show that Asian American students exhibit a higher level of anxiety and lower level of self-esteem; Asian women between the ages of fifteen to twenty-four have the highest rates of depression and suicide.[12] Their psychological pressure comes from not only their parents' expectation but also structural vulnerabilities outside the family. The tiger mom stereotype attributes Asian American success to overzealous and even oppressive parenting rather than individual effort. As Carolyn Chen puts it, "When Asian students succeed, their peers chalk it up to 'being Asian.'" They feel belittled and discredited by the double-bind "model minority" stereotypes in the society at large.[13]

Raising Global Families situates parents' personal troubles in global contexts, identifies the institutional roots of the cultural contradictions in their parenting practice, and exposes the landscape of social inequality behind it all. It is easier to think of inequality as "their" problems—by criticizing incapable parents or having sympathy for children in poverty—than facing the hard truth that their misfortune may have something to do with the ways we, the resourceful, raise our own children. My emphasis on the relational nature of class inequality does not aim to incur middle-class guilt but hopes to generate understanding, empathy, and solidarity across social differences.

To lift the burden from anxious parents and struggling families, we need to create more interdependence across class, racial, and gender divides instead of falling back on individualized security strategies. We need an educational system that respects the value and culture of the working class and ethnic minorities. It takes collective efforts from the whole village, including schools, workplaces, communities, governments, and transnational networks, to turn childrearing into a pathway to reach greater social equality and cultural diversity.

Appendix A: Research Methods

THE TAIWANESE PORTION of the study was carried out during 2010–2011 and 2012–2013. I conducted in-depth interviews with 80 parents from 57 households, including 51 mothers and 28 fathers. I followed previous scholars to recruit parents from four public elementary schools followed by in-depth interviews of parents and observation in selected households.[1] At each school, my research assistants and I started with observing a randomly assigned second-grade classroom and activities of parental participation, including field trips, school fairs, and parent-teacher meetings.

Two of the schools were located in metropolitan Taipei. Like most Asian cities, real estate in Taipei is most expensive in the city center and more affordable on the outskirts. Central School (pseudonym) was situated in a downtown neighborhood characterized by high-rise buildings and fashionably renovated apartments. The area near the campus gate was always crowded at the end of school hours, with homemaker mothers waiting in cars by the curbside and a few Filipina and Indonesian maids standing by the gate. Several vans from after-school institutions were ready to transport their young clients to a multitude of talent lessons. Students at this school were mostly Taiwanese origin, with only 4 percent of pupils born to immigrant mothers or white expatriates. The school lunch displayed multicultural flavors—including spaghetti, hamburgers, and Thai curry—to please the cosmopolitan taste buds of middle-class children. The school also respected children's opinions by allowing the pupils to have a collective vote to choose between three catering companies whose menus had already won the approval of school administrators and concerned parents.

The other urban school, Riverside School, was located on the outskirts of Taipei. The neighborhood was filled with worn-out, old buildings and small factories tucked away in allies. The parents at Riverside School were mostly factory workers and low-end service workers who dropped their children off at school on their motorcycles before rushing to work. Many children walked home by themselves or went to after-school programs before their parents got off work. At the time of the study, 14 percent of the pupils attending Riverside School were born to immigrant mothers from China or Southeast Asia. The school lunch was always Chinese cuisine. School administrators scrutinized the menu without much involvement of parents or students.

The other two schools were located in Yilan County in northeastern Taiwan. The area is famous for its picturesque rural scenery, marked by beautiful mountains and rice fields. It became much more accessible after a recently built tunnel shortened the travel time to central Taipei to one and a half hours. The third school, Seashore School, was located in a fishing village with a working-class and aging population. Many children at Seashore School were under the care of grandparents because their parents divorced or resided in the city to work. Because these cases involve quite different family dynamics, for the purpose of comparison, this book does not discuss Seashore School families in detail. At the time of the study, 20 percent of the pupils attending Seashore School were born to immigrant mothers from China or Southeast Asia. Most students there received free or subsidized lunch and the cuisine was simply Chinese.

The fourth school, Garden School, was a public charter school that provided an alternative curriculum based on European pedagogy, reflecting a broader trend toward alternative education in Taiwan. The school attracted a growing number of middle-class parents who emigrated from the city to the countryside so that their children could escape mainstream education. Many purchased a single-family home at a price less than the cost of a tiny apartment in Taipei. Garden School looked very different from an ordinary campus of public school. All the classrooms had wooden floors and curtains of gradient color that were hand-dyed by dedicated parents. The playground had no plastic slides but swings and tree houses made of natural materials. The school lunch was all vegetarian and made of organic produce. Many mothers of the pupils volunteered to work in the school kitchen.

The families recruited in this study are not intended to be a representative sample. Rather, they were selected to provide a range of viewpoints and experiences. Residential areas in Taiwan are not as class segregated as most American cities and suburbs, and a school district usually contains some variation in parents' socioeconomic status. I chose parents who matched the main socioeconomic profile at each school. I also interviewed one or two families who did not fit the main profile, such as working-class parents at Central School, for the purposes of comparison. In addition to parents who were recruited through public schools, I also found some upper-middle-class interviewees though snowball referrals. This sample included 11 parents from 9 households who sent their children to private schools in Taipei (four private schools in all).

For the Taiwanese middle-class informants, who were born between 1960 and 1979, I used a bachelor's degree as the benchmark of education for the measurement of class status. This generation of Taiwanese experienced intense competition in the college entrance exam before the expansion of higher education in the 1990s (see Chapter 1). About two-thirds of my interviewees fell into this group, including 33 mothers and 19 fathers from 36 households. The occupations of these parents included engineer, manager, professor, architect, lawyer, technician, teacher, public servant, and other office workers. The self-reported median incomes of the families I interviewed from this group were about 65,000 USD per year, slightly higher than the cutoff value of the second quintile group (the richest 40 percent of the population), but those who sent children to private school earned a median annual income above 100,000 USD, close to the cutoff value of the first quintile (the richest 20 percent).[2]

About one-third of the Taiwanese households fell into the working-class category, including 18 mothers and 9 fathers from 21 households. Eight mothers were immigrants from Southeast Asia and Mainland China. None of the parents in this category had a college degree, and they worked in factories, construction sites, restaurants, and grocery markets or as taxi drivers or street vendors. The self-reported median incomes of the families I interviewed from this group were less than 30,000 USD per year, which was lower than the cutoff value of the fifth quintile group (the poorest 20 percent).

From the pool of interviewees, I selected nine households (three from Central, three from Riverside, and three from Garden) for home observation as supplementary data. Because parents might have found it more difficult to ignore the presence of a professor, I sent two research assistants (one man and one woman, both in their late twenties) to observe family life. They spent a minimum of fifteen hours in each household, including two evenings during the week and two weekend mornings or afternoons. I attended some school field trips and family events.

During 2011–2012, I conducted research in the Boston area when I was a visiting scholar at Harvard University. Although there are significant differences between immigrants from Taiwan and China in terms of history and demography (see Chapter 1), I included both countries of origin to maintain sufficient class variation in the sample. The book focuses on social class as the primary social divide, but I also pay careful attention to variations in national background in my analysis of immigrant parents. The scope of this book did not allow me to conduct research with middle- and working-class parents in China, but I draw on a growing set of literature about parenting in contemporary China to situate my data in a broader context.[3]

In Boston, I did not have access to public schools to recruit parents as I did in Taiwan. Yet this did not impose a methodological challenge, because residential segregation by socioeconomic status was significant among ethnic Chinese immigrants in Boston area. Professional immigrants mostly own single-family homes in northern suburbs such as Brookline, Lexington, and Newton. These neighborhoods are home to many parks, lakes, and historical buildings; the real estate is expensive, at least in part because of the high-quality public schools. In 2014, the median value of housing units in these areas was over 700,000 USD.[4] As of 2010, around 80 percent of the population was white, but Asian residency in the area has grown substantially over the years; one often hears Mandarin, Korean, and Hindu spoken on the streets.[5] Suburban Chinese immigrants rarely visit Chinatown to access ethnic services; instead, they go to Asian supermarkets and restaurants in nearby suburbs that have better sanitation and increased prices.

Some working-class Chinese immigrants live in state-subsidized rental apartments (through Section 8 program) in neighborhoods of the city with a visible presence of racial minorities. Those who are financially better off own apartments or modest houses in less expensive southern suburbs such as Quincy and Malden. In 2014, the median value of housing units in these areas was slightly over 320,000 USD.[6] As of 2010, working-class whites constituted more than half of the population in these suburbs, but the working-class Asian population has also grown here in recent years. Quincy, for example, has the highest per capital concentration of Asians in Massachusetts, rising from 15 percent in 2000 to 24 percent in 2010.[7] The downtown streets are lined with Vietnamese and Chinese restaurants, grocery stores, and other service providers. The fast-growing Chinese population is mainly composed of recent immigrants from Fujian Province.[8] They take a direct subway line to Chinatown for work or they find jobs in Chinese restaurants throughout the Boston area.

In total, I conducted in-depth interviews with 56 ethnic Chinese immigrant parents (40 mothers and 16 fathers) of primary-school-aged children from 48 households. Thirty-one families, including two-thirds from Taiwan and one-third from China,[9] belonged to the professional middle class, which I define according to education and occupation in the United States. At least one of the parents had acquired a postgraduate degree, and when employed, their occupations fell into the categories of engineer, researcher, lawyer, accountant, medical doctor, and business manager. The self-reported median household income of the professional immigrants I interviewed from this group was about 125,000 USD.

I define working-class immigrants on the basis of their occupations in the receiving country, and 17 families (4 from Taiwan and 13 from China) belonged to this category. Many of these parents were high school graduates, although some had received college educations in their homelands. They were employed in the United States mostly as restaurant workers, elderly or child caretakers, cleaners, and other service workers. The self-reported median income of immigrant families I interviewed from this group was less than 35,000 USD.

I made initial contact with middle-class immigrants by going to two Chinese-language schools located in Boston's northern suburbs where children attended classes on Sunday and parents socialized in the cafeteria. I also joined a social group of Taiwanese immigrant mothers and posted advertisements for participants through other informal immigrant networks. I recruited about half of my working-class informants by attending community-based programs and activities held by a nongovernmental organization in Chinatown. I also made requests for interviews when I used services provided by immigrants in a hair salon or Chinese restaurant. I found the remaining informants through snowball referrals but limited each referral to one person to avoid sample bias.

All interviews were conducted in Mandarin Chinese and translated into English when quoted. The interviews lasted from two to four hours and were tape-recorded and fully transcribed. When possible, I interviewed both fathers and mothers and conducted the interviews separately. Yet in many cases, only one parent (usually the mother) agreed to be interviewed. The interviews were held at locations chosen by the participants. The middle-class informants preferred homes, coffee shops, restaurants, and the Chinese-language school cafeteria—comfortable settings located conveniently near their daily activities. By contrast, some working-class informants felt that their homes were too crowded or not tidy enough to accommodate guests, so they chose public places with free or inexpensive access, such as parks, public libraries, and fast-food restaurants.

To better understand the content and effect of parental education, I also conducted observations on three series of parental seminars. All the instructors and participants were aware of my identity and purpose of research. In Taiwan, I participated in a free parental workshop held by a local community center for immigrant mothers; it included sixteen two-hour seminars held twice a week. In Boston, I joined a free workshop held by a nongovernmental organization in Chinatown, where most attendants were working-class immigrants; we met three hours each week for twelve sessions. In addition, I attended three sessions in a paid course on parental education held in a suburban Chinese language school on Sundays for middle-class immigrants.

Along with trained research assistants, I analyze the data with a grounded theory approach. We started with "open coding" by closely reading all the interview transcripts in their entirety to gain a holistic understanding of these parents' experiences. Using themes that emerged from these readings, we generated codes to categorize the data ("focused coding") with qualitative data analysis software. This coding process allowed me to identify commonality and variation across cases and systematic differences across and within social class. I gradually developed concepts such as global pathway consumption and orchestrating natural growth to construct the ideal types of parenting styles. At a later stage of research, I developed the concept of global security projects to encompass a multitude of parenting strategies in this study and engage in theoretical dialogue with the existing literature.

Appendix B: Sample Characteristics

Table B1 Participating families in Taiwan

	Middle class	Working class
Number of households	36	21
Marital status		
Married	36	14
Divorced	0	7
Mother's country of birth		
Taiwan	36	13
China	0	3
Vietnam	0	2
Cambodia	0	1
Thailand	0	1
Indonesia	0	1
Father's country of birth		
Taiwan	36	21
Mother's education		
Middle school or less	0	11
High school	2	10
Bachelor's degree	25	0
Graduate degree	9	0
Father's education		
Middle school or less	0	8
High school	0	13
Bachelor's degree	25	0
Graduate degree	11	0
Employment status		
Dual earners	18	12
Employed father + full-time homemaker	18	2
Single mother	0	3
Single father	0	4

Table B2 Participating immigrant families in the United States

	Professional middle class	Working class
Number	31	17
Marital status		
Married	0	15
Divorced	0	2
Mother's country of birth		
Taiwan	20	4
China	11	13
Father's country of birth		
Taiwan	21	3
China	10	14
Mother's education		
Middle school or less	0	2
High school	0	15
Bachelor's degree	8	0
Graduated degree	23	0
Father's education		
Elementary school	0	0
Junior high school	0	1
High school	0	12
Bachelor's degree	4	4
Graduated degree	27	0
Employment status		
Dual earners	18	7
Employed father + full-time homemaker	13	7
Employed mother + full-time homemaker	0	1
Single mother	0	2

Appendix C: Demographic Profiles of Immigrants

Table C1 Demographic profiles of immigrants

	Taiwan born	China born	US national population
Population	358,460	1,601,147	309,349,689
Household median income	$76,893	$52,187	$50,046
Home ownership	72.0%	55.0%	65.1%
Family poverty rate	7.5%	12.2%	11.3%
Education			
Bachelor's degree and above	69.2%	43.9%	28.2%
Lower than high school	5.8%	25.8%	14.4%
Limited English proficiency	50.1%	65.5%	8.7%
Occupation			
Management, business, science, and art	64.0%	48.3%	35.9%
Service	9.2%	24.0%	18.0%
Sales and office	21.7%	16.7%	25.0%
Natural resources, construction, and maintenance	1.3%	3.0%	9.1%
Industry			
Education, health care, and social assistance	24.3%	21.9%	23.2%
Professional, scientific, management, and administrative	14.9%	12.4%	10.6%
Arts, entertainment, recreation, accommodation, and food services	7.6%	20.7%	9.2%
Manufacturing	14.5%	12.4%	10.4%
Finance, insurance, real estate, and leasing	8.6%	6.3%	6.7%
Retail trade	7.2%	7.3%	11.7%

Source: Data compiled from 2010 US Census.

Notes

Introduction

1. Chua 2011a.

2. Chua 2011b; Murphy Paul 2011.

3. *Wo zai meiguo zuo mama: Yelu faxueyuan jiaoshou de yurrjing*/我在美国做妈妈: 耶鲁法学院教授的育儿经 (Chua 2011c).

4. Douglass 2006: 423.

5. Chao 1994; Chao and Sue 1996; Wu 1996.

6. Lin and Fu 1990.

7. Way et al. 2013: 69.

8. A special issue of *Asian American Journal of Psychology* is dedicated to deconstructing the myth of the tiger mother using several empirical studies of Asian heritage families (Juang, Qin, and Park 2013). Also see Kang and Shih (2016) for a comprehensive review of the literature on Asian American parenting.

9. Here I follow Ann Swidler (1986) in using the term *cultural repertoire* to describe culture as a multiplicity of cultural resources and frameworks that people apply to particular situations to generate meanings and direct their actions

10. Chang 2010: 446.

11. Taiwan's nominal gross domestic product (GDP) grew fifteen times from 1960 to 1980 and became one of the "Four Asian Tigers," alongside Hong Kong, Singapore, and South Korea.

12. The total fertility rate dropped to 0.895 in 2010, the lowest in the world, and the rate in 2016 was 1.17. ROC Ministry of the Interior, http://www.ris.gov.tw/346, accessed November 22, 2017.

13. The traditional Chinese family invests more educational resources in sons to secure future returns for parents, but intrafamily gender inequality in schooling disappeared with shrinking family sizes in Taiwan (Yu and Su 2006).

14. Harvey 1989.

15. Hoffman and Zhao (2008) reveal a similar situation in China.

16. Zelizer 1985.

17. Buckingham 2007; Kincheloe 2002.

18. Freeman 2010: 578.

19. Roland Robertson's (1992) famous concept glocalization describes the simultaneity or co-presence of both universalizing and particularizing tendencies. I have also raised the concept of glocal entanglement to describe the global-local entanglements in the changing discourses of parenting in Taiwan (Lan 2014).

20. See Chung 2016 and Wu 2014 for a review of these narratives.

21. Espiritu 2010.

22. Portes and Zhou 1993; Zhou and Kim 2006.

23. Zhou 2009; Zhou and Bankston 1998.

24. Chen 2006, 2008; Yang 1999.

25. Lee and Zhou 2015.

26. Kasinitz 2016; Tran 2016. Also see Appendix C in this book.

27. Kasinitz 2016.

28. Tran 2016: 2402.

29. Coe 2014: 21–25.

30. Espiritu 2001.

31. Coe 2014; Waters and Sykes 2009.

32. Vivian Louie (2004) interviewed Chinese Americans who grew up in middle-class suburbs and in urban enclaves in New York City. Jamie Lew (2006) compares Korean Americans at an elite magnet high school in New York with those who dropped out of high school. Angie Chung (2016) interviewed second-generation Korean, Chinese, and Taiwanese Americans across the social class spectrum.

33. Shah, Dwyer, and Modood 2010.

34. Levitt and Waters 2002; V. Louie 2006.

35. Wolf (1997) uses this term to describe second-generation youths who battle with multiple understandings of cultural identities, including cultural expectations from their parents and even grandparents.

36. Chien-Juh Gu (2010) applies the concept of emotional transnationalism to examine the emotional struggles of Taiwanese immigrant mothers.

37. Hoang 2015.

38. Lee 2018; L. Wang 2016; Yamashiro 2017. See Chapter 1 for more details.

39. Bourdieu and Passeron 1990; Kohn 1959, 1963. Also see Friedman 2013; Smith and Sun 2016; Streib 2015; Weis, Cipollone, and Jenkins 2014.

40. Lareau 2011. For the class-specific ways of interacting with school, also see Lareau 1989; Calarco 2014.

41. Kusserow 2004.

42. Bourdieu 1977, 1984.

43. See the criticism of Irwin and Elley 2011; Vincent and Ball 2007; Reay 1998.

44. The middle class is divided along lines such as assets (organizational assets for managers or cultural capital for professionals), fields of production (material or symbolic) and sectors of employment (public or private sectors) (Power 2000).

45. See Lo 2015 for a review of the critique.

46. Archer 2007: 39, 47.

47. Sweetman (2003) calls this "reflexive habitus" or "habitual reflexivity."

48. Nelson 2010; Sandelowski 1991.

49. Reay, Crozier, and James 2011.

50. Wimmer and Schiller 2002.

51. Hall 1992; Lamont 1992.

52. Ong 1999.

53. Johanna Waters (2005) found that graduates who returned from Canada to Hong Kong gained advantages in the local job market that allowed them to reproduce their privileged lifestyles and social status, leaving behind the less mobile children of the lower class.

54. Lee and Koo 2006.

55. In 2016, in addition to the many kindergartens, there are forty-seven Waldorf (Steiner) elementary and secondary schools in Asia, including ten in South Korea, nine in Japan, and seven in China and India. Waldorf Worldwide, https://www.freunde-waldorf.de/en/waldorf-worldwide/waldorf-education/waldorf-world-list/, accessed Nov 17, 2016.

56. Gao 2015; Johnson 2014.

57. Carlson, Gerhards, and Hans 2017; Weenink 2008.

58. Cooper 2014; Pugh 2015; Villalobos 2014.

59. Cooper 2014. Ana Villalobos (2014: 9) coins a similar concept, security strategy, albeit with a more specific focus on mother-child bonding; she defines it as "an ideologically driven set of mothering practice intended to maximize the security derived from the mother-child relationship."

60. Although the term *strategy* connotes a certain degree of rationality and choice, recent sociological literature has expanded the concept to refer to modes of actions in which people negotiate structural constraints in the constitution of dynamic social relations; strategic conducts may involve practical consciousness and often produce unintended consequences (Giddens 1984).

61. Following the paradigm of critical realism, Bourdieu proposes the relational method in opposition to positivism and methodological individualism (Bourdieu and Wacquant 1992).

62. Gillies 2007; Skeggs 1997.

63. Reay 2017: loc. 2421 of 4452, Kindle.

64. Peggy Levitt and Nina Glick Schiller (2004) have used the concept of the transnational social field to describe that transnational exchanges of ideas, practices, and resources facilitate the simultaneity of family lives and kin networks lived across national borders. To avoid confusion, I instead use the term *transnational geography* to emphasize power relations and symbolic struggle among parents across geographic and class divides.

65. Massey 1994: 149.

66. Derné 2005; Koo 2016.

67. Silvey, Olson, and Truelove 2007.

68. Julie Chu (2010:4: 12) conducted an ethnography in Fuzhou, a Chinese border city that sends a large outflow of illicit migration to the United States.

69. Ehrenreich 1989.

70. Reay 1998.

71. Previous scholars have used this term with different meanings. Paul DiMaggio (1982) has proposed *cultural mobility theory* to describe that the participation in status culture (art, music, or literature) can help high school students, especially socially disadvantaged ones, to improve school success and prospect of class mobility. Michael Emmison (2003) also utilized this concept to describe individuals' omnivore tastes and capacities to consume cultural goods and services across divergent cultural fields. My definition of *cultural mobility* refers to the capacity to navigate multiple ethnic cultural realms. And, unlike Emmison, who views cultural consumers as "freely choosing subjects," I emphasize the structural constraints and power inequalities embedded in the practice of cultural mobility.

72. Pugh 2009.

73. Weininger and Lareau 2009.

74. Marcus 1995.

75. I follow Margaret Nelson's (2010: 5) definition of "the professional middle class" as "people with educational credentials beyond a bachelor's degree and, when employed, as people holding professional occupations."

76. I thank Ken Sun for this reminder.

77. The post-1965 waves of Chinese immigration in the United States, in particular, demonstrates a feature of "hyperselectivity" (Lee and Zhou 2015).

78. Gu 2006; Louie, V. 2004.

79. Kasinitz et al. 2008.

Chapter 1

1. Portes, Guarnizo, and Landolt 1999.

2. *Harvest* 1952a.

3. *Harvest* 1952b, 1952c, 1952d.

4. Hodgson 1988.

5. Chow 1970.

6. Tsai 2007.

7. Huang 2016.

8. Chang, Freedman, and Sun 1987.

9. Wang 2011.

10. Taiwan's infant mortality rate (under one year of age) was 44.7 in 1952 and 35 in 1960 per 1,000 live births. ROC Ministry of Health and Welfare, https://dep.mohw .gov.tw/DOS/cp-3443-34193-113.html, accessed March 9, 2018.

11. An 2010: 60–61.

12. Chiang (1951) 1990.

13. Huang 1991: 48.

14. Lu et al. 2007.

15. Lo 2002.

16. Sun Te-Hsiung (1978: 17–18), a leading policymaker involved in the program of family planning, said: "The program was started in rural townships and continued to lay its emphasis on these townships. . . . The program is reaching relatively more of those who are less likely to adopt contraception on their own."

17. Kuo 1998: 77.

18. Kuo 1998: 78.

19. Chen, Sun, and Li 2003.

20. Lee and Zhou 2015: 29.

21. Liu and Cheng 1994: 89.

22. Chang 1992: 35.

23. Gu 2006.

24. Chen 1992.

25. Ng 1998:18.

26. Chen 2008: 22.

27. Fong 2008: 32.

28. Kanjanapan 1995: 17.

29. ROC Ministry of Education, https://depart.moe.edu.tw/ed2500/News_Con tent.aspx?n=2D25F01E87D6EE17&sms=4061A6357922F45A&s=9548BB768A861B5E, accessed March 9, 2018.

30. Gu 2006: 106, 115.

31. On the basis of visa applications, some forty thousand children arrived in the US from Taiwan without parent accompaniment between 1980 and the mid-1990s, and the actual numbers of "parachute kids" are believed to be even larger (Zhou 2009: 203).

32. Chee 2005: 98.

33. Chang 1992.

34. Chang 2006: 54.

35. Ley 2010: 231.

36. Saxenian and Hsu 2001.

37. Chang 2006.

38. Naftali 2009, 2010.

39. Tseng 1996.

40. Hays 1996.

41. Ho and Hindley 2011.

42. In 1999, the Legislation Yuan modified the Educational Foundation Act and Primary and Junior High Education Act to open space for charter schools and allow parents to choose among their preferred education systems. In 2016, legal changes were added to three acts related to experimental education to further deregulate schooling.

43. See Lan 2014 for details.

44. Teresa Kuan (2015) also found that middle-class mothers in China are engaged in emotional work to attend to their children's psychological selves in order to raise a "high-quality [*suzhi*] child."

45. Some fathers still feel awkward about verbally expressing affection to their children. This is a gendered habit common among older generations of heterosexual men in Taiwan.

46. The Family Education Act, section 1.

47. Chen 2003.

48. This law was promulgated in 1973 as a symbolic display of the state's protection of children's welfare after UNICEF terminated its services in Taiwan after the country lost its seat in the United Nations. Yet the clause on the protection of children from abuse and neglect was not added until 1993.

49. As proposed, those parents who refuse to attend would be subject to a fine of 3,000–15,000 TWD (100–500 USD) (Hsueh 2008).

50. Lin 2008.

51. ROC Ministry of Education 2013: 5–6; ROC Legislative Yuan 2002.

52. The state-sponsored programs of parental education in the United Kingdom showed a similar tendency (Holloway and Pimlott-Wilson 2014: 97).

53. According to article 51 in the Protection of Children and Youth Welfare and Rights Act: "Parents, guardians, or other people looking after children and youth will not leave children alone in an environment that can easily cause danger or damage; children aged below six or children and youth that need special care will not be left alone or be looked after by improper people."

54. The Child and Youth Welfare and Rights Protection Act of 2012 protects children from "physical and mental mistreatment" (art. 49) but does not prohibit all corporal punishment. Corporal punishment is banned in all levels of schools in article 8 of the Fundamental Law of Education, as amended in 2006.

55. She 2017.

56. ROC Ministry of Health and Welfare 2015.

57. Yu 2014.

58. Tseng 2011

59. Li 2015.

60. Fu et al. 2016.

61. Lan and Wu 2016.

62. Taiwanese are eligible to multiple entry visas that are automatically approved for a year of residency. They can also apply for up to a five-year residency permit and can renew it upon the fulfillment of qualifications (Tseng and Wu 2011).

63. Shen 2014.

64. Li 2015.

65. Shen 2014.

66. Temporary labor migration from China is barred except for fishermen who are not allowed to land. Chinese students are subject to quota control, and they are not entitled to work and residency after they finish their studies.

67. Shih 1998: 294–295.

68. Statistics accumulated from 1998 to 2016, Department of Household Registration, ROC Ministry of the Interior, table C-3, http://www.ris.gov.tw/346, accessed on November 29, 2017.

69. Friedman 2015: 8–9.

70. Chao 2004; Friedman 2015.

71. ROC Ministry of the Interior, table B-03, http://www.ris.gov.tw/346.

72. With the declining fertility rate, the total number of children in primary and secondary schools dropped from 2,840,460 in 2004 to 2,129,050 in 2013. Children of new immigrants have increased from 46,411 to 209,784, rising proportionally from 1.63 percent to 9.85 percent. ROC Ministry of Education 2014.

73. Institute of International Education Open Doors Report 2015, http://www.iie.org/Research-and-Publications/Open-Doors/Data/International-Students/Leading-Places-of-Origin/2013-15, accessed April 12, 2016.

74. China is the top sending country of diploma-seeking secondary students in the United States. Chinese students account for 58 percent of international secondary students, and their numbers have grown each year from 2013 to 2016 (Farrugia 2017).

75. H-1B visa applicants included Indians and Chinese as the two largest national groups, and many were former international students in the US (Liu 2009).

76. In the US, an EB-5 visa holder is required to create ten jobs in the US in addition to having 1,000,000 USD in financial assets.

77. US Department of Homeland Security, "Profiles on Lawful Permanent Residents," https://www.dhs.gov/profiles-lawful-permanent-residents-2014-country, accessed September 9, 2016.

78. Passel and Cohn 2016.

79. Zhao 2010: 34–36.

80. Zhao 2010: 144.

81. Zhao 2010: 91.

82. Zhou 2009: 119.

83. V. Louie 2004.

84. Tuan 1998.

85. Waters 1990.

86. Portes and Zhou 1993; Zhou and Kim 2006.

87. Zhou, Chin, and Kim 2013: 362.

88. Li 1998.

89. Hwang 2005.

90. Jiménez and Horowitz 2013. The authors' research site, Cupertino, California, has some peculiar features: nearly half of residents are foreign born, and the immigrant population is highly selective in terms of education and income. Also, Cupertino is an Asian and white city with few blacks or Latinos.

91. Lee and Zhou 2015.

92. Zhou, Chin, and Kim 2013: 361.

93. Brittain 2002: 86.

94. Kanjanapan 1995: 30, table 4.

95. Schreckinger 2014.

96. Brittain 2002: 87.

97. Fox 2011.

98. See Gu 2006 for similar situations among Taiwanese immigrants in Chicago.

99. Levitt and Waters 2002.

100. Wang 2015.

101. A. Louie 2004.

102. Rumbaut 2002: 88.

103. L. Wang 2016; Wessendorf 2013.

104. Jain 2013; Lee 2018; Nguyen-Akbar 2014; Yamashiro 2017.

105. Yan, Lam, and Lauer 2014.

106. Chiang and Liao 2008.

107. Ley and Kobayashi 2005; Waters 2006.

108. Ip 2006.

109. Ley and Kobayashi 2005.

110. For instance, in Hong Kong, those growing up in North America are considered more outgoing and communicative as opposed to introverted Hong Kong students who were educated through rote memorization (Waters 2006: 186).

111. Yan, Lam, and Lauer 2014.

112. L. Wang 2016; Ley and Kobayashi 2005.

113. Ranks of US students were 36 in math, 28 in reading, and 24 in science. British students did slightly better, at 26 in math, 20 in reading, and 23 in science.

114. Paten 2013.

115. BBC News 2016.

116. Zhao 2015.

Chapter 2

1. Yu and Su 2008.

2. All the names for respondents are pseudonyms; their quotes were originally in Mandarin Chinese and translated by me into English.

3. Hays 1996: 45.

4. Bourdieu 1977, 1984.

5. Archer 2007.

6. Giddens 1984.

7. Wang 2003.

8. ROC Ministry of Education, http://www.edu.tw/pages/detail.aspx?Node=3973&Page=20272&WID=31d75a44-efff-4c44-a075-15a9eb7aecdf, accessed May 20, 2014.

9. See Chapter 3 for statistics on unemployment by educational level.

10. The number of Taiwanese high school graduates attending foreign universities has increased over the years. According to the Department of Education, the number of Taiwanese high school graduates who went on to study abroad was only 550 in 2009 (0.22 percent) and doubled to 1,067 in 2012 (0.42 percent) (Chen 2014).

11. According to the investigation of *Education, Parenting and Lifestyle,* there are 104 experimental schools and institutions around the country, including eighteen Waldorf schools. These numbers include small-scale educational institutions primarily run by parents (Chen and Chen 2018).

12. Alternative school enrollment for primary and secondary school increased rapidly from 392 in 2003 to 4856 in 2016. ROC Ministry of Education 2017, table A1-10.

13. All school names in this book are pseudonyms. See Appendix A for more details about the schools from which I recruited parents.

14. Chen and Huang 2007, 124, quoting the Taiwanese businessman Daniel M. Tsai.

15. Koo 2016: 443.

16. Derné 2005: 181.

17. Dan 2013: 128, 134, 136.

18. Chen 2007a.

19. Chen 2007a: 77.

20. Pugh (2009: 178) uses this term to describe that parents spend on opportunities and social contexts, including neighborhoods, schools, day care, camps, that shape children's trajectories.

21. Reay, Crozier, and James 2011.

22. Khan 2011.

23. Carlson, Gerhards, and Hans 2017; Weenink 2008.

24. Aihwa Ong (1999) describes Asian elite families' acquisition of foreign passports as a strategy of "flexible citizenship."

25. The family spends roughly USD 700–800 dollars per month on talent lessons (not including private school tuition), nearly one-sixth of the total household income.

26. Bourdieu 1986. Also see Shih 2010 for a discussion of "raising an international child" in Taiwan.

27. Pugh 2015: 170.

28. Private school tuitions vary, ranging from to USD 2000 to 5500 per semester (nonboarding).

29. Such as applying for International Baccalaureate (IB) accreditation or certification from the American Western Association of Schools and Colleges (WASC).

30. Overall, 3 percent of Taiwanese students attend private elementary schools, but in Taipei City, the number attending stands at nearly 9 percent. ROC Bureau of Statistics, Ministry of Education, http://depart.moe.edu.tw/ED4500/cp.aspx?n =1B58E0B736635285&s=D04C74553DB60CAD, accessed March 8, 2018.

31. Yi-Ping Shih and Chin-Chun Yi (2014) analyzed 2000–2001 survey data from the Taiwan Youth Project.

32. Friedman 2013.

33. For a similar observation, see Shih 2010: 201.

34. Chen 2007b, 127.

35. In 2016, about 28 percent of married Taiwanese women age twenty-five to forty-nine were not gainfully employed. For women of all age groups with a college degree or above, 34.5 percent were not gainfully employed (ROC Bureau of Statistics 2017).

36. Amy Brainer (2017), in her study of Taiwanese families with LGBT children, found many mothers doing emotional work to negotiate with children's gender and sexuality, usually without involving fathers at all.

37. Ho et al. 2011.

38. Lareau 2011.

39. On average, Taiwanese employees work about 2,200 hours annually, 20 percent more than workers in the US and 50 percent more than workers in Germany (Sui 2012).

40. According to Hsiu-Hua Shen (2014: 272), as a result of increasing competition from local talents, expatriate packages for Taiwanese in recent years are not as generous as in the past, but working in China is still considered a pathway to career advancement and future economic gain.

41. Connell (1987) raises the influential concept of "hegemonic masculinity" to describe the configuration of gender practices that sustain men's domination over women.

42. Connell (1998) suggests that global capitalism and multinational companies' practice of sending out top male employees perpetuate "transnational business masculinity," which is a transformed pattern of business masculinity achieving a hegemonic position in global gender relations.

43. Hondagneu-Sotelo and Avila 1997.

44. Parents may have more relaxed attitudes toward their children's future if they are raising daughters instead of sons. I asked Jason if he would have similar expectations if he were raising sons. He paused and said: "Maybe not. Society would ask a boy to take on more responsibility."

45. I borrow the term "Transitional" from Arlie Hochschild (1989), who uses it to refers to fathers who share an egalitarian gender ideology but still leave a lot of family work to their wives.

46. Sayer 2005.

47. Bobel 2010; Cairns, Johnston, and MacKendrick 2013; MacKendrick 2014; Reich 2014.

48. Apple 2006.

49. Cooper 2014.

Chapter 3

1. Yahoo-Kimo Knowledge, https://tw.knowledge.yahoo.com/question/question?qid=1511121702491, accessed November 3, 2014. The original post is longer and in Chinese. The quote has been extracted and translated by the author. I thank She Keng-Jen for directing me to this quote.

2. Shieh 1992.

3. Lin 2015.

4. See Lan 2006. ROC Ministry of Labor Statistics, http://statdb.mol.gov.tw/statis/jspProxy.aspx?sys=210&kind=21&type=1&funid=q13016&rdm=lpbijrlp, accessed August 8, 2017.

5. The unemployment rate in Taiwan was as low as 1.45 percent in 1993 but rose to 4.57 percent in 2001 and 5.85 percent in 2009. Men's unemployment became significantly higher than women's after 2001; the gap was biggest in 2002 (5.91 percent versus 4.1 percent) and also substantial in 2009 (6.53 percent versus 4.96 percent). Directorate General of Budget, Accounting and Statistics, ROC Executive Yuan, 2016, "Employment and Unemployment Query System." http://win.dgbas.gov.tw/dgbas04/bc4/timeser/more_f.asp, accessed June 21, 2016.

6. In 2013, for men with college degrees, the unemployment rate in the twenty-five to twenty-nine age group was as high as 8.4 percent, but the rate dropped to 4.09 percent in the thirty to thirty-four age group and 3.11 percent in the thirty-five to forty age group. Yet for men without a high school diploma, the unemployment rate was high across all ages (8.16 percent for those aged twenty-five to twenty-nine, 8.17 for those aged thirty to thirty-four, and 6.17 percent for those aged thirty-five to

thirty-nine). Directorate General of Budget, Accounting and Statistics, ROC Executive Yuan, 2016, "Employment and Unemployment Query System." http://win.dgbas .gov.tw/dgbas04/bc4/timeser/more_f.asp, accessed June 21, 2016.

7. According to government data, men in the lower socioeconomic classes are more likely to enter into transnational marriage. Men with an average monthly salary between 20,000 and 30,000 TWD have the highest rates of transnational marriage, followed by those with an average monthly salary between 30,000 and 40,000 TWD. The most common occupations for men with foreign spouses are technical and other related workers (23.8 percent), service and retail industry worker (18.5 percent), and nontechnical laborer (17.2 percent). ROC Ministry of the Interior 2009.

8. Hsia 1997; Lan 2008.

9. According to Yen-Hsin Cheng (2016), the divorce differentials by education reversed in the early 1990s for men and in the early 1980s for women; the recent climbing of the divorce rate was mainly driven by the tremendous growth in marital disruption among the less educated.

10. Constable 2005.

11. According to article 31 in the Protection of Children and Youth Welfare and Rights Act: "The government will establish an assessment mechanism for the development of children aged below six, offering special care for early prevention, medical, schooling and family support for developmental delays in children as needed."

12. Tseng 2008.

13. Tang and Hong 2015.

14. The Ministry of Education initiated a program called Education and Counseling Program for Foreign and Mainland Chinese Spouses and Children in 2006. Each school that applies to the program can receive 25,000 to 60,000 TWD (800–2000 USD) in funding to provide expert-run parenting seminars for foreign and mainland Chinese spouses.

15. Lareau 2011.

16. Gillies 2005: 847–848.

17. Sousa 2015.

18. Hughes, Valle-Riestra, and Arguelles 2008.

19. Because of his busy work schedule and his quiet personality, Wu-long isn't used to interacting with strangers. We were unable to formally interview him during our research.

20. Leaving children alone at home, especially for those under six, is now seen as an act of neglect. See Chapter 1 for more details.

21. Wu-long's salary, including overtime, totals about 30,000 TWD (1000 USD) per month. Grandma Chen currently makes a minimum salary, about 22,000 TWD per month. Grandma Chen estimates that they spend 50,000 to 60,000 TWD a month, including a mortgage of 22,000 TWD.

22. Pugh 2009: 145–147.

23. Even among Western families, the nuclear family model serves as an ideological construct and overlooks social differences (Smith 1993).

24. According to a government survey in 2013, 37 percent of married women relied on grandparents to care for children under the age of three; the proportion rose to 44 percent among mothers with college degrees or higher (ROC Bureau of Statistics 2014). The latter proportion is higher because more college-educated women stay in the workforce.

25. Parents with a child under age two can receive a monthly childcare subsidy of 3,000–5,000 TWD (95–160 USD) to hire a licensed nanny and a kin child caregiver (parent or grandparent) can receive a monthly allowance of 2,000–4,000 TWD (65–130 USD) after completing sixty hours of training.

26. Kohn 1959, 1963.

27. The minimum hourly wage was 103 TWD (3.5 USD) at the time of research (in 2011), but the amount rose to 140 TWD starting from January 2018.

28. Mullainathan and Shafir 2013.

29. Friedman 2015: 19, 151.

30. Kim 2014. Cheng, Yeoh, and Zhang (2014) also reveal similar dynamics in Singapore.

31. This concept builds on Pugh 2009 and contrasts with the middle-class strategy of global pathway consumption in Chapter 2.

32. Bourdieu 1984.

33. Lareau 2011.

34. Hsung 2014.

35. Shih 2010: 167–168.

36. Article 51, Protection of Children and Youth Welfare and Rights Act.

37. Allison Pugh (2009: 200) coins the term *exposed childhood* to describe that "parents choose contexts for children that present challenges of adaption to them, because of their contrasting racial or class composition."

38. The law specifies that for a divorced Chinese spouse who had received child custody, the child had to reside in Taiwan for more than 183 days per year; otherwise, the Chinese parent's residency status would be revoked. The immigration bureaucrats interviewed by Sara Friedman explained the rationale behind the regulation was to minimize "the undesirable result of making a Taiwanese child into a Mainland child through the force of family socialization and exposure to the Chinese education system" (Friedman 2014: 301).

39. Yang et al. 2012.

40. In 2015, the divorce rate for cross-border unions was 21.97 per 1,000 married couples, compared to 8.84 for local couples. ROC Ministry of the Interior, http://www.moi.gov.tw/stat/news_content.aspx?sn=10664, accessed July 1, 2016.

41. Friedman (2015: 214) observed these seminars in which the gender etiquettes instructed is intended to erase Chinese women's undesirable differences and attune them to "proper" femininity.

42. Hwang 2014.

43. The *New Immigrant Parental Education Curriculum* published by ROC Ministry of Education in 2015 (Family Education Center, National Chiayi University, 2015) is more sensitive to the cultures of immigrants' home countries, but even this curriculum tends to essentialize Southeast Asian customs in a reductive manner.

44. Friedman 2015: 145.

45. Hsia 2009.

46. Li 2013.

47. Ministry of Education, the New Southbound Talent Development Program, https://ws.moe.edu.tw/001/Upload/7/relfile/8053/51384/5fd31e54-beb7-48c1-b018 -22ccf3de1e19.pdf, accessed October 16, 2017.

48. New Taipei City Government, http://epaper.ntpc.edu.tw/index/EpaSubShow .aspx?CDE=EPS20170307170813KKS&e=EPA201612091115522O6, accessed October 16, 2017.

49. Hale 2005; Melamed 2006.

50. Kymlicka 2012: 111.

51. A participant spoke at the forum "Human-Based New South-Turn Policy: Cultivating Southeast Talents for Taiwan," May 17, 2016.

Chapter 4

1. Hwang 2005.

2. Spencer 2015.

3. Lee and Zhou 2015.

4. Chen 2008.

5. Xiao Baiyou (2011), a Chinese father, coined the term *wolf dad* in his memoir published in the PRC. The book promotes his disciplinary style of childrearing, which is based on the argument that up to age twelve, children express an animal side and cannot be educated gently through a reward system.

6. See Chapter 2.

7. Connell 1995; Espiritu 2008.

8. Cooper 2000: 381.

9. ASCEND, an Asian American professional organization, analyzed 2013 data from the Equal Employment Opportunity Commission that were collected from HP, Google, Intel, LinkedIn, and Yahoo (Chin 2016).

10. Compared to their counterparts from Taiwan, professional women from the PRC are more determined to continue their careers after giving birth and more likely to invite the grandparents to cohabitate in the US and help with childcare. In Com-

munist China, housewifery was considered a feudalist heritage that impeded women's emancipation, but this cultural norm has changed since China marched into capitalism. Some among the younger generations of Chinese women aspire full-time motherhood as a symbol of luxury and status (Rofel 1999).

11. Gu 2010.

12. Karabel 2005.

13. Stevens 2007.

14. Jiménez and Horowitz 2013; Lee and Zhou 2015. See Chapter 1 for more details.

15. Unz 2013.

16. At highly competitive public colleges, the acceptance rate for Asian students is 46 percent, compared to 54 percent for statistically equivalent white students, 57 percent for Hispanics, and 80 percent for blacks (Espenshade and Radford 2009: 128).

17. Yang 2011.

18. According to Alba and Nee (2003), immigrant assimilation no longer requires an erasure of ethnicity; instead, ethnicity is negotiated as a social boundary by ethnic individuals or groups by narrowing the social distance that separates them from the mainstream and its opportunities.

19. Lee and Zhou 2015: 57.

20. Chen (2006) made a similar observation on Taiwanese Christian communities in California.

21. Stevens 2007.

22. Lareau 2011.

23. Chu 2008.

24. Kao 2000; Peguero and Williams 2011.

25. Osajima 1993: 82.

26. Whether students of ethnic minorities can successfully develop cross-racial networks as their parents expect is an open question. The existing research suggests that racial minority students face substantial barriers to penetrate the white, Anglo-Saxon Protestant social circle that dominates elite universities in the US, and especially to gain admittance into exclusive social organizations such as fraternities (Khan 2011; Rivera 2015).

27. Rivera 2015.

28. Lareau 2011: 59.

29. Kang and Larson (2014) found that a "sense of indebtedness toward parents" helps Korean American emerging adults to normalize cross-generational conflicts and strengthen a sense of filial obligation in the postadolescent years.

30. Min Zhou (2009: 12–13) has used the term *ethnic capital* to refer to an interplay of financial, human, and social capital in an identifiable ethnic community. I use

the term in a slightly different way, without emphasizing spatial embeddedness but highlighting cultural negotiation around ethnic boundaries.

31. Erel (2010) criticizes the "rucksack approach" of ethnic capital for overlooking the social process in which migrants actively bargain with institutions to validate particular cultural resources as capital.

32. Neckerman, Carter, and Lee 1999.

33. Vallejo 2012.

34. Stanly Sue and Sumie Okazaki (2009) have argued that Asian American parents invest in their children's education because they perceive "blocked opportunities" for Asians in areas outside of education such as career, sports, and politics. Also see Lee and Zhou 2015 and V. Louie 2004 for similar findings.

35. Chen 2006; Yang 1999.

36. Stevenson and Lee 1990; Lee and Zhou 2015.

37. Music training toward the goal of competitions can be very expensive. One family I interviewed spent as much as 4,800 USD per month for their daughter's lessons in piano, flute, and ballet.

38. Lu 2013: 15.

39. Wang 2015: 53.

40. Unlike the ethnic system of supplementary education in Chinatown (see Chapter 5), these after-school programs are not necessarily ethnic institutions and are often geographically dispersed.

41. A. Louie 2015.

42. Kibria 2002; Purkayastha 2005.

43. Zhou 2009.

44. Kasinitz et al. 2008.

45. Angie Chung (2016: 199–200) made a similar remark in the conclusion of her book.

46. For instance, several participants in this web discussion advise that Chinese American students should take foreign-language courses other than Chinese; otherwise they will "look bad" when they apply to college. See http://talk.collegeconfidential .com/college-admissions/670446-will-chinese-student-born-in-usa-taking-chinese -as-world-language-hurt-his-apps.html, accessed 12/18/2015.

47. Parents from Taiwan feel more ambivalent about the rise of China. On the one hand, they appreciate the increasing recognition of the Chinese language and culture, but on the other hand, they feel a sense of distance from or even hostility toward China, which still claims sovereignty over Taiwan and threatens a military takeover if Taiwan declares independence. They tend to describe immigrant parents from China as "more authoritarian," "not as open," and "less democratic" toward their children. My interviews actually do not suggest substantial difference between Chinese and Taiwanese immigrant parents in terms of parenting styles. Instead, Taiwanese im-

migrants use this rhetoric to reclaim a symbolic hierarchy between Taiwan's open democracy and China's closed, authoritarian regime.

48. Chung 2016: 194, 7.

49. Lo and Nguyen 2018.

Chapter 5

1. Their educational backgrounds vary to some extent. Most parents are high school graduates, but two men had a bachelor degree in China and one with an associate degree. See Appendix B for more details.

2. Glenn 1986.

3. Some of my informants, such as a locksmith and a beautician, are able to continue their careers after immigration and actually earn higher wages in the US.

4. Chinese immigrants coined the term *American filial son* to describe the fact that elderly benefits in the US have partly replaced children's filial duty to take care of aging parents (Lan 2002).

5. V. Louie 2004.

6. Bourdieu 1990.

7. Coe 2014; Zhou and Bankston 1998.

8. Waters and Sykes 2009: 75.

9. In 1968, 94 percent of Americans approved of spanking a child, but the percentage of approval dropped to 68 percent in 1994. The decline in approval was greatest among the white, the highly educated, and among people who did not live in the South (Straus and Mathur 1996). According to a survey conducted in 1995, 94 percent of American parents said that during the previous twelve months they had used some type of corporal punishment (usually hand slapping or spanking) with their toddler children, especially among parents with lower socioeconomic status (Straus and Stewart 1999: 64).

10. The tutoring sessions at the cram school cost 20 USD an hour, but Chinese-language lessons and cultural programs are mostly free, offered by cultural centers in Chinatown.

11. Portes and Zhou 1993; Zhou 1997.

12. Pyke 2000.

13. Orellana 2009; Katz 2014.

14. Lisa Park (2005: 66) defines it as "the placement of an individual who is socially considered a child (as indicated by age and developmental level) in adultlike roles with adult responsibilities.

15. Orellana 2009.

16. Pyke 2000: 247.

17. Chung 2013: 299.

18. V. Louie 2004; Lee and Zhou 2015.

19. Lee and Zhou 2015.

20. BPS Parent University, http://www.bpsfamilies.org/parentuniversity, accessed June 10, 2016.

21. Low 2014: 165.

22. Lisa Park (2005: 66), in her study of the children of immigrant entrepreneurs, uses the term *prolonged childhood* to describe "the placement of an individual who is socially considered an adult in child-like roles with child-like responsibilities."

23. Silva 2013: 19.

24. Ibid. Also see Illouz 2008.

25. Hochschild 1983.

26. Silva 2013: 22.

27. Bourdieu 1984.

28. Rohner and Pettengill 1985.

29. Zhou and Kim 2006.

30. Lu 2013.

31. Chen 2008.

32. Bohr and Tse 2009.

33. Liu et al. 2017.

34. Bohr and Tse 2009.

35. Yoshikawa 2011: 57.

36. Liu et al. 2017.

37. The video and description are available at http://www.theatlantic.com/video/index/491843/the-confusing-lives-of-chinese-american-satellite-babies/.

38. China's rapid growth of rural-to-urban migration has created a population of "left-behind children" which is estimated to be more than 60 million and equals to one-fifth of all children in China (Sudworth 2016).

39. Bohr and Tse 2009.

40. The attachment theory postulates that it is essential for infants to experience consistent and predictable protection and comfort from a primary caregiver. See Bohr 2010 and Liu et al. 2017 for an assessment of culture-specific theoretical assumptions in the context of transnational separation.

41. For instance, a growing literature has examined how migrant mothers maintain emotional ties with children left behind, especially through the use of information and communication technology (ICT) (e.g., Parreñas 2001; Madianou 2012).

42. Orellana et al. 2001: 584.

43. Immigrant parents were not necessarily aware that childrearing and disciplinary norms in Ghana have since changed, including new regulations banning corporal punishment (Coe 2014: 135, 152).

44. Lareau 2011: 67. However, as working-class children grow into their teenage years and gain easier access to institutions outside the family, they fulfill similar roles

to immigrant children in many ways, including "translating" material that requires a certain type or level of education to understand. I thank Jessica Cobb for this insight.

45. Jennifer Hochschild (1995) made a similar point in her study of African Americans. She argues that middle-class African Americans are more skeptical of the American dream than their working-class counterparts because they have experienced struggles with racial discrimination in their pursuit of upward mobility. In contrast, economically disadvantaged African Americans who lack similar opportunities tend to downplay the harsh racial and economic realities.

Conclusion

1. Nelson 2010.

2. Tavangar 2009; Gross-Loh 2014.

3. Carlson, Gerhards, and Hans 2017; Weenink 2008.

4. Bellafante 2006, Weise 2007.

5. I thank Nicole Constable for inspiring my thinking here.

6. Reich (2014) describes upper-middle-class American mothers who strive to defend their entitlement to *choices*—such as selecting schools or refusing vaccinations—to achieve optimization in raising children.

7. Naftali 2009.

8. Reich 2014: 562.

9. Tuan 1998; Lee and Zhou 2015; Wang 2015.

10. Gillies 2007: 25.

11. Also see Chang 2010 for the case of South Korea.

12. Qin 2006.

13. Chen 2012.

Appendix A

1. Lareau 1989, 2011; Pugh 2009.

2. Most of these interviews were conducted in Taiwan in 2011 and 2013, so I used the 2012 statistics as benchmarks (Department of Budget, Accounting and Statistics, Taipei City Government 2013).

3. Fong 2006; Kuan 2015; Naftali 2009, 2010; Woronov 2007.

4. According to the 2010 US Census, the median household income was 93,640 USD in Brookline, 118,639 in Newton, and 137,456 Lexington, American FactFinder, https://factfinder.census.gov/faces/nav/jsf/pages/index.xhtml, accessed November 16 2016.

5. According to the 2010 US Census, the population of Brookline included 76.7 percent whites and 15.6 percent Asians; similarly, Newton accommodated 82 percent whites and 11.5 percent Asians. The Asian population in Lexington was more substantial (19.9 percent), but whites still occupy the vast majority (75.5 percent).

6. According to the 2010 US Census, the median household income was 62,710 USD in Quincy and 55,523 USD in Malden.

7. As of 2010, the population of Quincy was 24 percent Asian, in contrast to 67.3 percent white and 4.6 percent black. The Asian population in Malden was 20 percent, in contrast to 56.7 percent white and 14.8 percent black (data from the US Census).

8. Eschbacher 2003.

9. Most couples who participated in this study share the same country of origin, except for one middle-class couple composed of a mother born in China and a father born in Taiwan and one working-class single mother whose daughter's father is of PRC origin.

Bibliography

Alba, Richard, and Victor Nee. 2003. *Remaking the American Mainstream: Assimilation and Contemporary Immigration.* Cambridge, MA: Harvard University Press.

An Hou-Wei. 2010. *U.S. Aid and Vocational Education in Taiwan (1950–1965).* [In Chinese.] Taipei City: Academia Historica.

Apple, Rima D. 2006. *Perfect Motherhood: Science and Childrearing in America.* New Brunswick, NJ: Rutgers University Press.

Archer, Margaret. S. 2007. *Making Our Way Through the World: Human Reflexivity and Social Mobility.* Cambridge: Cambridge University Press.

BBC News. 2016. "Asian Maths Method Offered to Schools." *BBC News*, July 12. http://www.bbc.com/news/education-36772954.

Bellafante, Ginia. 2006. "To Give Children an Edge, Au Pairs From China." *New York Times*, September 5.

Bobel, Chris. 2010. *Paradox of Natural Mothering.* Philadelphia: Temple University Press.

Bohr, Yvonne. 2010. "Transnational Infancy: A New Context for Attachment and the Need for Better Models." *Child Development Perspectives* 4 (3): 189–196.

Bohr, Yvonne, and Connie Tse. 2009. "Satellite Babies in Transnational Families: A Study of Parents' Decision to Separate from Their Infants." *Infant Mental Health Journal* 30 (3): 265–286.

Bourdieu, Pierre. 1977. *Outline of a Theory of Practice.* Cambridge: Cambridge University Press.

———. 1984. *Distinction: A Social Critique of the Judgment of Taste.* Cambridge, MA: Harvard University Press.

———. 1990. *In Other Words: Essays Towards a Reflexive Sociology.* Stanford, CA: Stanford University Press.

Bourdieu, Pierre, and Jean Claude Passeron. 1990. *Reproduction in Education, Society and Culture*. Translated by Richard Nice. London: Sage Publications.

Bourdieu, Pierre, and Loïc J. D. Wacquant. 1992. *An Invitation to Reflexive Sociology*. Chicago: University of Chicago Press.

Brainer, Amy. 2017. "Mothering Gender and Sexually Nonconforming Children in Taiwan." *Journal of Family Issues* 38 (7): 921–947.

Brittain, Carmina. 2002. *Transnational Messages: Experiences of Chinese and Mexican Immigrants in American Schools*. New York: LFB Scholarly Publishing.

Buckingham, David. 2007. "Childhood in the Age of Global Media." *Children's Geographies* 5 (1): 43–54.

Cairns, Kate, Josee Johnston, and Norah MacKendrick. 2013. "Feeding the 'Organic Child': Mothering Through Ethical Consumption." *Journal of Consumer Culture* 13 (2): 97–118.

Calarco, Jessica McCrory. 2014. "Coached for the Classroom: Parents' Cultural Transmission and Children's Reproduction of Educational Inequalities." *American Sociological Review* 79 (5): 1015–1037.

Carlson, Sören, Jürgen Gerhards, and Silke Hans. 2017. "Educating Children in Times of Globalisation: Class-Specific Child-rearing Practices and the Acquisition of Transnational Cultural Capital." *Sociology* 51 (4): 749–765.

Chang, Kyung-Sup. 2010. *South Korea Under Compressed Modernity: Familial Political Economy in Transition*. London: Routledge.

Chang, Ming-Cheng, Ronald Freedman, and Te-Hsiung Sun. 1987. "Trends in Fertility, Family Size Preferences, and Family Planning Practices in Taiwan, 1961–85." *Studies in Family Planning* 18 (6): 320–337.

Chang, Shenglin. 2006. *The Global Silicon Valley Home: Lives and Landscapes Within Taiwanese-American Trans-Pacific Culture*. Stanford, CA: Stanford University Press.

Chang, Shirley L. 1992. "Causes of Brain Drain and Solutions: The Taiwan Experience." *Studies in Comparative International Development* 27 (1): 27–43.

Chao, Antonia. 2004. "The Modern State, Citizenship, and the Intimate Life: A Case Study of Taiwan's Glorious Citizens and Their Mainland Wives." [In Chinese.] *Taiwanese Sociology* 8: 1–41.

Chao, Ruth K. 1994. "Beyond Parental Control and Authoritarian Parenting Style: Understanding Chinese Parenting Through the Cultural Notion of Training." *Child Development* 65 (4): 1111–1119.

Chao, Ruth K., and Stanley Sue. 1996. "Chinese Parental Influence and Their Children's School Success: A Paradox in the Literature on Parenting Styles." In *Growing Up the Chinese Way: Chinese Child and Adolescent Development*, edited by Sing Lau, 93–230. Hong Kong: Chinese University Press.

Chee, Maria W. L. 2005. *Taiwanese American Transnational Families: Women and Kin Work*. New York: Routledge.

Chen, Carolyn. 2006. "From Filial Piety to Religious Piety: Evangelical Christianity Reconstructing Taiwanese Immigrant Families in the United States." *International Migration Review* 40 (3): 573–602.

———. 2008. *Getting Saved in America: Taiwanese Immigration and Religious Experience.* Princeton, NJ: Princeton University Press.

———. 2012. "Asians: Too Smart for Their Own Good?" *New York Times*, December 19.

Chen Chao-Nan, Sun Te-Hsiung, and Li Dong-Ming. 2003. *Taiwan's Demographic Miracle: Research on the Success of Family Planning Policy.* [In Chinese.] Taipei City: Linking Publishing.

Chen, Hsiang-Shui. 1992. *Chinatown No More: Taiwanese Immigrants in Contemporary New York.* Ithaca, NY: Cornell University Press.

Chen Jhih-Hua. 2014. "Going Abroad Straight out of High School: Population in Thousands for the First Time." [In Chinese.] *United Daily News*, March 5.

Chen Min-Fong. 2003. "The Third Reading of New Family Legislation: Lowering Divorce Rates, Reducing Broken Families, and Preventing Adolescent Delinquency." [In Chinese.] *Min Sheng Daily*, January 8, A1.

Chen Ya-Hui, and Chen Hsiu-Ju. 2018. "A List of 177 Experimental Schools and Institutions in Taiwan." [In Chinese.] *Education, Parenting, Family Lifestyle* 98 (March): 138–146.

Chen Ya-Ling. 2007a. "The Future Number Ones." [In Chinese.] *Business Weekly (Taiwan)*, March 5, 71–78.

———. 2007b. "More Than 50% of Families Use Money to Buy Talent." [In Chinese.] *Business Weekly (Taiwan)*, August 20, 126–127.

Chen Ya-Ling, and Huang You-Ning. 2007. "Cultivating Uniqueness in Pursuit of High Scores." [In Chinese.] *Business Weekly (Taiwan)*, August 20, 120–123.

Cheng, Yen-Hsin. 2016. "More Education, Fewer Divorce? Shifting Education Differentials of Divorce in Taiwan from 1975 to 2010." *Demographic Research* 34 (33): 927–942.

Cheng, Yi'En, Brenda S. A. Yeoh, and Juan Zhang. 2014. "Still 'Breadwinners' and 'Providers': Singaporean Husbands, Money and Masculinity in Transnational Marriages." *Gender, Place & Culture* 22 (6): 867–883.

Chiang Monlin. 1990 (1951). *An Examination of JCRR's Work Progress.* [In Chinese.] Taipei: Council of Agriculture, ROC.

Chiang, Nora Lan-Hung, and Sunny Pei-Chun Liao. 2008. "Back to Taiwan: Adaptation and Self-Identity of Young Taiwanese Return Migrants from Australia." *Journal of Population Studies* 36: 99–135.

Chin, Margaret M. 2016. "Asian Americans, Bamboo Ceilings, and Affirmative Action." *Contexts* 15 (1): 70–73.

Chow, L. P. 1970. "Family Planning in Taiwan, ROC: Progress and Prospects." *Population Studies* 24 (3): 339–352.

Chu, Bryan. 2008. "Asian Americans Remain Rare in Men's College Basketball." *San Francisco Chronicle*, December 16.

Chu, Julie Y. 2010. *Cosmologies of Credit: Transnational Mobility and the Politics of Destination in China*. Durham, NC: Duke University Press.

Chua, Amy. 2011a. *Battle Hymn of the Tiger Mother*. New York: Penguin Press.

———. 2011b. "Why Chinese Mothers Are Superior." *Wall Street Journal*, January 8.

———. 2011c. *Wo zai meiguo zuo mama, Yelu faxueyuan jiaoshou de yurrjing* 我在美国做妈妈：耶鲁法学院教授的育儿经 [The ways I mother in the US: Childrearing advice from a Yale law professor]. Beijing: CITIC Press.

Chung, Angie Y. 2013. "From Caregivers to Caretakers: The Impact of Family Roles on Ethnicity Among Children of Korean and Chinese Immigrant Families." *Qualitative Sociology* 36 (3): 279–302.

———. 2016. *Saving Face: The Emotional Costs of the Asian Immigrant Family Myth*. New Brunswick, NJ: Rutgers University Press.

Coe, Cati. 2014. *The Scattered Family: Parenting, African Migrants, and Global Inequality*. Chicago: University of Chicago Press.

Connell, R. W. 1987. *Gender and Power: Society, the Person, and Sexual Politics*. Stanford, CA: Stanford University Press.

———. 1995. *Masculinities*. Berkeley: University of California Press.

———. 1998. "Masculinities and Globalization." *Men and Masculinities* 1 (1): 3–23.

Constable, Nicole. 2005. *Cross-Border Marriages: Gender and Mobility in Transnational Asia*. Philadelphia: University of Pennsylvania Press.

Cooper, Marianne. 2000. "Being the 'Go-To Guy': Fatherhood, Masculinity, and the Organization of Work in Silicon Valley." *Qualitative Sociology* 23 (4): 379–405.

———. 2014. *Cut Adrift: Families in Insecure Times*. Berkeley: University of California Press.

Dan Siao-Yi. 2013. "Multiple Entrance Is an Informational Battle, Not a Financial One." [In Chinese.] *Business Weekly (Taiwan)*, May 13, 128–136.

Department of Budget, Accounting, and Statistics, Taipei City Government. 2013. *Report on the Family Income and Expenditure Survey in Taipei*. [In Chinese.] http://w2.dbas.taipei.gov.tw/eng/family/2013.pdf.

Derné, Steve. 2005. "Globalization and the Making of a Transnational Middle Class: Implications for Class Analysis." In *Critical Globalization Studies*, edited by Richard P. Appelbaum and William I. Robertson, 177–186. New York: Routledge.

DiMaggio, Paul. 1982. "Cultural Capital and School Success: The Impact of Status Culture Participation on the Grades of US High School Students." *American Sociological Review* 47 (2): 189–201.

Douglass, Mike. 2006. "Global Householding in Pacific Asia." *International Development Planning Review* 28 (4): 421–446.

Ehrenreich, Barbara. 1989. *Fear of Falling: The Inner Life of the Middle Class*. New York: HarperCollins.

Emmison, Michael. 2003. "Social Class and Cultural Mobility: Reconfiguring the Cultural Omnivore Thesis." *Journal of Sociology* 39 (3): 211–230.

Erel, Umut. 2010. "Migrating Cultural Capital: Bourdieu in Migration Studies." *Sociology* 44 (4): 642–660.

Eschbacher, Karen. 2003. "Chinatown South: A Special Report in *The Patriot Ledger*." http://www.southofboston.net/specialreports/chinatown/day1-trends.html. Accessed November 17, 2016.

Espenshade, Thomas J., and Alexandria Walton Radford. 2009. *No Longer Separate, Not Yet Equal: Race and Class in Elite College Admission and Campus Life.* Princeton, NJ: Princeton University Press.

Espiritu, Yen Le. 2001. "We Don't Sleep Around Like White Girls Do: Family, Culture, and Gender in Filipina American Lives." *Signs* 26 (2): 415–440.

———. 2008. *Asian American Women and Men: Labor, Laws, and Love.* Lanham, MD: Rowman and Littlefield.

———. 2010. "Migration and Cultures." In *Handbook of Cultural Sociology*, edited by John Hall, Laura Grindstaff, and Ming-Cheng Lo, 659–667. London: Routledge.

Family Education Center, National Chiayi University. 2015. *New Immigrant Parental Education Curriculum.* [In Chinese.] Taipei: Ministry of Education, ROC. https://moe .familyedu.moe.gov.tw/Pages/Detail.aspx?nodeid=352&pid=4464.

Farrugia, Christine. 2017. "Globally Mobile Youth: Trends in International Secondary Students in the United States, 2013–2016." IIE Center for Academic Mobility Research and Impact. https://www.iie.org/en/Research-and-Insights/Publications/ Globally-Mobile-Youth-2013-2016.

Fong, Timothy P. 2008. *The Contemporary Asian American Experience: Beyond the Model Minority.* 3rd ed. Upper Saddle River, NJ: Pearson.

Fong, Vanessa L. 2006. *Only Hope: Coming of Age Under China's One-Child Policy.* Stanford, CA: Stanford University Press.

Fox, Jeremy C. 2011. "Downtown, Malden, Quincy: Chinese Population Expanding in Boston Suburb." http://www.boston.com/yourtown/news/downtown/2011/05/ chinese_american_population_ex.html. Accessed October 12, 2016.

Freeman, Carla. 2010. "Analyzing Culture Through Globalization." In *Handbook of Cultural Sociology*, edited by John Hall, Laura Grindstaff and Ming-Cheng Lo, 577–587. London: Routledge.

Friedman, Hilary Levey. 2013. *Playing to Win: Raising Children in a Competitive Culture.* Berkeley: University of California Press.

Friedman, Sara L. 2014. "Marital Borders: Gender, Population, and Sovereignty across the Taiwan Strait." In *Wives, Husbands, and Lovers: Marriage and Sexuality in Hong Kong, Taiwan, and Urban China*, edited by Deborah S. Davis and Sara L. Friedman, 285–311. Stanford, CA: Stanford University Press.

———. 2015. *Exceptional States: Chinese Immigrants and Taiwanese Sovereignty*. Berkeley: University of California Press.

Fu Yang-Chih, Chang Ying-Hwa, Tu Su-Hao, and Liao Pei-Shan. 2016. *Taiwan Social Change Survey, Seventh Phase, First Wave Research Report*. [In Chinese.] Taipei: Institute of Sociology, Academia Sinica.

Gao, Helen. 2015. "China's Wealthy Parents Are Fed Up with State-Run Education." *Foreign Policy Magazine*, February 10.

Giddens, Anthony. 1984. *The Constitution of Society: Outline of the Theory of Structuration*. Berkeley: University of California Press.

Gillies, Val. 2005. "Raising the 'Meritocracy': Parenting and the Individualization of Social Class." *Sociology* 39 (5): 835–853.

———. 2007. *Marginalised Mothers: Exploring Working-Class Experiences of Parenting*. London: Routledge.

Glenn, Evelyn Nakano. 1986. *Issei, Nisei, War Bride: Three Generations of Japanese American Women in Domestic Service*. Philadelphia: Temple University Press.

Gross-Loh, Christine. 2014. *Parenting Without Borders: Surprising Lessons Parents Around the World Can Teach Us*. New York: Penguin.

Gu, Chien-Juh. 2006. *Mental Health Among Taiwanese Americans: Gender, Immigration, and Transnational Struggles*. New York: New York: LFB Scholarly Publishing.

———. 2010. "Culture, Emotional Transnationalism and Mental Distress: Family Relations and Well-Being Among Taiwanese Immigrant Women." *Gender, Place and Culture* 17 (6): 687–704.

Hale, Charles R. 2005. "Neoliberal Multiculturalism: The Remaking of Cultural Rights and Racial Dominance in Central America." *Political and Legal Anthropology Review* 28 (1): 10–28.

Hall, John R. 1992. "The Capital(s) of Cultures: A Nonholistic Approach to Status Situations, Class, Gender, and Ethnicity." In *Cultivating Differences: Symbolic Boundaries and the Making of Inequality*, edited by Michèle Lamont and Marcel Fournier, 257–285. Chicago: University of Chicago Press.

Harvest. 1952a. "Children's Day." [In Chinese.] April 1.

———. 1952b. "Working Children." [In Chinese.] April 1.

———. 1952c. "Children's Obedience Problem." [In Chinese.] December 15.

———. 1952d. "Scouts of China." [In Chinese.] March 1.

Harvey, David. 1989. *The Condition of Postmodernity: An Enquiry into the Origins of Cultural Change*. Oxford, UK: Blackwell.

Hays, Sharon. 1996. *The Cultural Contradictions of Motherhood*. New Haven, CT: Yale University Press.

Ho, Hsiu-Zu, Connie Tran, Chu-Ting Ko, Jessica Phillips, Alma Boutin-Martinez, Carol Dixon, and Wei-Wen Chen. 2011. "Parent Involvement: Voices of Taiwanese Fathers." *International Journal* 5 (2): 35–42.

Ho, Ming-Sho, and Jane Hindley. 2011. "The Humanist Challenge in Taiwan's Education: Liberation, Social Justice and Ecology." *Capitalism Nature Socialism* 22 (1): 76–94.

Hoang, Kimberly Kay. 2015. *Dealing in Desire: Asian Ascendancy, Western Decline, and the Hidden Currencies of Global Sex Work*. Berkeley: University of California Press.

Hochschild, Arlie Russell. 1983. *The Managed Heart: Commercialization of Human Feeling*. Berkeley: University of California Press.

———. 1989. *The Second Shift: Working Parents and the Revolution at Home*. New York: Avon Books.

Hochschild, Jennifer L. 1995. *Facing Up to the American Dream: Race, Class, and the Soul of the Nation*. Princeton, NJ: Princeton University Press.

Hodgson, Dennis. 1988. "Orthodoxy and Revisionism in American Demography." *Population and Development Review* 14 (4): 541–569.

Hoffman, Diane M., and Guoping Zhao. 2008. "Global Convergence and Divergence in Childhood Ideologies and the Marginalisation of Children." In *Education and Social Inequality in the Global Culture*, edited by Joseph I. Zajda, Karen Biraimah, and William Gaudelli, 1–16. New York: Springer.

Holloway, Sarah L., and Helena Pimlott-Wilson. 2014. "'Any Advice Is Welcome, Isn't It?': Neoliberal Parenting Education, Local Mothering Cultures, and Social Class." *Environment and Planning A* 46 (1): 94–111.

Hondagneu-Sotelo, Pierrette, and Ernestine Avila. 1997. "'I Am Here, but I Am There': The Meanings of Latina Transnational Motherhood." *Gender and Society* 11 (5): 548–571.

Hsia, Hsiao-Chuan. 1997. "SELFing and OTHERing in the 'Foreign Bride' Phenomenon: A Study of Class, Gender, and Ethnicity in the Transnational Marriage Between Taiwanese Men and Indonesian Women." PhD diss., University of Florida.

———. 2009. "Foreign Brides, Multiple Citizenship and the Immigrant Movement in Taiwan." *Asian and Pacific Migration Journal* 18 (1): 17–46.

Hsueh He-Yu. 2008. "Parents Refuse to Attend Family Education Courses, Penalties Proposed." [In Chinese.] *United Daily News*, June 24, C4.

Hsung, Ray-May. 2014. "Social Capital and Trust: Reflections on Data from the East Asia Social Capital Survey." [In Chinese.] *Taiwanese Journal of Sociology* 54: 1–30.

Huang Chun-Chieh. 1991. *Joint Commission on Rural Reconstruction and Taiwan Experience 1949–1979*. [In Chinese.] Taipei City: San Min Book.

Huang, Yu-Ling. 2016. "Biopolitical Knowledge in the Making: Population Politics and Fertility Studies in Early Cold War Taiwan East Asian Science." *East Asian Science, Technology and Society: An International Journal* 10: 377–399.

Hughes, Marie Tejero, Diana Martinez Valle-Riestra, and Maria Elena Arguelles. 2008. "The Voices of Latino Families Raising Children with Special Needs." *Journal of Latinos and Education* 7 (3): 241–257.

Hwang, Shann Hwa. 2014. "Family Policies in Taiwan: Development, Implementation, and Assessment." In *Handbook of Family Policies Across the Globe*, edited by Mihaela Robila, 273–287. New York: Springer New York.

Hwang, Suein. 2005. "The New White Flight: In Silicon Valley, Two High Schools with Outstanding Academic Reputations are Losing White Students as Asian Students Move In. Why?" *Wall Street Journal*, November 19.

Illouz, Eva. 2008. *Saving the Modern Soul: Therapy, Emotions, and the Culture of Self-Help*. Berkeley: University of California Press.

Ip, Manying. 2006. "Returnees and Transnationals: Evolving Identities of Chinese (PRC) Immigrants in New Zealand." *Journal of Population Studies* 33: 61–102.

Irwin, Sarah, and Sharon Elley. 2011. "Concerted Cultivation? Parenting Values, Education and Class Diversity." *Sociology* 45 (3): 480–495.

Jain, Sonali. 2013. "For Love and Money: Second-Generation Indian-Americans 'Return' to India." *Ethnic and Racial Studies* 36 (5): 896–914.

Jiménez, Tomás R., and Adam L. Horowitz. 2013. "When White Is Just Alright: How Immigrants Redefine Achievement and Reconfigure the Ethnoracial Hierarchy." *American Sociological Review* 78 (5): 849–871.

Johnson, Ian. 2014. "Class Consciousness: China's New Bourgeoisie Discovers Alternative Education." *New Yorker*, February 3.

Juang, Linda P., Desiree Baolin Qin, and Irene J. K. Park. 2013. "Deconstructing the Myth of the 'Tiger Mother': An Introduction to the Special Issue on Tiger Parenting, Asian-Heritage Families, and Child/Adolescent Well-Being." *Asian American Journal of Psychology* 4 (1): 1–6.

Kang, Hyeyoung, and Reed W. Larson. 2014. "Sense of Indebtedness Toward Parents: Korean American Young Adults' Narratives of Parental Sacrifice." *Journal of Adolescent Research* 29 (4): 561–581.

Kang, Hyeyoung, and Kristy Shih. 2016. ""Actions Speak Louder Than Words": Korean American Emerging Adults' Perceptions and Meaning Making of Their Parents' Instrumental Aspects of Parenting." *Journal of Family Issues*. https://doi.org/10.1177/0192513X16676856.

Kanjanapan, Wilawan. 1995. "The Immigration of Asian Professionals to the United States: 1988–1990." *International Migration Review* 29 (1): 7–32.

Kao, Grace. 2000. "Group Images and Possible Selves Among Adolescents: Linking Stereotypes to Expectations by Race and Ethnicity." *Sociological Forum* 15 (3): 407–430.

Karabel, Jerome. 2005. *The Chosen: The Hidden History of Admission and Exclusion at Harvard, Yale, and Princeton*. Boston: Houghton Mifflin.

Kasinitz, Philip. 2016. "Explaining Asian American Achievement." *Ethnic and Racial Studies* 39 (13): 2391–2397.

Kasinitz, Philip, John H. Mollenkopf, Mary C. Waters, and Jennifer Holdaway. 2008. *Inheriting the City: The Children of Immigrants Come of Age*. New York: Russell Sage Foundation.

Katz, Vikki S. 2014. *Kids in the Middle: How Children of Immigrants Negotiate Community Interactions for Their Families, Rutgers Series in Childhood Studies*. New Brunswick, NJ: Rutgers University Press.

Khan, Shamus Rahman. 2011. *Privilege: The Making of an Adolescent Elite at St. Paul's School*. Princeton, NJ: Princeton University Press.

Kibria, Nazli. 2002. *Becoming Asian American: Second-Generation Chinese and Korean American Identities*. Baltimore: Johns Hopkins University Press.

Kim, Minjeong. 2014. "South Korean Rural Husbands, Compensatory Masculinity, and International Marriage." *Journal of Korean Studies* 19 (2): 291–325.

Kincheloe, Joe L. 2002. "The Complex Politics of McDonald's and the New Childhood: Colonizing Kidworld." In *Kidworld: Childhood Studies, Global Perspectives, and Education*, edited by Gaile Sloan Cannella and Joe L. Kincheloe, 75–122. New York: Peter Lang.

Kohn, Melvin L. 1959. "Social Class and Parental Values." *American Journal of Sociology* 64 (4): 337–351.

———. 1963. "Social Class and Parent-Child Relationships: An Interpretation." *American Journal of Sociology* 68 (4): 471–480.

Koo, Hagen. 2016. "The Global Middle Class: How Is It Made, What Does It Represent?" *Globalizations* 13 (4): 440–453.

Kuan, Teresa. 2015. *Love's Uncertainty: The Politics and Ethics of Child Rearing in Contemporary China*. Berkeley: University of California Press.

Kuo Wen-Hua. 1998. "Politicizing Family Planning and Medicalizing Reproductive Bodies: US Backed Population Control in 1960s Taiwan." [In Chinese.] *Taiwan: A Radical Quarterly in Social Studies* (32): 39–82.

Kusserow, Adrie S. 2004. *American Individualisms: Child Rearing and Social Class in Three Neighborhoods, Culture, Mind, and Society*. New York: Palgrave Macmillan.

Kymlicka, Will. 2012. Neoliberal Multiculturalism? *In Social Resilience in the Neoliberal Era*, edited by Peter Hall & Michèle Lamont, 99–126. Cambridge: Cambridge University Press.

Lamont, Michèle. 1992. *Money, Morals and Manners: The Culture of the French and the American Upper-Middle Class*. Chicago: University of Chicago Press.

Lan, Pei-Chia. 2002. "Subcontracting Filial Piety: Elder Care in Ethnic Chinese Immigrant Families in California." *Journal of Family Issues* 23 (7): 812–835.

———. 2006. *Global Cinderellas: Migrant Domestics and Newly Rich Employers in Taiwan* Durham, NC: Duke University Press.

———. 2008. "Migrant Women's Bodies as Boundary Markers: Reproductive Crisis and Sexual Control in the New Ethnic Frontiers of Taiwan." *Signs: Journal of Women in Culture and Society* 33 (4): 833–861.

———. 2014. "Compressed Modernity and Glocal Entanglement: The Contested Transformation of Parenting Discourses in Postwar Taiwan." *Current Sociology* 62 (4): 531–549.

Lan, Pei-Chia, and Yi-Fan Wu. 2016. "Exceptional Membership and Liminal Space of Identity: Student Migration from Taiwan to China." *International Sociology* 31 (6): 742–763.

Lareau, Annette. 1989. *Home Advantage: Social Class and Parental Intervention in Elementary Education.* London: Falmer Press.

———. 2011. *Unequal Childhoods: Class, Race, and Family Life.* Berkeley: University of California Press.

Lee, Helene K. 2018. *Between Foreign and Family: Return Migration and Identity Construction Among Korean Americans and Korean Chinese, Asian American Studies Today.* New Brunswick, NJ: Rutgers University Press.

Lee, Jennifer, and Min Zhou. 2015. *The Asian American Achievement Paradox.* New York: Russell Sage Foundation.

Lee, Yean-Ju, and Hagen Koo. 2006. "'Wild Geese Fathers' and a Globalised Family Strategy for Education in Korea." *International Development Planning Review* 28 (4): 533–553.

Levitt, Peggy, and Nina Glick Schiller. 2004. "Conceptualizing Simultaneity: A Transnational Social Field Perspective on Society." *International Migration Review* 38 (3): 1002–1039.

Levitt, Peggy, and Mary C. Waters, eds. 2002. *The Changing Face of Home: The Transnational Lives of the Second Generation.* New York: Russell Sage Foundation.

Lew, Jamie. 2006. *Asian Americans in Class: Charting the Achievement Gap among Korean American Youth.* New York: Teachers College Press.

Ley, David. 2010. *Millionaire Migrants: Trans-Pacific Life Lines.* West Sussex, UK: John Wiley & Sons.

Ley, David, and Audrey Kobayashi. 2005. "Back to Hong Kong: Return Migration or Transnational Sojourn?" *Global Networks* 5 (2): 111–127.

Li Cheng-Yu. 2013. "VTC Bureau Chief: The Next Generation of Taiwan Possesses More South East Asian Capital." [In Chinese.] *United Daily News*, July 3.

Li Shiue li. 2015. "The Happiness and Sorrow of 'Left-Behind Families.'" [In Chinese.] *Common Wealth*, December 8.

Li, Wei. 1998. "Anatomy of a New Ethnic Settlement: The Chinese Ethnoburb in Los Angeles." *Urban Studies* 35 (3): 479–501.

Lin, Chin-Yau Cindy, and Victoria R. Fu. 1990. "A Comparison of Child-Rearing Practices Among Chinese, Immigrant Chinese, and Caucasian-American Parents." *Child Development* 61 (2): 429–433.

Lin Chia-Chi. 2008. "Parental Negligence Fines Prompt United Protests." [In Chinese.] *United Daily News*, June 29, C3.

Lin, Thung Hong. 2015. "Causes and Consequences of Increasing Class Inequality in Taiwan." *Taiwan Economic Forecast and Policy* 45 (2): 45–68.

Liu, Cindy H., Stephen H. Chen, Yvonne Bohr, Leslie Wang, and Ed Tronick. 2017. "Exploring the Assumptions of Attachment Theory Across Cultures: The Practice of

Transnational Separation among Chinese Immigrant Parents and Children." In *The Cultural Nature of Attachment: Contextualizing Relationships and Development*, edited by Heidi Keller and Kim A. Bard, 171–192. Cambridge, MA: MIT Press.

Liu, John M., and Lucie Cheng. 1994. "Pacific Rim Development and the Duality of Post-1965 Asian Immigration to the United States." In *The New Asian Immigration in Los Angeles and Global Restructuring*, edited by Paul Ong, Edna Bonacich, and Lucie Cheng, 74–99. Philadelphia: Temple University Press.

Liu, Lisong. 2009. "Mobility, Community and Identity: Chinese Student/Professional Migration to the United States Since 1978 and Transnational Citizenship." PhD diss., University of Minnesota.

Lo, Ming-Cheng. 2002. *Doctors Within Borders: Profession, Ethnicity, and Modernity in Colonial Taiwan*. Berkeley: University of California Press.

———. 2015. "Conceptualizing 'Unrecognized Cultural Currency': Bourdieu and Everyday Resistance Among the Dominated." *Theory and Society* 44 (2): 125–152.

Lo, Ming-Cheng, and Emerald T. Nguyen. 2018. "Caring and Carrying the Cost: Bicultural Latina Nurses' Challenges and Strategies for Working with Coethnic Patients." *Russell Sage Foundation Journal of the Social Science* 4 (1). https://doi.org/10.7758/RSF.2018.41.09.

Louie, Andrea. 2004. *Chineseness Across Borders: Renegotiating Chinese Identities in China and the United States*. Durham, NC: Duke University Press.

———. 2015. *How Chinese Are You? Adopted Chinese Youth and Their Families Negotiate Identity and Culture*. New York: New York University Press.

Louie, Vivian. 2004. *Compelled to Excel: Immigration, Education, and Opportunity Among Chinese Americans*. Stanford, CA: Stanford University Press.

———. 2006. "Growing Up Ethnic in Transnational Worlds: Identities Among Second-Generation Chinese and Dominicans." *Identities: Global Studies in Culture and Power* 13 (3): 363–394.

Low, Yiu Tsang. 2014. "Parents' Perception of Effective Components of a Parenting Programme for Parents of Adolescents in Hong Kong." *Revista de cercetare si interventie sociala* 46: 162–181.

Lu Hsin-Mi, Liang Fei-Yi, and Tsai Duujian. 2007. *The Foundation and Development of Taiwan's Family Planning Program: Interviews with Prof. L. P. Chow*. [In Chinese.] Taichung: National Health Bureau.

Lu, Wei-Ting. 2013. "Confucius or Mozart? Community Cultural Wealth and Upward Mobility Among Children of Chinese Immigrants." *Qualitative Sociology* 36 (3): 303–321.

MacKendrick, Norah. 2014. "More Work for Mother: Chemical Body Burdens as a Maternal Responsibility." *Gender & Society* 28 (5): 705–728.

Madianou, Mirca. 2012. "Migration and the Accentuated Ambivalence of Motherhood: The Role of ICTs in Filipino Transnational Families." *Global Networks* 12 (3): 277–295.

Marcus, George E. 1995. "Ethnography in/of the World System: The Emergence of Multi-Sited Ethnography." *Annual Review of Anthropology* 24: 95–117.

Massey, Doreen. 1994. "A Global Sense of Place." In *Space, Place, and Gender*, edited by Doreen Massey, 146–156. Cambridge, UK: Polity Press.

Melamed, Jodi. 2006. "The Spirit of Neoliberalism: From Racial Liberalism to Neoliberal Multiculturalism." *Social Text* 24 (4): 1–24.

Mullainathan, Sendhil, and Eldar Shafir. 2013. *Scarcity: Why Having Too Little Means So Much*. New York: Macmillan.

Murphy Paul, Annie. 2011. "Tiger Moms: Is Tough Parenting Really the Answer?" *Time*, January 20.

Naftali, Orna. 2009. "Empowering the Child: Children's Rights, Citizenship and the State in Contemporary China." *China Journal* 61: 79–103.

———. 2010. "Recovering Childhood: Play, Pedagogy, and the Rise of Psychological Knowledge in Contemporary Urban China." *Modern China* 36 (6): 589–616.

Neckerman, Kathryn M., Prudence Carter, and Jennifer Lee. 1999. "Segmented Assimilation and Minority Cultures of Mobility." *Ethnic and Racial Studies* 22 (6): 945–965.

Nelson, Margaret K. 2010. *Parenting Out of Control: Anxious Parents in Uncertain Times*. New York: New York University Press.

Ng, Franklin. 1998. *The Taiwanese Americans*. Westport, CT: Greenwood Press.

Nguyen-Akbar, Mytoan. 2014. "Ambivalent 'Returns': High-Skilled Migration and Social Change in Ho Chi Minh City, Vietnam." PhD diss., University of Wisconsin–Madison.

Ong, Aihwa. 1999. *Flexible Citizenship: The Cultural Logics of Transnationality*. Durham, NC: Duke University Press.

Orellana, Marjorie Faulstich. 2009. *Translating Childhoods: Immigrant Youth, Language, and Culture*. New Brunswick, NJ: Rutgers University Press.

Orellana, Marjorie Faulstich, Barrie Thorne, Anna Chee, and Wan Shun Eva Lam. 2001. "Transnational Childhoods: The Participation of Children in Processes of Family Migration." *Social Problems* 48 (4): 572–591.

Osajima, Keith. 1993. "The Hidden Injuries of Race." In *Bearing Dreams, Shaping Visions: Asian Pacific American Perspectives*, edited by Linda A. Revilla, Shirley Hune, and Gail M. Nomura, 81–91. Pullman: Washington State University.

Park, Lisa Sun-Hee. 2005. *Consuming Citizenship: Children of Asian Immigrant Entrepreneurs*. Stanford, CA: Stanford University Press.

Parreñas, Rhacel Salazar. 2001. *Servants of Globalization: Women, Migration and Domestic Work*. Stanford, CA: Stanford University Press.

Passel, Jeffrey, and D'Vera Cohn. 2016. "Overall Number of U.S. Unauthorized Immigrants Holds Steady Since 2009." *Pew Research Center: Hispanic Trends*. http://www.pewhispanic.org/2016/09/20/overall-number-of-u-s-unauthorized-immigrants-holds-steady-since-2009/.

Paten, Graeme. 2013. "Cut Length of School Holidays, Says Michael Gove." *The Telegraph*, April 18.

Peguero, Anthony A., and Lisa M. Williams. 2011. "Racial and Ethnic Stereotypes and Bullying Victimization." *Youth and Society* 45 (4): 545–564.

Portes, Alejandro, Luis E. Guarnizo, and Patricia Landolt. 1999. "The Study of Transnationalism: Pitfalls and Promise of an Emergent Research Field." *Ethnic and Racial Studies* 22 (2): 217–237.

Portes, Alejandro, and Rubén Rumbaut. 2001. *Legacies: The Story of the Second Generation*. Berkeley: University of California Press.

Portes, Alejandro, and Min Zhou. 1993. "The New Second Generation: Segmented Assimilation and Its Variants." *Annals of the American Academy of Political and Social Science* 530: 74–96.

Power, Sally. 2000. "Educational Pathways into the Middle Class(es)." *British Journal of Sociology of Education* 21 (2): 133–145.

Pugh, Allison J. 2009. *Longing and Belonging: Parents, Children, and Consumer Culture*. Berkeley: University of California Press.

———. 2015. *The Tumbleweed Society: Working and Caring in an Age of Insecurity*. Oxford: Oxford University Press.

Purkayastha, Bandana. 2005. *Negotiating Ethnicity: Second-Generation South Asian Americans Traverse a Transnational World*. New Brunswick, NJ: Rutgers University Press.

Pyke, Karen. 2000. "'The Normal American Family' as an Interpretive Structure of Family Life Among Grown Children of Korean and Vietnamese Immigrants." *Journal of Marriage and Family* 62 (1): 240–255.

Qin, Desiree Baolian. 2006. "'Our Child Doesn't Talk to us Anymore': Alienation in Immigrant Chinese Families." *Anthropology and Education Quarterly* 37 (2): 162–179.

Reay, Diane. 1998. *Class Work: Mothers' Involvement in Their Children's Primary Schooling*. London: UCL Press.

———. 2017. *Miseducation: Inequality, Education and the Working Class*. Bristol, UK: Policy Press.

Reay, Diane, Gill Crozier, and David James. 2011. *White Middle Class Identities and Urban Schooling*. London: Palgrave Macmillan.

Reich, Jennifer A. 2014. "Neoliberal Mothering and Vaccine Refusal: Imagined Gated Communities and the Privilege of Choice." *Gender & Society* 28 (5): 679–704.

Rivera, Lauren A. 2015. *How Elite Students Get Elite Jobs*. Princeton, NJ: Princeton University Press.

Robertson, Roland. 1992. *Globalization: Social Theory and Global Culture*. London: Sage Publications.

ROC Bureau of Statistics. 2017. *Report on Women's Marriage, Fertility, and Employment*. [In Chinese.] Taipei: National Statistics, ROC.

ROC Legislative Yuan. 2002. *Education and Culture Committee Conference Record*. [In Chinese.] Taipei: Legislative Yuan.

ROC Ministry of Education. 2013. *The Family Education Act*. [In Chinese.] Taipei: Legislative Yuan, ROC.

———. 2014. *A Demographic Overview of Elementary and Middle School Age Children of New Immigrants*. [In Chinese.] Taipei: Executive Yuan, ROC.

———. 2017. "Education Statistics ROC 2017." [In Chinese.] http://stats.moe.gov.tw/files/ebook/Education_Statistics/106/106edu.pdf. Accessed January 2, 2018.

ROC Ministry of Health and Welfare. 2015. *The Protection of Children and Youths Welfare and Rights Act*. [In Chinese.] Taipei: Executive Yuan, ROC.

ROC Ministry of Interior. 2009. *The 2008 Investigation of the Living Condition of Foreign and Mainland Spouses*. [In Chinese.] Taipei: Executive Yuan, ROC.

Rofel, Lisa. 1999. *Other Modernities: Gendered Yearnings in China After Socialism*. Berkeley: University of California Press.

Rohner, Ronald P., and Sandra M. Pettengill. 1985. "Perceived Parental Acceptance Rejection and Parental Control Among Korean Adolescents." *Child Development* 56 (2): 524–528.

Rumbaut, Rubén G. 2002. "Severed or Sustained Attachments? Language, Identity, and Imagined Communities in the Post-Immigrant Generation." In *The Changing Face of Home: The Transnational Lives of the Second Generation*, edited by Peggy Levitt and Mary C. Waters, 43–95. New York: Russell Sage Foundation.

Sandelowski, Margarete. 1991. "Telling Stories: Narrative Approaches in Qualitative Research." *Journal of Nursing Scholarship* 23 (3): 161–166.

Saxenian, AnnaLee, and Jinn-Yuh Hsu. 2001. "The Silicon Valley-Hsinchu Connection: Technical Communities and Industrial Upgrading." *Industrial and Corporate Change* 10 (4): 893–920.

Sayer, Andrew. 2005. *The Moral Significance of Class*. Cambridge: Cambridge University Press.

Schreckinger, Ben. 2014. "China's Town: The Priciest Homes, the Best Schools, the Hottest Handbags: From Newbury Street to the Waterfront, Big-Money Chinese Buyers Are Spending Millions. Are We Cashing in or Selling Out?" *Boston Magazine*, September 30. http://www.bostonmagazine.com/news/2014/09/30/chinese-real-estate-boston/.

Shah, Bindi, Claire Dwyer and Tariq Modood. 2010. "Explaining Educational Achievement and Career Aspirations among Young British Pakistanis." *Sociology* 44 (6): 1109–1127.

She Keng-Jen. 2017. "Managing Whose Risks? Child Abuse Substantiation Practices in Taiwan." [In Chinese.] Master's thesis, National Taiwan University.

Shen, Hsiu-Hua. 2014. "Staying in Marriage Across the Taiwan Strait: Gender, Migration, and Transnational Family." In *Wives, Husbands, and Lovers: Marriage and Sexuality in Hong Kong, Taiwan, and Urban China*, edited by Deborah S. Davis and Sara L. Friedman, 262–284 Stanford, CA: Stanford University Press.

Shieh, Gwo-Shyong. 1992. *"Boss" Island: The Subcontracting Network and Micro-entrepreneurship in Taiwan's Development.* New York: Peter Lang.

Shih, Shu-Mei. 1998. "Gender and a New Geopolitics of Desire: The Seduction of Mainland Women in Taiwan and Hong Kong Media." *Signs* 23 (2): 287–319.

Shih, Yi-Ping. 2010. "Raising an International Child: Parenting, Class and Social Boundaries in Taiwan." PhD diss., State University of New York at Buffalo.

Shih, Yi-Ping, and Chin-Chun Yi. 2014. "Cultivating the Difference: Social Class, Parental Values, Cultural Capital and Children's After-School Activities in Taiwan." *Journal of Comparative Family Studies* 45 (1): 55–76.

Silva, Jennifer M. 2013. *Coming Up Short: Working Class Adulthood in an Age of Uncertainty.* Oxford: Oxford University Press.

Silvey, Rachel, Elizabeth A. Olson, and Yaffa Truelove. 2007. "Transnationalism and (Im)mobility: the Politics of Border Crossings." In *The Sage Handbook of Political Geography,* edited by Kevin R. Cox, Murray Low, and Jennifer Robinson, 483–491. London: Sage Publications.

Skeggs, Beverley. 1997. *Formations of Class and Gender: Becoming Respectable.* Thousand Oaks, CA: Sage Publications.

Smith, Dorothy E. 1993. "The Standard North American Family: SNAF as an Ideological Code." *Journal of Family Issues* 14 (1): 50–65.

Smith, Jill M., and Ken Chih-Yan Sun. 2016. "Privileged American Families and Independent Academic Consultants They Employ." *Sociological Forum* 31 (1): 159–180.

Sousa, Amy C. 2015. "'Crying Doesn't Work': Emotion and Parental Involvement of Working Class Mothers Raising Children with Developmental Disabilities." *Disability Studies Quarterly* 35 (1). http://dx.doi.org/10.18061/dsq.v35i1.3966.

Spencer, Kyle. 2015. "New Jersey School District Eases Pressure on Students, Baring and Ethnic Divide." *New York Times,* December 25.

Stevens, Mitchell L. 2007. *Creating a Class: College Admissions and the Education of Elites.* Cambridge, MA: Harvard University Press.

Stevenson, Harold W., and Shin-Ying Lee. 1990. "Contexts of Achievement: A Study of American, Chinese, and Japanese Children." *Monographs of the Society for Research in Child Development* 55 (1–2): 1–123.

Straus, Murray A., and Anita K. Mathur. 1996. "Social Change and Trends in Approval of Corporal Punishment by Parents from 1968 to 1994." In *Family Violence Against Children: A Challenge for Society,* edited by Detlev Frehsee, Wiebke Horn, and Kai-D Bussmann, 91–105. Berlin: Walter de Gruyter.

Straus, Murray A., and Julie H. Stewart. 1999. "Corporal Punishment by American Parents: National Data on Prevalence, Chronicity, Severity, and Duration, in Relation to Child and Family Characteristics." *Clinical Child and Family Psychology Review* 2 (2): 55–70.

Streib, Jessi. 2015. *The Power of the Past: Understanding Cross-Class Marriages.* Oxford: Oxford University Press.

Sudworth, John. 2016. "Counting the Cost of China's Left-Behind Children." *BBC News, Beijing*, April 12.

Sue, Stanley, and Sumie Okazaki. 2009. "Asian-American Educational Achievements: A Phenomenon in Search of an Explanation." *Asian American Journal of Psychology* S (1): 45–55.

Sui, Cindy. 2012. "Deaths Spotlight Taiwan's 'Overwork' Culture." *BBC News Asia*, March 20.

Sun, Te-Hsiung. 1978. "Demographic Evaluation of Taiwan's Family Planning Program." *Industry of Free China* 49 (5): 11–27.

Sweetman, Paul. 2003. "Twenty-first Century Disease? Habitual Reflexivity or the Reflexive Habitus." *The Sociological Review* 51 (4): 528–549.

Swidler, Ann. 1986. "Culture in Action: Symbols and Strategies." *American Sociological Review* 51 (2): 273–286.

Tang Jheng-Yu and Hong Min-Lyong. 2015. "Number of Child Abuse Cases Surpasses Ten Thousand, Even More Helpless Victims Unreported." [In Chinese.] *Apple Daily*, July 17.

Tavangar, Homa Sabet. 2009. *Growing Up Global: Raising Children to Be at Home in the World*. New York: Ballantine Books.

Tsai Hung-Jeng. 2007. "Historical Formation of Population Policy in Taiwan." [In Chinese.] *Taiwanese Journal of Sociology* 39: 65–106.

Tseng Ching-Yan. 1996. "Dangerous Parenting Style: Please Stop Harmful Love and Understand That Love Requires Knowledge and Efforts." [In Chinese.] *United Daily News*, October 13.

Tseng Fan-Tzu. 2008. "Discovering the 'Developmentally Delayed': Scientific Knowledge, Power Techniques, and Social Ordering." [In Chinese.] *Taiwanese Sociology* 15: 165–215.

Tseng, Yen-Fen. 2011. "Shanghai Rush: Skilled Migrants in a Fantasy City." *Journal of Ethnic and Migration Studies* 37 (5): 765–784.

Tseng, Yen-Fen, and Jieh-Min Wu. 2011. "Reconfiguring Citizenship and Nationality: Dual Citizenship of Taiwanese Migrants in China." *Citizenship Studies* 15 (2): 265–282.

Tran, Van C. 2016. "Ethnic Culture and Social Mobility among Second-Generation Asian Americans." *Ethnic and Racial Studies* 39 (13): 2398–2403.

Tuan, Mia. 1998. *Forever Foreigners or Honorary Whites? The Asian Ethnic Experience Today*. New Brunswick, NJ: Rutgers University Press.

Unz, Ron. 2013. "Statistics Indicate an Ivy League Asian Quota." *New York Times*, December 12.

Vallejo, Jody Agius. 2012. *Barrios to Burbs: The Making of the Mexican American Middle Class*. Stanford, CA: Stanford University Press.

Villalobos, Ana. 2014. *Motherload: Making It All Better in Insecure Times*. Berkeley: University of California Press.

Vincent, Carol, and Stephen J. Ball. 2007. "'Making Up' the Middle-Class Child: Families, Activities and Class Dispositions." *Sociology* 41 (6): 1061–1077.

Wang, Grace. 2015. *Soundtracks of Asian America: Navigating Race Through Musical Performance*. Durham, NC: Duke University Press.

Wang, Leslie K. 2016. "The Benefits of In-Betweenness: Return Migration of Second Generation Chinese American Professionals to China." *Journal of Ethnic and Migration Studies* 42 (12): 1941–1958.

Wang, Ru-jer. 2003. "From Elitism to Mass Higher Education in Taiwan: The Problems Faced." *Higher Education* 46 (3): 216–287.

Wang Wen-Yue. 2011. "The HARVEST Rural Periodical and Agricultural Extension in Early Post-War Taiwan (1951~1954)." [In Chinese.] *Kaohsiung Normal University Journal* (30): 1–22.

Waters, Johanna L. 2005. "Transnational Family Strategies and Education in the Contemporary Chinese Diaspora." *Global Networks* 5 (4): 359–377.

———. 2006. "Geographies of Cultural Capital: Education, International Migration and Family Strategies Between Hong Kong and Canada." *Transactions of the Institute of British Geographers* 31 (2): 179–192.

Waters, Mary C. 1990. *Ethnic Options: Choosing Identities in America*. Berkeley: University of California Press.

Waters, Mary C., and Jennifer Sykes. 2009. "Spare the Rod, Ruin the Child? First- and Second-Generation West Indian Child-Rearing Practices." In *Across Generations: Immigrant Families in America*, edited by Nancy Foner, 72–92. New York: New York University Press.

Way, Niobe, Sumie Okazaki, Jing Zhao, Joanna J. Kim, Xinyin Chen, Hirokazu Yoshikawa, Yueming Jia, and Huihua Deng. 2013. "Social and Emotional Parenting: Mothering in a Changing Chinese Society." *Asian American Journal of Psychology* 4 (1): 61–70.

Weenink, Don. 2008. "Cosmopolitanism as a Form of Capital: Parents Preparing Their Children for a Globalizing World." *Sociology* 42 (6): 1089–1106.

Weininger, Elliot B., and Annette Lareau. 2009. "Paradoxical Pathways: An Ethnographic Extension of Kohn's Findings on Class and Childrearing." *Journal of Marriage and Family* 71 (3): 680–695.

Weis, Lois, Kristin Cipollone, and Heather Jenkins. 2014. *Class Warfare: Class, Race, and College Admissions in Top-Tier Secondary Schools*. Chicago: University of Chicago Press.

Weise, Elizabeth. 2007. "As China Booms, So Does Mandarin in U.S. Schools." *USA Today*, November 19.

Wessendorf, Susanne. 2013. *Second Generation Transnationalism and Roots Migration: Cross-Border Lives*. Surrey, UK: Ashgate Publishing.

Wimmer, Andreas, and Nina G. Schiller. 2002. "Methodological Nationalism and Beyond: Nation-State Building, Migration and the Social Science." *Global Networks* 2 (4): 301–334.

Wolf, Diane L. 1997. "Family Secrets: Transnational Struggles Among Children of Filipino Immigrants." *Sociological Perspectives* 40 (3): 457–482.

Woronov, Terry E. 2007. "Chinese Children, American Education: Globalizing Child Rearing in Contemporary China." In *Generations and Globalization: Youth, Age, and Family in the New World Economy*, edited by Jennifer Cole and Deborah Durham, 29–51. Bloomington: Indiana University Press.

Wu, David Y. H. 1996. "Parental Control: Psychocultural Interpretations of Chinese Patterns of Socialization." In *Growing Up the Chinese Way: Chinese Child and Adolescent Development*, edited by Sing Lau, 1–28. Hong Kong: Chinese University Press.

Wu, Ellen D. 2014. *The Color of Success: Asian Americans and the Origins of the Model Minority*. Princeton, NJ: Princeton University Press.

Xiao Baiyou. 2011. *So, Brothers and Sisters of Peking University*. [In Chinese.] Shanghai: Shanghai Joint Publishing.

Yamashiro, Jane H. 2017. *Redefining Japaneseness: Japanese Americans in the Ancestral Homeland, Asian American Studies Today*. New Brunswick, NJ: Rutgers University Press.

Yan, Miu Chung, Ching Man Lam, and Sean Lauer. 2014. "Return Migrant or Diaspora: An Exploratory Study of New-Generation Chinese-Canadian Youth Working in Hong Kong." *International Migration and Integration* 15 (2): 179–196.

Yang Ching-Li, Huang I-Chi, Tsai Hung-Jeng, and Wang Hsiang-Ping. 2012. "Comparisons of Fertility Rate and Birth Quality Between Native and Foreign-Born Women in Taiwan." [In Chinese.] *Taiwanese Journal of Social Sciences and Philosophy* 24 (1): 83–120.

Yang, Fenggang. 1999. *Chinese Christians in America: Conversion, Assimilation, and Adhesive Identities*. University Park, PA: Penn State University Press.

Yang, Wesley. 2011. "Paper Tigers." *New York*, May 8. http://nymag.com/news/features/asian-americans-2011-5/.

Yoshikawa, Hirokazu. 2011. *Immigrants Raising Citizens: Undocumented Parents and Their Children*. New York: Russell Sage Foundation.

Yosso, Tara J. 2005. "Whose Culture Has Capital? A Critical Race Theory Discussion of Community Cultural Wealth." *Race, Ethnicity, and Education* 8 (1): 69–91.

Yu Hon-Yei Annie. 2014. "Changing Child Protection in Taiwan: The Impact for Projects for Families at High Risk." [In Chinese.] *Taiwan: A Radical Quarterly in Social Science* 96: 137–173.

Yu, Wei-Hsin, and Kuo-Hsien Su. 2006. "Gender, Sibship Structure, and Educational Inequality in Taiwan: Son Preference Revisited." *Journal of Marriage and Family* 68 (4): 1057–1068.

Yu, Wei-Hsin, and Kuo-Hsien Su. 2008. "Intergenerational Mobility Patterns in Taiwan: The Case of a Rapidly Industrializing Economy." In *Social Stratification and Social Mobility in Late-Industrializing Countries*, edited by Hiroshi Ishida, 49–78. Tokyo: 2005 SSM Research Committee.

Zelizer, Viviana A. 1985. *Pricing the Priceless Child: The Changing Social Value of Children*. New York: Basic Books.

Zhao, Xiaojian. 2010. *The New Chinese America: Class, Economy, and Social Hierarchy.* New Brunswick, NJ: Rutgers University Press.

Zhao, Yong. 2015. "Lessons That Matter: What Should We Learn from Asia's School Systems?" *Mitchell Institute,* June 19. http://zhaolearning.com/2015/06/19/lessons -that-matter-what-should-we-learn-from-asia%E2%80%99s-school-systems/.

Zhou, Min. 1997. "Growing Up American: The Challenge Confronting Immigrant Children and Children of Immigrants." *Annual Review of Sociology* 23: 63–95.

———. 2009. *Contemporary Chinese America: Immigration, Ethnicity, and Community Transformation.* Philadelphia: Temple University Press.

Zhou, Min, and Carl L. Bankston. 1998. *Growing Up American: How Vietnamese Children Adapt to Life in the United States.* New York: Russell Sage Foundation.

Zhou, Min, Margaret M. Chin, and Rebecca Y. Kim. 2013. "The Transformation of Chinese American Communities: New York vs. Los Angeles." In *New York and Los Angeles: The Uncertain Future,* edited by David Halle and Andrew A. Beveridge, 358– 382. Oxford: Oxford University Press.

Zhou, Min, and Susan S. Kim. 2006. "Community Forces, Social Capital, and Educational Achievement: The Case of Supplementary Education in the Chinese and Korean Immigrant Communities." *Harvard Educational Review* 76 (1): 1–29.

Index

Affirmative action, 114, 139
Alba, Richard and Victor Nee, 115
Alternative education, 11, 18, 65–76; Garden
    School, 182; statistics, 50, 201n12
American education: view of middle-class
    immigrants, 109, 113–114, 117, 133; view
    of working-class immigrants, 141, 149,
    154
American racism, 41, 121–123, 126, 128, 129,
    133, 134–135, 151, 170, 207n6
Asian American, 22, 39, 41, 176; academic
    success, 7, 39, 109, 113, 117, 137, 158,
    164; bamboo ceiling, 112, 113, 173;
    blocked opportunities, 122, 208n34;
    class bifurcation, 8, 40, 156–159; forever
    foreignness, 39, 134; hyperselectivity,
    7, 18, 26, 196n77; model minority, 7,
    15, 138, 158–159, 170, 176, 178–179;
    stereotype, 39, 41, 112, 122–123, 132, 137,
    158–159
Asian quota, 41, 113, 133, 136, 143, 173, 178
Assimilation, 39, 104, 114, 129, 138, 142;
    competitive, 110, 115–126, 130, 139, 173,
    178; cultural, 3, 21, 142, 154, 170, 174;
    downward, 151; narrating, 153–156, 164;
    segmented, 6, 19, 39, 113–114, 127, 138

Bohr, Yvonne, 165, 210n32, 210n34,
    210nn39–40
Boston, 17–19, 40, 113, 115, 134, 184–186
Bourdieu, Pierre, 9–11, 12, 45, 48, 147, 162,
    194n39, 195n42, 195n61, 201n4, 202n26,
    205n32, 209n6, 210n27

Brain circulation, 28, 54, 112
Brain drain, 28, 54

Chang, Kyung-Sup, 5, 193n10, 211n11
Chang, Shenglin, 29, 198n34, 198n37
Chee, Maria, 28, 197n32
Chen, Carolyn, 111, 180, 194n24, 197n26,
    206n4, 207n20, 208n35, 210n31, 211n13
Childhood: American, 2, 57, 58, 158, 165;
    commercial, 6, 57–58, 73, 75; competitive,
    58; exposed, 99, 101, 205n37; global
    convergence, 5; happy, 30, 47, 50, 63, 66,
    75, 77, 115, 119, 176, 178; innocent, 48;
    lost, 46–47, 77, 173, 178; sacralization of, 6
Child welfare system, 151, 152, 157, 168
Chinatown, 39, 40; English classes, 146,
    152; ethnic economy for parents'
    employment, 38, 152, 157, 162, 165;
    ethnic institution for children's
    enrichment, 7, 39–40, 135, 164–165,
    209n9; parental education seminar, 141,
    144, 146, 159–162; research methods, 20,
    184–186
Chinese Americans, 4, 38–42, 57, 134,
    137, 148, 165–166, 194n32, 208n46;
    geographic distribution, 40
Chinese culture: collectivism, 77; Confucian
    heritage, 6–7, 77, 118, 120; immigrant
    assimilation, 118; immigrants find it
    useless, 145; immigrants reinforcing
    traditions, 130–134, 137, 140, 164–169;
    interaction with structure, 6. *See also*
    Chinese parenting